HER HONOR, THE JUDGE

The Iowa State University Press, Ames ● 1 9 8 0

HER HONOR, THE JUDGE

the story of Reva Beck Bosone

BEVERLY B. CLOPTON

To my loving husband Jim
who is foremost in my thoughts
and
to the memory of my
beloved mother, Hazel Cutler Beck

Composed and printed by The Iowa State University Press, Ames, Iowa 50010

Library of Congress Cataloging in Publication Data

Clopton, Beverly B
    Her honor, the judge.

    Includes index.
    1. Bosone, Reva Beck. 2. Legislators—United States—Biography. 3. United States. Congress. House—Biography. 4. Law—Utah—history and criticism. 5. Judges—Utah—Biography. 6. Utah—Biography. I. Title.
E748.B723C56   328.73′092′4 [B]   80–12996

ISBN 0–8138–0565–1

CONTENTS

69814

FOREWORD

"EVERY MAN'S LIFE TOUCHES ME." Among those who have passed this way none has touched me more, few have been so noble in character, so exemplary in conduct, so illustrative of the human potential than Reva Beck Bosone. The life of this wonderful woman should, in my opinion, touch everyone. This is why the story of her life should be made a matter of permanent record. This is why it pleases me so much that a biography of this great friend is now being written.

I have known Reva Beck Bosone since the day she was sworn in as a member of the House of Representatives. The first woman ever to be elected to Congress from her State of Utah, she is a woman who has won many "firsts" throughout her life.

But it was not only her accomplishments as a woman that impressed her colleagues. As a legislator and as a human being she met every test of talent, integrity, and greatness. She knew why she was in Congress and what to do to achieve her goals. She came to the House of Representatives because she loved people and believed that she could serve many human needs as a member of the House. She set her goals and she attained them.

I have never known a more dedicated, respected, or knowledgeable person in all my years in Congress than Reva Bosone. Her wit, charm, and judgment were evident at every stage of our legislative proceedings. More than that, she was big in mind and heart, kind to every colleague, and above all compassionate with all her fellow human beings, large and small.

The story of Reva Beck Bosone's life and service is a great human treasure that must not be lost. That is why this biography had to be written.

CARL ALBERT

PREFACE

ALMOST EVERYONE has an aunt who is off the norm! Maybe she's an intellectual, a kleptomaniac, philanthropist, powermonger, bigot, benefactor, religious fanatic, or humanitarian. An aunt can be like any of us.

My aunt is especially off the norm. A Boston publishing house wanted Reva Beck Bosone to do her story for them in 1952, but like so many other achievers, she was just too busy living her life; huge contributions to society had put her in a class by herself.

Inasmuch as her achievements have been accruing since the 1950s, her story is long overdue. Today in semiretirement, as she urges others on to lofty ends, makes speeches, and corresponds with hundreds of loyal friends and associates, she must thoroughly enjoy the unquenchable glow of that goal she aspired to years ago—to justify her existence.

Warm words of praise have come from many people. This is what they have said:

John W. McCormack, former Speaker of the United States House of Representatives: "I consider her to be one of the ablest, most dedicated and courageous members of Congress I served with during my long service in the House."

Mike Mansfield, former majority leader, United States Senate: "Her ability as a congresswoman was excellent. She voted her conscience and was very well accepted."

Marguerite Rawalt, attorney, former national president of Business and Professional Women's Club, former president of the District of Columbia Federal Bar Association: "A woman of character. One of the great women of achievement of this country."

Harry S. Truman, late former president of the United States: "I wish we had more people with her ability and enthusiasm."

William A. Duvall, judge, chief hearing examiner, United States Post Office Department: "She had an interesting facet, I thought, to her decisions; she injected more of the human side than the legalistic side."

Frank E. Moss, former senator from Utah (judicial colleague in the 1940s): "Friendly, helpful, willing to give of her time. She was positive, never negative."

Kenneth R. Harding, sergeant at arms, United States House of Representatives: "Just the mention of her name triggers pleasant memories of admiration and respect. She made a great record back here."

Bernard L. (Barney) Flanagan, eminent pressman, former Bosone staff member, former writer with U.S. Fish and Wildlife Service: "She always looked for the good in people rather than the bad. Her part was to help put in motion forces that would offer hope and aid to those who needed it while there was still time."

J. Edward Day, attorney, former postmaster general, United States Post Office Department: "A very capable woman! My wife and I and Reva became good friends."

James W. Dixon, former director of Project Planning, Bureau of Reclamation, Department of the Interior: "One of my favorite congressmen. One of my favorites as a person. She's smart; she persevered!"

John E. Moss, former congressman from California: "Highly regarded by the members I knew."

Garff B. Wilson, professor of rhetoric and dramatic art, University of California, Berkeley, author, authority on American theatre and drama: "During all the years of my own education, I have encountered many good teachers, a few excellent teachers, and two or three outstanding teachers who have left a lasting imprint on my life. Reva Beck belongs in the last category."

BEVERLY BECK CLOPTON

PROLOGUE

FROM THE AGE OF SEVEN, when she first enrolled in school (traditional starting age), Reva Beck sensed being pushed aside by her contemporaries—perhaps due to her basic shyness or a reserve developed from the rejection of her red hair, freckles, and extreme height. She was convinced that she fit part of the fringe watching the scene from the background.

Many years and heartaches later she managed to partially overcome this reticence. Friends in adult years have found it hard to believe, viewing her apparent self-assurance, that Reva was ever beleaguered by a lack of self-confidence. But the inside struggle throughout much of her life was always kept from view.

Reva, the youngster, whether one of a few or one of a crowd, vowed that she would not be shunned, disregarded, or ignored forever! She vowed, in fact, that one day she would distinguish herself by accomplishing great deeds.

THE WARM ATMOSPHERE belied its source—the primordial fireball was sitting on the podium, not in the sky, that bright spring day of May 25, 1974. With the verve of a comet, red-haired Reva Beck Bosone addressed the graduating class of Westminster College in the Dane Hansen Memorial Stadium in Salt Lake City with the admonition that money and power without a conscience are disrupting government; polluting the air, water, and soil; and depleting the natural resources that are vital for the protection of the well-being of future generations.

With the sounds of bush-swept breezes, chittering birds, and thunderous jets punctuating her well-modulated tones, she counseled, "If life is to continue on this planet, you young people must stand up and be counted!"

Those black-gowned, mortarboard-clad students, each looking to his own ultimate day of accomplishment, were thoughtful in comprehension. They saw before them on the stand an original's original; a self-starting reformer who upholds the underdog and downgrades the elevated scrub; a leader for soul rights, a follower of the small voice; a doer for justice and damn the consequences!

The officials of Westminster, a junior college when Mrs. Bosone (pronounced Bozz-oh-nee) attended, were now assessing the career of a great teacher, lawyer, state legislator, judge, and congresswoman and respecting the merits of a life that has been dedicated to enriching people. They were conferring an honorary Doctor of Humanities degree with love and devotion and much sunshine. Mrs. Bosone's fair complexion was the only loser on that beautiful, cloudless occasion. Despite the effects of the sun, a woman stood tall, unwavering, and—above all—triumphant, with a conscience free of compromises.

HER HONOR, THE JUDGE

the story of Reva Beck Bosone

On the Bench

THE WOMAN, tall and straight, with natural red to strawberry blonde hair set softly above her ears, a splash of freckles across the cheekbones, owl glasses framing green eyes, straightened the jacket of her brown pinstripe wool suit and fluffed the bow of her blouse.

After receiving an exuberant hug for success from her husband, she made her way toward the bench, quite glad she had rejected the suggestion that she wear a robe. The formality didn't appeal; better to appear this first day like the "gal" the people had elected.

The large courtroom, ordinarily busy but seldom packed, seemed turgid with standing well-wishers and the curious. They pulled back from her pathway as she stepped up to the bench which, at the moment, was presenting an incongruous sight. A handsomely designed piece of courtroom furniture, ordinarily it held folders and papers, perhaps a book or two, and the traditional gavel. But on this auspicious winter day it was all but covered with baskets and bouquets of roses, chrysanthemums, and

PHOTO: *On the bench in the 1930s.*

greenery—delighting the nostrils and most certainly providing an unusual reversal of the courtroom scene.

The clerk pronounced the court in session. As Judge Reva Beck Bosone sat down in that high-backed black leather chair, her vision of the faces of smiling friends, lawyers, and the accused from whom she soon would hear was obscured for a moment until she rearranged the flowers directly in front of her. The flowers pushed aside, but not the choking knot in her throat, the Judge made the first vow—to herself: No one coming into her Salt Lake City courtroom would ever have cause to accuse her of unfair practices! This accomplished, she heard Case No. 1.

The first woman to be elected a judge in the State of Utah—year 1936—was holding court.

THAT IMPRESSIVE MOMENT could not help but induce memories of early struggles. It also seemed to portend even greater moments for her future, although she scarcely imagined that her mark on the West would work unprecedented changes in the systems of education, legislation, and adjudication.

Ever since graduation from high school, where she had campaigned for the post of president (ending up as vice-president), she had pushed her sights higher and wider. Improving each corner of her world as she moved upward, she was a hell-raiser when necessary and a placater when necessary, but Judge Bosone did it all her way—with dash and integrity.

Which niche of her life is considered most noteworthy? Which contribution has been most enriching to the human family? Which was the most satisfying personally and professionally? It has been said that each of her major accomplishments ranks with the next one. None takes precedence over the other.

The seven years she served as an Ogden High School teacher are memorable for establishing new standards in debate, oratory, and drama while maintaining the special rapport between teacher and students that has lasted over two generations.

As a lawyer Reva Beck Bosone continued a general practice for ten years, was appointed legal counsel for the Subcommittee on Safety and Compensation of the United States House of Representatives Committee on Education and Labor, and filled the position of judicial officer of the Post Office Department, its highest ranking woman. There she rendered legal decisions in the final appeals. Either of these appointments could be the apex of a career.

As a state legislator her important labor statutes for women and children are indelible on the pages of Utah history. She pushed aside the discriminatory barriers by becoming the first woman floor leader of the majority party and the first woman chairperson of the Sifting Committee.

As "Her Honor, the Judge," for twelve years she saw her sweeping reforms stand as a monument to her tireless efforts. As a leader who initiated programs in Utah for greater traffic safety on the road, she influenced other programs in the country. As director of the State Board on Alcoholism she rewrote the system on education on alcoholism. Recognition was widespread when she gave keynote convention speeches in the nation on both subjects. Experiences in these areas piled up memories to last a lifetime.

As a radio and television moderator her programs earned prestigious awards for her community.

As a United States congresswoman, the first and only one from Utah, she served as a member of the House Interior Committee and on two other major committees, among other duties, and introduced many important measures.

Taken individually, each of these pursuits could have pointed the direction of a career. In this case, however, they led to one woman whose life goal was to justify her existence. And her good deeds were never more oriented toward helping the human condition than in the Police and Traffic Court of the middle 1930s.

"UTAH MOTORISTS DIE AT FASTEST RATE IN HISTORY," headlined a gory article in the *Salt Lake Telegram*. There was no doubt that the town occupied one of the most dangerous traffic spots in the United States in 1936, ranking sixth highest in the nation for its size in fatalities, injuries, and damages.

And into this situation stepped Judge Bosone in December, a month ahead of schedule because of the death of Judge C. F. Dalby.

"These are not fatalities," the new magistrate declared, "these are proclaimed killings!" The motorized caldron was the No. 1 blot on the police blotter. If anyone, let alone a woman, could rectify such a fiery condition, it would be a test of ingenuity, patience, and fortitude.

A comprehensive study of traffic records was undertaken by the Judge as one of her first tasks on the bench; for the first three months she levied the customary low traffic fines while gaining time to figure out a new system. She was very aware that when a change was made, it had better be workable and effective or her tenderfoot reputation would be razzed. So, after careful deliberation, she decided to boost the fine and forfeiture level to $10. But it seemed to have no apparent effect on speeders, a fact that amazed the Judge. After all, this was the bumper end of the depression and the average monthly wage was $65.

So, shortly after, in the spring of 1937, Judge Bosone gave two weeks' notice to the newspapers that traffic fines would be upped to $25 for the three chief hazards on the highway: speeding, stop sign, and red light violations. The dent in the wallet would be deep and the hurt excruciating to the budget. Reaction? Outrage! She was warned that her lustrous career would be "all washed up" if she proceeded on this course. Lawyers jumped on the plan as nonjuristic and inequitable. It would even be discriminatory.

Determined to "chill the thrill of reckless driving," Reva Beck Bosone was not to be daunted. How could a compassionate judge, she reasoned, review 125 offenses for speeding in one 24-hour period—Memorial Day—a staggering number for a city the size of Salt Lake City, and remain unmoved to take severe measures? After all, police court was her baby; the other judges had offered her her choice of the four courts in the city. Generally regarded as the most distasteful, this assignment was the most interesting to Reva who said, "It gives the judge the opportunity not only to render justice but to help hundreds of people in many ways. It is a spot where tremendous good can be done for one's fellowman."

The drastic, radical program, as the Judge described it, of high fines resulted in an immediate reduction of violations, actually from near the top of the nation's toll ladder to almost the bottom, thereby ultimately pushing car insurance rates down. It also rocked the nation's safety boats; eventually her program was to be emulated by other cities and her counsel sought at illustrious conferences in the nation—but not before she struggled through a lifetime of other people's troubles.

Judge Bosone's relationship with the police force took on enormous importance when she was elected to the bench. One could envision a department of hardened (in coping with problems of broken social values) law enforcers suddenly faced with a gentle-mannered but sure-voiced, owl-bespectacled, red-thatched, black-robed member of the distaff, those who were hitherto considered at their peak in the kitchen or bedroom.

At first these men were curious to perceive her reactions to the wide range of situations making the police court an arena of pandemonium. Reva gives credit to the training she experienced at home growing up with three brothers. Giving in to emotions was next to cataclysmic, she had long ago concluded; she was only too aware that men like to feel comfortable.

"When they would come in to have a conference with me," she admitted, "and I could see they were ill at ease, I would drop a 'hell' or a 'damn' in my conversation and the ice would crack up quickly! As the days passed, I got well acquainted with the members of the force and became fond of most of them. They were a fine and conscientious group. To be a good law enforcer one has to be dedicated to his job and most of them were.

"I found that the majority of the policemen tried to weigh the facts as best they could before they made an arrest. It was not unusual to see one of them come into my chambers later, after an arrest, and explain that he could have made a mistake. Some of them, after they had cited criminal or traffic offenders and had heard the circumstances surrounding the defendant, felt sorry. They had good hearts with the job they had to do. Oh, it wasn't long before I had the ones pegged who took a delight in making an arrest. But most of them tried their best." And proof of their respect has been evident in their reunions of "Bosone Days."

In a sense it was a two-way judgment court; the Judge had a putty heart for the unfortunates and a steel fist for the irresponsible. The arresting officer learned, sometimes dearly, that if there were mitigating circumstances, he should save his breath and his time in writing up a ticket. But in the case of the selfish, reckless driver who created the slaughter on the streets, she had no pity.

For the wayward, nondriving, harmful-only-to-himself alcoholic, the Judge could be counted on to try every type of rehabilitation available by phoning or personally hunting up a job, a guardian, counseling, or medical help. But for the show-off with a hot right foot, she lowered the boom and raised the bail!

In September William D. Rishel, head of the Automobile Association of Utah and chairman of the Safety Committee of the Chamber of Commerce, asked the lady jurist to address a luncheon of the chamber.

"When I learned that Judge Bosone was assigned to the Police and Traffic Court," he said in his luncheon introduction, "I called the Safety Committee of the Chamber of Commerce together and told them, 'Well, we have a skirt in the traffic court as a judge. We will just forget everything we have been working on and that is too bad.' " He went on to admit that in reading the newspapers each day he commenced to think that maybe he was wrong about that skirt on the bench. He then called her "the person who has done the most for safety in this city." Capping that compliment, he turned to her and promised, " Judge Bosone, if you ever run for president of the United States I shall vote for you."

Most gratified for being so recognized, Reva opened her remarks by stressing speed as the chief cause of traffic deaths. Outlining her past program and the reasons for it, she proposed other policies to cut the accident rate: a stronger traffic force, a change in the driver's license law, additional speed limit signing. She decried the small number of patrolmen—three shifts, eight men to a shift, four men patrolling the highways and four others on duty—to protect the safety of 150,000 people!

Repeated applause by 150 members and civic leaders was her reward that fall day as her drastic measures were given their approval.

The National Safety Council, hearing sounds of revolution in Salt

Lake City's traffic court, sent their representatives to Utah to check them out. Their report was publicized in an article in the *National Public Safety Magazine* of January 1938, "She's Tough on Violators":

> When this No. 1 woman traffic judge of the country took over the Salt Lake City Police Court December 6, 1936, she declared war on violators, announced a schedule of stern, impartial penalties, outlawed fixing and launched a campaign for traffic safety that has won plaudits from the safety forces of the Utah city.
>
> With a severity that has stricken roadhogs and signal light crashers with terror, with heavy fines for habitual offenders and prison sentences where the occasion demands, Judge Bosone has established a record for herself that eventually may establish one for Salt Lake City. . . .
>
> A feature of her campaign is a traffic school where convicted offenders may take a test on laws and rules of traffic. If they succeed in the examination, a part of the fine is suspended. She started this plan because so many offenders displayed a woeful lack of knowledge of the laws governing traffic. . . .

The examination innovation eased the burden on offenders by saving them money, at the same time increasing their driving acumen and making it possible for them to fulfill their obligation in a positive manner. The school system has thrived for decades, but the present program does not call for a written examination.

"The public little realizes how far-reaching and how uniformly disseminated the impact of traffic accidents are throughout society," states the Judge who has witnessed indescribable misery. A case in particular focuses on the sorrow and hopelessness.

An automobile accident has injured an eighteen-year-old youth and he is near death from a broken neck. His family is at his hospital bedside. The doctor reports that the victim has little chance of recovery because his spinal cord was severed and he is completely paralyzed. The young man's mother, a waitress from Chicago, sold all her possessions to be able to hurry to her son's bedside. Her other son, seventeen, an army paratrooper, spent his last cent to reach his brother from Fort Benning, Georgia. The father, from Chicago, divorced from his wife, used up his savings to make the trip.

"Traffic accidents are circuitous," the Judge asserts. "The effect never ends. Aside from the waste of money, there are the desolate heartaches and worry. Nothing," she stresses, "seems to be any more horrible than the hundreds of uncalled-for accidents."

How fortunate was another boy, according to his mother's testimony in her card to the Judge, when he was reprimanded while there was still time for him to live his life. Whenever the mother would scold the boy for his lawless driving, she was met with a "phooey." But the stern medicine of high fines prescribed by Judge Bosone could have been the reason this youth was saved from a similar fate of the permanently paralyzed patient.

Proceeding on the theory that a successful experiment is worth a hundred ideas, Judge Bosone kept innovating—new fines, new ways to improve traffic conditions—and, surprisingly, she found new friends. Screams for a massive deterrent for the traffic slaughter which had turned into screams of "uncle" were being subdued and reconsidered—the public was beginning to accept those unheard-of fines.

The business manager of the Bell Telephone Company was the recipient of a speeding ticket. A good friend of the Judge, he paid her a visit in her chambers shortly thereafter, expecting a reprieve. Following her policy of uniform fines, she informed him that if he was guilty he would be liable for the $25 fine. He promptly objected, whereupon she asked him whether he wanted to smear her conscience by forcing her to make him an exception. Answering in the negative, he sulked out and paid his fine at the counter—and refused to speak to her for six months!

Being of the mind that she was "doing right," the Judge had a clear conscience but regretted his reaction. Then one day they encountered each other in the Telephone Building. Extending both arms to her in a gesture of friendship, he apologized for his attitude. "I hated to pay that $25 but I want to tell you, Judge Bosone, that anyone who says a high fine doesn't make a better driver is plain crazy. My wife says it is the best thing that ever happened to me." Reva then asked if she could quote him, and he gave his immediate consent.

Not all those sentenced in her court agreed with her, however. Typed in caps, an explicit postcard message—angry yet with a touch of pathos—arrived one day:

> DEAR JUDGE:
>   IT SEEMS TO ME YOU HAVE MADE YOUR BENCH A THRONE AND YOUR SELF A DICTATORIAL QUEEN LIKE UNTO CATHERINE. SOMETHING SHOULD BE DONE TO REMIND YOU THAT YOU ARE DEALING WITH HUMAN BEINGS. THINK HOW AUTOCRATIC YOU ARE. NO HUMAN IS ALLOWED TO SAY A SINGLE WORD BEFORE YOUR THRONE, IF THEY DO OFF GOES THEIR HEAD. BE A LITTLE HUMAN AND LOOK UPON YOUR "SUBJECTS" AS HUMAN. HAVE A HEART AND SOME MERCY AND YOU WILL BE REMEMBERED.

Judge Bosone's system of uniform fines in particular was in contention; in and out of Utah were judges who would not agree with her. She maintained that if the offense were the same, the fine should be the same.

The defense heard in court for almost every speed charge was, "I didn't realize how fast I was going" or "I thought I was on a through highway." For the stop sign, "I didn't see it" or "I shifted gears." For the semaphore, "I thought I could make it."

The Judge challenged the comments of her opposition, "Now you tell me why a brunette needs to a pay a greater fine than a blonde! You may ask why a poor boy should pay more (proportionately) than the bank president. Well, the bank president, believe it or not, will howl more about losing $25 than the poor man. Anyway, traffic judges are not the judges of finances—it isn't fair to have the punishment for the same crime differ."

With no discrimination in her new traffic program, cooperation between the traffic officers, court attachés, and the Judge improved. Favoritism gone, the healthful atmosphere was conducive to productive effort and high-level rapport. Ticket fixing was passé, and the job of invoking uniform fines, those that fell upon the offender who had no excuse for his hazarding life on the highways, became easier. However, where there were extenuating circumstances, sentences have been entirely suspended in the Bosone court. Each case was judged separately.

Considering that during the first ten months of her first term she reviewed and rendered decisions in more than 15,000 cases, her action accounted for a lot of merit judging. Speeding, reckless driving, drunken driving, hit-and-run, and overparking violations constituted the majority of offenses. Fines of $56,509 collected during the first eleven months meant a substantial increase over the preceding period. In the year 1938, 3,728 traffic cases, excluding parking violations, came to her attention, with a 90 percent record of conviction.

But unlike a predecessor who bragged to her about the number of defendants he had held guilty (Reva thought no judge should behave like a prosecutor), she gave every defendant an opportunity to make a plea. Her desire to administer justice was the spur for the constant comment that she was a *fair* judge. In line with the statement of the late associate justice of the Supreme Court, Benjamin N. Cardozo, "Justice remains to some extent, when all is said and done, the synonym of an aspiration, a mood of exaltation, a yearning for what is fine and high," Judge Bosone's aspiration was to right what is wrong with mankind.

A VIRTUE that manifested itself early in Reva's life was compassion. Her spirits were uplifted when those of others around her were as high. As a youngster she would never let a girl watch as a bystander while she herself was participating in an activity; the reticent one would always be pulled into the fold. Cruelty in any form was difficult for her to comprehend. This probity was not given the same value by many in her peer group.

The very young girl, exceptionally tall for her age, with red hair, freckles, and woebegone eyes dragged her sagging body into the hotel her mother managed in American Fork; the school day, as every other school day, had gone miserably. Shy and sensitive to a point of desperation, Reva Beck concluded that she was destined to live a shadow life.

"Why can't I be little and cute and named Dorothy?" she lamented. Every night young Reva would wish upon a star through that high window in her room, knowing it was hopeless, but not knowing that there was a star up there somewhere with her name on it. Mother Zilpha would then begin the routine that was called upon all the way through her daughter's tender years.

"Reva, red hair is beautiful! Do you know who in history had red hair?"

Reva, who had heard it all before, was peculiarly consoled, "Who, mama?"

"Thomas Jefferson, Sarah Bernhardt, Jesus Christ! That's who!" But if that didn't suffice—"And for heaven's sake, who ever heard of a short queen?" Queens, of course, were the acme. "Now you take Queen Victoria!" A real shortie, but who was to know?

So with confidence restored, Reva would trot off to school in the morning—chest out, head up, eyes bright. And every afternoon, she would slink back home—shoulders forward, head down, completely dispirited. Unkind remarks had undercut the buoyancy. So once again mama would wind up her pep talk record. No wonder Zilpha Beck is a revered name in Reva's own Hall of Fame.

Young Reva would occasionally be encouraged by one of the many salesmen guests at the Grant Hotel. One affable gentleman and avowed friend would assure her in their conversations in the lobby that the slope shoulders she so desired were not those of glamorous motion picture actresses.

" Just look at their square shoulders the next time you see a motion picture." And right he was. But then another time he would say, "You're tall, Reva, because you have a good heritage. Your forebears ate good food!"

Reva listened well and ate less.

Any rangy person knows that school photographs (forever included in family albums) are a drag! Especially were they for Reva who was always assigned the back row and consequently obliterated by some boy almost as tall in front of her. So, being ingenious then as now, she soon learned the habit of holding up her hand. Showing the class picture to family and friends, she would point to an apparently disembodied hand gaily waving from behind scores of smiling faces.

"See, that's me," she would pipe.

As a teacher, Reva decided to make a few changes in the system for her tall girl students. Instead of standing them in the back row, she seated them in the front.

In this day of high rises of practically everything, Reva's five feet nine and one-quarter inches (in adulthood) make her just mildly statuesque. Several Miss Americas have been in that bracket or even taller, but in Reva's youth there were but two other girls in American Fork as lofty. Although Reva had the edge on both, scholastically and in such skills as dancing, acting, and debating, her inferiority complex held her like invisible chains. Hanging back because of her height became a way of life. But she recalls with a shiver how an aunt threatened her daughter with a brick on her head if the cousin continued to grow, and Reva was grateful that her mama had no such false pride.

Reva was born a year old! One might say this child, thirteen pounds at birth, entered the world in a stimulating atmosphere with a head start. Reva hailed from an age of babies of uninhibited size, proving in her case that big babies do presage a higher potential. But at the age of five, a tragedy marked Reva with long-lasting effects.

While playing out-of-doors, she was so terrified that a big dog following her might attack that she ran from him to the point of exhaustion and unconsciousness. Bedded for days, she later learned that her heart had been impaired and limitations would always be placed on immoderate physical activity. In fact, her mother was warned that Reva's life prognosis had been shortened.

The townsfolk became aware of Reva's health problem and protected her from herself; whenever she ran or skipped down the street, some kindly benefactor would restrain her. And she was never permitted to engage in strenuous athletics, although no one could dissuade her from her hobby of dancing. It not only preoccupied Reva during her early years but the thought of not dancing was so devastating that her mother indulged her for happiness' sake while, in her opinion, Reva was able to enjoy it.

In time, however, the blood vessels of her heart built by-passes, the frightening murmur became less noticeable, and little by little various restrictions were lifted. Years later a normal schedule was resumed; compensation had taken place.

"When I was grown," Reva says, "I remember hearing my mother tell a friend that when I was a child, she wondered when I was away from her whether she would see me alive again. I'm convinced that I'm alive only because she used such good sense in rearing me. She'd be happy if she could see how long I have lived, and expect to live—God willing.''

In favoring the body processes, Reva's quiet inclinations toward drawing, painting, singing, emoting, and playing the piano were given resolute encouragement; the trifling hours of gossip and games and just plain lolling were discouraged. Of course, energetic sports were not in her routine, anyway; hence talents grew. Over those tethered years, the motivation to excel, to make golden each hour, to be the best possible, to top the competition became paramount and no amount of nonathletic effort was too great to harness the goal.

Added to that will power was a mother instinct that has dominated her life. "I have mothered everybody and everything," she explains. "This is good judgment in many instances and bad in others! I have long since mothered issues, people with whom I have worked, and my friends—even my men friends. It has caused me to take a personal interest which often has gotten me all involved and worn out. But I'm glad I have that instinct, and I can't cry about its dominating me. If it has caused me trouble it has done so only because of wrong judgment."

Reva's motherly touch was evidenced in frequent letters to her brother Horace when he was away from home in Salt Lake City after high school. The eighth grader wrote:

> Ruth says in her letters that you never come to see them anymore, now Horace I want you to go and see Ruth for my sake. . . . There for a while when you didn't go to see Margaret [a mutual friend] she was blue and she told Mrs. Steel that you didn't come anymore, you bet she likes you. . . . Horace, don't you think you could do without using so much money. I think you could, we aren't doing a very good business, so be careful. . . . Tell Clarence to write, he hasn't answered my letter yet. . . . Goodbye with love to Clarence, but keep a good share for yourself. Yours, Reva.

An expression of that proneness to mothering was Reva's passion for dolls. The rag doll given her on her first birthday was so lovingly cared for that her mother wished she had selected one of more quality for her "first." Reva's last doll gift was on her fifteenth birthday!

So compassion in her developing years served her well, and on the bench it was a consoling companion of her keen mind in handing down judgments, as a January 1939 newspaper editorial pointed out: " Judge Bosone has shown that she is peculiarly fit temperamentally to meet the onerous responsibilities confronting her in the dual post of police judge and traffic judge."

The editorial further explained:

> Though they [the dual judgeship] are combined into one, the law and the testimony can be her only guide, her ability to respond to distinct philosophies has enabled her to appreciate that a traffic court has a special problem. Her wisdom and discrimination in imposing penalties, in upholding the traffic code, in backing enforcement agencies, in maintaining public respect for the law, her court, and the police have won for her widespread esteem.
>
> She has been a wholesome and potent force here. She may take justifiable pride in the minimum number of successful appeals from her judgments. Her continuance in her accustomed place meets with the approbation of law respecting citizens, if not completely satisfying to some others who are unable to analyze her job as she has done, and yet others who might wish for a "soft" judge in her place.

At the end of her first year on the Police and Traffic Court, Reva had expected to move to another jurisdiction, one of the civil courts, but requests by the city commissioners, Chamber of Commerce, and other civic organizations convinced her that she was bordering on the indispensable—anyway, certainly fulfilling a vital need. And so she remained at that post for three more years, rotating the rest of her tenure as judge, twelve years in all. (In 1946 she again became the magistrate of the Police and Traffic Court.)

Understandably, not all action was solemn, lachrymose, or chastening in the Bosone court, which never lacked for listeners. Not all judgments went by the book when she felt justice could not be served by sticking with orthodox decisions. Judge Cardozo was reported to have said, "In the long run, there is no guarantee of justice except the personality of a judge."

A young woman pled guilty to a speeding charge, explaining that the car behind her late at night imitated her every move and so by trying to escape from it by accelerating she had drawn the attention of a patrolman. Another young woman pled guilty for running a stop sign the day after she had attended the funeral of her mother. An engineer at a local hospital was issued a ticket for speeding; he had received a call at home that the boiler in the hospital furnace system was acting peculiarly and had rushed to correct a dangerous situation. The three cases were analyzed—critically and humanely—then dismissed. And soon the officers learned it was useless to arrest drivers who could prove extenuating circumstances.

But excuseless defendants were made to toe the line if they determined to beat the rap. One Joe Bosone didn't show at the appointed time for an overparking charge, whereupon his wife instructed the clerk to notify him to appear immediately or she would issue a bench warrant. He came and he paid. One surmises this $2 addition to the police court revenue did not help domestic relations much, but one also surmises that

Judge Bosone regarded her action as the only honorable one in her Fair Deal bench program. Husbands would just have to understand, and Joe did—most of the time! Eventually, the whole family learned that ticket fixing was a definite no-no. A brother had to fork over his parking fine the same as everyone else. One Christmas season the Judge even served her own sentence and dug up the change on being issued a parking citation.

As may be imagined, the Bosone traffic bench tactics were not without humor. "Friends of mine used to say as they approached a stop sign," the Judge remembers, "that they could see a picture of me, and my image made them stop. Men said that when they were driving with their wives they were warned to slow down or Bosone would get them. The accelerator was even reported by a cautious driver to shout, 'Bosone, Bosone, Bosone!' " The conscientious Judge knew it wasn't she they were most aware of but rather the painful $25 that acted as the needle to enforce safety.

But the really hurtful incidences involved sentencing of friends and business and professional acquaintances. There were a few whose friendship she lost by being forced to levy the established fines in lieu of mitigating circumstances. Others took their medicine with fine fettle and an open mind. The reaction of the sentenced was unpredictable. But through all the conflict and turmoil on the bench the Judge strove for reasonableness and impartiality. "I made darn good and sure I could sleep nights," she emphasized.

Reva was a practicing attorney when she first suspected that the only gambling houses in town subject to being raided were those that didn't make a payoff to police. After becoming municipal judge she clarified her views with the police chief that she would continue the sentences of defendants running those establishments until all offenders were brought before her. Her policy was stated from the bench; she definitely would not allow her court to act as a whip to a payoff!

Salt Lake City criminal lawyer Ray McCarty was asked to compile a list of these suspected gambling houses. As each defendant was arraigned and his plea entered in court, his name was checked off McCarty's list. Unknown to her, the city attorney also was compiling a list.

Judge Bosone recalls the startling incident when one afternoon the mayor, also head of the Public Safety Department, stormed into her chambers.

"What are you trying to do to the police," he roared, "by ignoring their arrests at gambling joints? You are not going to run the police department!"

"I am running the court," she explained after recovering from the verbal assault, "and I have jurisdiction only of the court, but what happens to gamblers there is my business. The court will not be a whip to a payoff. I should think you would approve of my policy; in fact, I'm surprised at your attitude!''

Flying out of her chambers and downtairs, he denounced the Judge all the way in a loud voice. Lee Acomb, police court clerk, walked in just then with the comment that the mayor's raving looked mighty suspect! The Judge did not detect his meaning at the moment, not connecting the distinguished city father with hanky-panky.

Weeks later a seething gambling situation erupted and Reva's policy stirred up an investigation wherein she was called to explain her reason for adopting it. In March (1938) the already spectacular police and vice investigations were compounded when Acomb reported that the docket sheets and complaints on several gambling cases had apparently been stolen from his office. Soon a full-blown scandal unfolded, with emblazoned headlines instrumental in indicting and convicting the mayor, police chief, and others for taking payoffs!

When the city's top official, with, as the Judge said, a reputation of honor and expertise in business and fiscal matters, had been elected, he had expressed a preference to head the City Finance Department but was delegated instead to the Public Safety Department. Judge Bosone likes to think that if his first wish had been granted, he would not have become corrupted, dashing an upstanding respectability. ''I felt very sorry that a man of his age and stature could be involved in a racket!''

The imbroglio of one department reverberated in others, which rattled and shook the straight-laced town. When the indicted mayor resigned, an appointed successor was the new order of the city commissioners. John M. Wallace, vice-president of Walker Bank and Trust Company, was named, touching off a skirmish in which the name of Reva Beck Bosone emerged again in the middle.

Women's groups and political and labor organizations which had sought the appointment of Judge Bosone as mayor immediately pressured the City Commission for a ''rehearing'' and threatened to contest the Wallace appointment. On February 19, 1938, early in the day of the protests, Paul M. Peterson, president of the Utah State Federation of Labor, presented petitions representing 10,000 citizens in behalf of Reva stating that '' Judge Bosone is not the champion of any group or clique. She does not fear the political graveyard that is the job of commissioner of public safety. We feel our candidate is more qualified than anyone who has been or will be considered.''

Among the aroused supporters speaking up in opposition to the sudden decision of the mayoralty appointment and the refusal of their efforts to be heard were Mrs. Mary Halloran Soules, financial director and treasurer of the Democratic party in Utah, who was the most vocal in her challenge; Mrs. C. O. Bonner, president of the Women's Democratic

Club; Mrs. Anthony C. Lund, state senator and president of the Women's Chamber of Commerce; Mrs. Margaret M. McQuilkin, U.S. collector of customs and a Democratic leader; County Clerk William J. Korth, Democratic leader; Fred Kohlenberg, president of local 68, Brotherhood of Locomotive Firemen and Enginemen; and Mrs. James H. Wolfe, regional adviser of the women's division, Democratic National Committee.

After an official meeting was called at 10:00 A.M., Bosone supporters were heard in heavy accusations. Brickbats of unfair tactics were tossed. At its conclusion the evidence obviously did not deter the four commissioners from their determination to seat John Wallace, who had previously expressed unwillingness to serve, and, according to the *Salt Lake Telegram* "it is believed he virtually was drafted to the post." As soon as the delegation had departed, Commissioner Murdock moved for the appointment of Wallace who was given the oath of office.

The *Salt Lake Telegram,* making traffic safety a civic enterprise, called for an immediate approach to solving the dilemma of record accidents. A traffic safety commission was formed under the direction of the new mayor, and the services of a National Safety Council engineer, Rufus Jasper, were solicited.

At the end of 1939 the *Telegram* editorialized on the situation, listing positive results of the "city's safest traffic year since 1925," due to the commission's efforts, and lauded Mayor Wallace; Chief of Police William C. Webb; Sergeant Harvey C. Peirce, head of the police traffic division; C. G. Woolley, assistant city engineer; Judge Bosone; George French, secretary of the traffic commission; and the city commissioners.

In 1939, when Reva anticipated running for either the mayoralty or a city commission post, the *Post-Sentinel* reported on September 7 that the Judge had not yet made a definite decision which office she would seek. "It is interesting to speculate upon what would happen if Her Honor Judge Bosone should win in the election. For nearly four years she has presided in police court and seldom given ground, maintaining her position with sincerity and conviction. Her efforts to help the Salt Lake City traffic situation have probably done more than a dozen Rufus Jasper reports and the Salt Lake City Safety Commission put together."

A specialized function of the judgeship posed a surprise for Reva— she had just never considered her right to perform marriage ceremonies. So in 1937 with the request from the chief of police for her to officiate the next day at the wedding of Jack Dawn, head makeup artist of MGM, and movie actress Marla Shelton at the Hotel Utah, she was intrigued but flustered. "I didn't know a ceremony from a scuttle of coal," she admits.

The Judge called in Lee Acomb, an active church-goer, inviting his ideas. Keeping them in mind she raced, typically conscientious, to the city library to bone up on all kinds of marriage ceremonies. She mixed them up and stirred in her own thoughts, motivated to create a true and lasting bond for this talented couple. Rushing back to court, Judge Bosone practiced her newly penned vows on Acomb and Earl Loury, an assistant in the clerk's office, the "bride and groom"—a Mack Sennett interlude in a couple of emotion-packed days.

"Late the next afternoon," the Judge recalls, "Zilpha [her daughter] and I met the attractive Jack Dawn and the perfectly lovely Marla Shelton at the hotel. The police chief acted as one of the witnesses. I performed my duty and then made a bit of a speech to the Dawns immediately after. The newly married couple assured me they had never heard a more beautiful ceremony, for which I was grateful. My heart was in it, believe me!

"In 1939 Jack and Marla entertained Zilpha and me in their spacious home in California one evening. Jack had spent the day showing us the movie lot. It was a wonderful experience for me since at one time in my young life I had aspired to become an actress."

Judge Bosone rues the fact, unfortunately, that they were one of only two couples who were divorced after a Bosone knot-tying.

The Judge performed many more ceremonies but of only one does she avoid the memory. A dear friend had expressed the hope that Reva would preside at her wedding, whenever. In this case the bridegroom-to-be had the reputation of being a big tippler and the fact disturbed the Judge who abhorred the idea of joining the two in matrimony, even though she had promised her friend.

On the date set, Reva found herself in the middle of the ceremony weeping on the bride's shoulder. What could possibly be more embarrassing? A funereal silence! Not a cough, not a murmur! A few moments later she regained her composure and concluded the ceremony. Apologies by the Judge were in order, of course, but how could she announce to the happy crowd her displeasure at uniting a beloved friend to a tiddly suitor? However, the consensus of the guests was that the slip of control enhanced the tenderness of the occasion.

Reva kept the reason secret. Years later she decided she could confide in her friend about her dismay that sentimental day; she had observed the wife's exceedingly happy marriage with the husband who had discarded his bachelor drinking habits on taking his vows. The friend greeted the confession with a good-natured laugh and Reva was off the hook.

Earl Loury, with an ambition to become a detective, would occasionally make the night rounds in a police car. One morning he reported to Judge Bosone that he had just doused an ugly rumor.

A bartender had deplored the fact to Loury that a young woman claiming to be Judge Bosone's daughter had been getting plastered to the gills every night in his beer tavern. (Under Utah liquor laws, only beer was served over the counter.)

"How old is she?" Earl asked him.

"Oh, twenty, twenty-two."

"Well," Earl explained, "the Judge's daughter is ten years old and is always with her mother when she isn't at home with an attendant!"

The bartender's reaction was amazement, according to Loury. He had believed the phony barfly. On hearing this story, the Judge wondered how many others had believed the imposter as she made her alcoholic rounds. But eventually Reva resolved her feelings to expect similar displays of invidiousness.

The inevitable threatening letter arrived a year and a half after Reva was elected to the bench.

"We are hired to get you and we will," it read.

The chief inspector wasn't too concerned when the Judge showed it to him. But later when she received another threat from Los Angeles signed with skull and bones warning her to get off the bench or they would "take your kid," he gave Reva strict survival instructions and then quizzed her about her desire to stay on the job under the circumstances.

"Nobody is going to tell me what I can and can't do!" she announced. "If some gangster thinks he is scaring me, he isn't!" All of which was reiterated by Uncle Jack Beck in the hometown, "Reva won't get off the bench. She'll stay!" But she asked for a bodyguard for young Zilpha and a houseguard around the clock. The chief inspector, with the support of the city commissioners, provided a bodyguard for the Judge for a month. Her daughter was ultimately protected for three years. And as an added safeguard, the newspapers refrained from breaking the news at the outset.

Reva avoided frightening Zilpha with the alleged kidnap details and sidestepped her question, "Mama, why does Roy have to be with me all the time?" Judge Bosone reflects painfully on the penalties of being a public official; to this day, if she fails to meet her daughter at a preestablished time, Zilpha is most disquieted.

The Steady Begetting

IN 1973 the dean of the College of Law at the University of Utah, Samuel D. Thurman, who has since retired from that post, wrote Reva Bosone, "You are my number one example of what women can accomplish in this world."

To gain insight if not complete understanding as to why one woman combines so many of the winning virtues to enhance the quality of life for so many, it would be necessary to harken to her precursors.

Reva's Great-grandfather Stephen Chipman (mother's side) and his wife, Amanda Washburn Chipman, were among the immigrants who began arriving in the Great Salt Lake valley during late September 1847, two months after Brigham Young made his July 24th pronouncement to his advance company (called the Pioneers): "This is the place!" The second contingent was described by Orson F. Whitney in his *Popular History of Utah* as including four large companies numbering 1500 men, women, and children, 560 wagons, and 5,000 head of stock. Joseph Smith, founder of the Church of Jesus Christ of Latter Day Saints, had been assassinated in Illinois and Brigham Young had been made the leader of the courageous travelers.

PHOTO: *The Grant Hotel, American Fork, Utah.*

In due course, President Young directed the Chipmans, the Motts, and the Adamses (Maude Adams, the great actress, was a descendant) to inhabit an area that came to be known as American Fork, thirty-three miles south of Salt Lake City.

The head of the Mormons was practicing polygamy, as he had before arriving in the Great Salt Lake valley, so the brethren who could afford it were taking extra wives, as their leader directed them to, although it was said there were those in the membership at that time who were not convinced of the rightness of the plural marriage precept.

The advantages of this new religion were numerous: vigorous family participation, healthful doctrines, purported sainthood in this world, and the chance of reaching celestial glory in the next. But polygamy was something else—especially could it be ignoble and the greatest putdown for the first wife. Many wives cooperated, of course, but many never dreamed the "Principle" would eventually involve them!

When Stephen announced one day that he had seen a pretty immigrant girl named Phoebe Davis whom he planned to marry and bring home, Amanda, of strong rockbound Massachusetts forebears, told him to go float a log.

"You take an extra wife, Stephen, and come through the front door with her, and I will take my five children and go out the back door."

Stephen did, and Amanda did, and never did the twain get together again. Her action was defiance of the institution of the Church in a culture with inhibited divorce laws. (Stephen, to his credit, did support his first wife and children.)

Courage was in long supply for the Mormons, and problems—internal or external—had beset those whose lifestyle was radically different from the mores of the day. Historian Whitney said that Abraham Lincoln "was well-acquainted with the people who had founded Utah, having known them in Illinois, and they looked upon him as a friend. When asked, after his election in 1860, what he proposed to do with the 'Mormons,' Lincoln answered: 'I propose to let them alone.' He compared the Utah question to a green hemlock log on a newly cleared frontier farm—'too heavy to move, too knotty to split, and too wet to burn.' He proposed to 'plow around it.' "

One of Amanda's children, William Henry (Reva's grandfather), made himself wealthy in the cattle and sheep business. A widower with two children, he married Eliza Adams Filcher, daughter of one of the first school teachers in Utah. Eliza's family had emigrated from England as converts to the Church, but when her parents grew to realize they could not sustain a belief in polygamy, they deserted Zion for California. Prior to their departure, Henry had promised to follow soon with Eliza and the children. But an attractive girl on an immigration train of handcarts and wagons gave a different perspective to his life and changed Henry's mind; he made Sarah Binns his second wife and the enlarged family remained in Utah, much to the everlasting regrets of Eliza's people in California.

Eliza seemed to accept her life, however. She taught her husband and his second wife to read and write. Besides the care of her nine children, she accepted the responsibility of dividing the food and home supplies between the two households. At age thirty-eight she died with the birth of her tenth child, who succumbed with her.

Meanwhile, back at the California ranches, Eliza's parents, three brothers, and a sister prospered and were content in their new environments of Auburn, Marysville, Pacific Grove, and San Francisco. Their progeny were fewer and accomplishments more pronounced. Her brother Joseph, for one (whom Reva is said to resemble), became a newspaper editor and later president of the State Board of Trade, representing California at world's fairs. He disavowed his Mormon beliefs and denied his Utah residency because of polygamy.

Reva's mother, Zilpha Ann Chipman, was number five in the family of nine and was but nine years old when her mother Eliza died. Sarah, her stepmother (or the other wife), bore four more than Eliza's ten; fourteen plus nine (one died) plus two (Henry's children from his first marriage) made a houseful! Zilpha opined that she used to feel about as important as a chicken!

Nonconformity, as exemplified in Amanda and later in Reva, was showing up clearly in Zilpha, who was the only one of either set of children who did not become a devout Mormon. She continually recoiled at hearing, "If you see a woman you want to marry, marry her," or "If you see a man you want to marry, ask him." She demonstrated the independence of progenitor John Howland who had arrived in this country on the *Mayflower*.

After being restrained from studying music at home, Zilpha received encouragement from a couple living across the street; they gave her access to their organ and she became proficient in organ and voice. Zilpha's father, though wealthy, did not subscribe to extensive education for his children, especially for his daughters, which resulted in his daughters' well-founded resentment later in their lives. His prejudice was most noticeable in his will, which specified that his daughters each receive 600 sheep but his sons were to receive not only more than 600 sheep each but also wealth of money and property. Ironically, the brothers' good fortune ran out in the economic panic of 1921 and the daughters enjoyed the affluence of the family.

Zilpha matured believing that the development of a woman's mind gave her the edge in serving humankind. Although shy in formal education she was determined to improve herself, reading the Bible, Book of

Mormon and all the books of the Mormon doctrine, books on Buddhism and Mohammedanism, the Harvard Classics, H. G. Wells, Rousseau, Voltaire, Thomas Jefferson, and the newspapers, always. And for lighter reading her favorite poets were Robert Burns and Walt Whitman. Through strong-jawed discipline, she creditably educated herself. As she read, writers became her most admired class of people. She avoided novels, but relented, however, in the 1920s and read *Main Street* by Sinclair Lewis because she was told she resembled a main character.

The dark-haired, gray-eyed Zilpha grew to womanhood gracefully. At a dance at the Opera House a handsome bachelor, Christian Mateus Beck, fixed his sights on the willowy Zilpha and demanded of a friend, "Make me acquainted with that girl with the pretty legs."

Legs have always been exceptional in this family. Women for generations have been highly favored. The saying, "Legs, not diamonds, are a girl's best friend!" would be fitting here.

Anyway, they stood Zilpha in good stead; in 1889, when she was twenty-one, she married Chris, thirty-three, who had not hurried his selection of a mate. They set up housekeeping in the wildly picturesque small town of Alpine, just north of American Fork. Alpine was chosen because of the Mormon bishop's aversion to polygamy. In fact, he was known to discourage the practice among the members, advising the husbands to take care of the wife they had.

The Beck's first child, Clarence, was born in that foothill village. When a move to American Fork was contemplated, Zilpha offered for sale the 600 sheep left to her by her father so Chris, whose vocation was raising and training fancy horses, could buy a livery stable. In American Fork, Chris, who was handy with his tools, built a four-room house for his budding family.

Chris's genealogy is rooted in Denmark, where Reva's Great-grandfather Jacob Stephenson Beck, born in Hune Hjorring, was a schoolmaster. Four of his eight children emigrated from Denmark as converts to the Mormon church: Frederic, Christian, Stephen Jensen Beck (Reva's grandfather, who was born in Salturm and was skilled as a carpenter) and a daughter, Lucy.

Unbelievable adversity tagged her grandparents (Stephen and his wife Kirstine) after leaving their homeland in 1862 with their five sons, Jacob, Peter, Stephen, Theodore, and Christian (Reva's father). They made the fateful decision after listening to proselyting missionaries and were reinforced in that decision by Kirstine's conviction that they should abdicate their old way of life for a freer one in the new world.

It was Kirstine, however, who felt the first flogging of fate. The ship on which the religious converts set sail, the *Franklin,* carried 600 passengers, and in that wash of humanity and discomfort in steerage class, daily compromises with hopes and dreams must have been endured. Under those presumably cold, chaotic, restrictive, and always physically harsh conditions, Kirstine gave birth to her sixth son, August, who survived only briefly; malnutrition haunted that ship like an unknown sea monster. Besides lack of good food, an outbreak of measles proved devastating.

Peter, Chris's older brother who was twelve at the time, related: "Over fifty deaths occurred during the sea voyage and as was customary at that time the bodies were rolled in canvas or burlap, weighted, and dumped overboard. I was a young boy and inexperienced, very homesick, and the impression made on my mind of this gruesome sight will never be erased from my memory."

After the weakened family arrived in America they continued, via cattle cars, to Winter Quarters (now Florence, Nebraska), where they joined a company readying to cross the plains. Working their way past the country of the sly but generally friendly Pawnees and Sioux along the north bank of the Platte River, now known as "The Old Mormon Trail," most of the ablebodied, including Stephen and his barefoot sons, walked the thousand miles from the Missouri River to the Great Salt Lake valley. The Beck family then moved thirty-one miles south to Lehi. Having few resources, they could see that their lot would be marked by deprivation.

The proposed fulfillments of the gospel made day-to-day hardships bearable. Great granddaughter Cora Beck Adamson relates an incident when Kirstine with several of her children spent long hours gleaning what heads of wheat they could find in a field left by a farmer just to be able to make a loaf of bread for her hungry brood. Then along came the farmer and confiscated her meager bundle.

Chris, at age eight, took charge of sheep at the Point of the Mountain, a windy remote bend in the straight route from Salt Lake to points southeast. The howl of the coyotes was unsettling to the gritty little boy, left on his own to stand staunch against the fears of the endless nights. The responsibility for the sheep was his contribution to the family's finances. Relieving the pressure of the solitude was the sight of an occasional stagecoach rounding the infamous bend in the distance and once an actual stagecoach robbery! The witnessing of that holdup made storytelling for his own children an exciting adventure.

Stephen F. Beck tells how his father, Jacob (Chris's oldest brother), pitched hay barefoot all one summer and when he collected his due, which was paid in products instead of money, his tender consisted of one old sheep, a shotgun, and five gallons of molasses. And a bitter pill was the forfeit of one-half the molasses for a ride to his home in Lehi!

Despite the religious influence that had resulted in the upheaval of spirit and body from everything familiar in Denmark, all was not placid for Kirstine in Utah. After enduring trials more severe than can be imagined in a push-button society, she left the faith after two years, informing the missionaries that the Church was not as they had depicted it.

The family then settled permanently in Alpine, six miles to the north, where Stephen built a stout house, still standing, and drove the mail route. Kirstine, over the years, gave birth to two more sons and one daughter— John, Dan, and Laura—the youngest two having the benefit of a substantial education which was then not the custom. Kirstine, who excelled as a seamstress, kept a rather casual house, blamed on the fact that she always had a book on her lap. But she was highly respected in the community and her children contributed much to the area's well-being.

Several years after the move to American Fork, the Chris Becks had increased their family to include Horace and Reva. Wanting to build up the family income, Zilpha convinced Chris that they should invest in the Grant Hotel in American Fork, a large one for so small a town, which she would manage with the additional help of two cooks and three maids. Reva recalls at age three accompanying her mother on a visit to the hotel, which was built in 1890, when the purchase was being considered. It included a large lobby, a parlor, salesmen's conference rooms, a dining room, and twenty-five bedrooms. The previous owners had run the establishment into the red, so the Beck family moved into an apartment in the hotel to give it their full attention. Chris, meantime, had become the first manager of the Bell Telephone Company in town and the representative of Standard Oil Company in North Utah County. Zilpha's ability in hotel management and Chris's business acumen eventually netted the Becks a plenteous income. Fourth child, Filcher, named after his mother's prominent relatives in California, completed the family.

By the time Reva was seven her mother and father had fortified their savings account, having built up the hotel to a prosperous status, so they decided to sell and move back to the frame house, one-half block south. Two years later Chris built an eight-room pressed brick house beside the original home, but the family enjoyed its roominess and convenience for only four years because the Becks were forced to shift their residence back to the hotel in one of several similar moves caused by the buyers' mismanagement. Repeatedly, Mother Zilpha would pull the floundering hostelry from exhausted resources only to confront the same situation in a few years.

"Mother, with the business ability of the Chipman family, could roll out ten cents and have it come back twenty-five cents, always!" said Reva.

William Gladstone wrote: "Any man can stand up to his opponents; give me the man who can stand up to his friends." The Becks could paraphrase the quote, "Give me the man who can stand up to his relatives!" The relationship with the Chipmans would have to be documented in any biographical account of the Becks because of its impact on the family's life for several generations. In recent times, for example, with the exception of one cousin, Manda, certainly no overt support has ever been rendered Reva, the family luminary, by the Chipmans.

Chris and Zilpha were leery of having the cousins privy to their income data, and rightly so, but they were helpless to do otherwise. While the hotel was prospering, Zilpha's cousins were operating the town's Big Red Store and the only bank in town. One day one of those cousins commanded Chris to sell the livery stable to a brother, Fon, or they would set up opposition. Zilpha, realizing they were being squeezed out of American Fork's livery stable business, called the cousin what he was. Reva says, "Mother and Harry Truman concurred in calling a spade a spade." Zilpha was not in the slightest impressed by the Chipman worldly goods. Chris felt compelled to sell, but being an expert carpenter, he and his wife agreed that he should construct another livery across town. In time, Fon found he was no match for the competition.

Later Chris leased a corner lot across the street from the hotel and once again built a livery stable—for the convenience of the guests. When the ten-year lease expired, the bank cousins again called in Chris. They explained that they had a chance to sell the ground but if he wanted to buy it for $3,000, he had the option. In those days, $3,000 amounted to a big-time double cross. Reva has a vivid recollection of her parents in agitated discussion at the hotel over this outrageous turn of events!

"Chris, what about the lot back of the hotel?" Zilpha was pondering the size for a proposed livery. After a measuring job, they concluded it was big enough and Chris commenced to tear down the livery stable on the corner and build behind the Grant Hotel. The anxious expression on the faces of the Chipman cousins as they watched each two-by-four being yanked away is well etched in Reva's memory. The bank received the consequences—a vacant lot which remained that way for ten years!

The Becks would have preferred to heed the old English proverb paraphrased, "If a man plays you a dirty trick, shame on him. If he does it the second time, shame on you." But the cousins controlled the only bank in town. Eventually another bank, Peoples State Bank, opened its door and the Becks then divided their deposits; however, the mouthwash of time, almost three generations, has not dissipated the bitter taste.

Reva was just a tot when the Becks saw an opportunity to buy the Pioneer Opera House, an impressive structure with thick adobe-lined walls and an expansive stage, second only in size in Utah to the venerable Salt Lake Theatre. With roomy dressing rooms, a gallery, and an audience floor that could be raised to meet the stage level for town dances, then lowered to accommodate an orchestra, it had been the hub of all community entertainment even before Reva was born. After the Becks acquired it, Chris managed it successfully for fifteen years and renowned theatrical companies would schedule American Fork appearances there because of its eminent reputation.

Throughout Reva's young life she danced, sang, and acted in home-town productions in this opera house. How did this shy girl whose hair and height made her so vulnerable rise above remarks such as, "Get in the back of the line, Red!" and "You big lummox!" to perform in public? The foremost reason was that Reva, being no dummy, knew she was good—far and away above the competition. Requiring little direction, she was classified a natural, adept at learning anything quickly—lines, dance steps, song verse. In fact, her memorizing abilities were judged phenomenal! When a woman vaudeville director visiting from New York heard that nine-year-old Reva had learned sixteen dance steps in one af-ternoon in preparation for an appearance before her, she urged her mother to allow Reva to accompany her back to New York City for a career in dancing, an offer Mrs. Beck sensibly declined since her daughter's heart was incapable of such strain.

Reva's love affair with the theatre was strengthened after an oc-currence when she was twelve. Gilmore Brown, who later became famous as the manager of the Pasadena Playhouse in California, arrived in town with his company for an engagement at the Pioneer Opera House, Staying at Mrs. Beck's Grant Hotel, he bemoaned the sudden loss of one of his leading ladies who had left the cast of "Pygmalion" because of a death in her family. Brown's mother, who was acting as his manager, inquired of Mrs. Beck the availability of any local talent who could substitute on such short notice. Recognizing a golden opportunity for her only daughter she suggested Reva.

"Why she's just a child—how could she?" Mrs. Brown was in-credulous.

"But she's tall," countered Zilpha Beck. "Arrange her red hair on top of her head and put her in a long dress—she'll look the part!" And know-ing the drive of her multitalented offspring, she proclaimed, "I guarantee she will know the part by tomorrow night!"

Mrs. Brown really had no options. Besides, she was intrigued, so it was a deal.

With the supreme willpower this youngster possessed, she se-questered herself in her room until each line was performance perfect. And she carried it off with such finesse that Gilmore Brown suggested that Zilpha Beck send Reva to him for tutoring—wherever he was on the road, that is—after she had finished her schooling which was to include the American School of Dramatic Art in New York City. However, nine years later Reva lost her faculty for quick memorization, influencing her choice of another career.

Young Abilities

THE TEENS INTRODUCED a new world; the stultifying self-consciousness disappeared as Reva's face showed beautiful beginnings and her body filled out in the appropriate places. Red hair became a distinctive feature. Freckles tended to fade, revealing a delicate complexion that was to her advantage a whole lifetime. A surprisingly vibrant personality emerged; free of cloying hangups, she concentrated on relationships with people.

Soon she found herself with the lead reins in her hand, serving as Girls' Association president and vice-president of her high school, winning the first debating cup for her high school, even directing the senior play—with the approval of the students—while taking the leading role!

Academically, Reva learned easily and with her spirited, compassionate manner she related well to her instructors. Her first boyfriend, Bert Duncan, was also cerebrally well endowed—school was just a walkaway for Bert, who felt no necessity for home study even for top grades.

PHOTO: *A 16-year-old "queen."*

The two students were ambling down the hill from American Fork High one afternoon. The building, looking down on the town, hasn't changed much from the sturdy three-story red brick building constructed in 1912—except for a few additions to the east. It has other uses these days, but the expansive view of Mahogany Mountain, spread directly in front of Timpanogos to the north, and silvery Utah Lake, three miles to the south, is still there. And the same locust and maple trees stand at the entrance.

This day the two teenagers, engrossed in conversation, looked down at their shoes shuffling in the dropped poplar leaves that frisked in the air at the motion. It was their once-a-day opportunity to settle the great issues of the world—often in heated argument. Bert, with six strapped library books slung over his shoulder, looked up and out toward the far peak of Mt. Nebo.

"You have to remember the Greek citizen in the great age had to have a certain amount of leisure to pursue knowledge."

"Sure, and do you know what Euripedes said?"

"Tell me."

" 'A slave is he who cannot speak his thought.' " Reflecting on the somber meaning, Reva added, "We never want to be slaves, Bert, to *any-body*. Submission to a potentate—how horrible! The ancient Egyptians were so suppressed."

"In a world of the spirit," Bert explained.

"Instead of in a world of reason."

"Well, it can't happen here, Reva, in our democracy."

"It would be more difficult right around here, anyway, in our Rocky Mountains," quipped Reva, "because rebels could hide out and absolute monarchs don't like that. They like a flatter land, they say, where they can watch over and whip their subjects into shape."

"You have a point. You know, the ancient Greeks just loved life. Art . . ."

"And sports," which led into a rollicking discussion of the Olympics. And quite suddenly they found themselves at the turning of their separate ways. "See you tomorrow."

Now, walking solo, Reva caught herself up short and mouthed, "Huh, we didn't argue even once!"

Having an insatiable curiosity, it is likely she drew the best from her teachers, one of whom was E. A. Morgan, one of those rare individuals students revere through their lives. Reva has felt gratitude that their paths crossed, she as his student. A tiny man with the inspirational grandeur of Mt. Timpanogos, says Reva, he instilled a devotion for English and American literature in his high school students that was hard to match in any college. He later moved to Brigham Young University, owned and operated by the Mormons, to continue his profession with inordinate dedication. Unfortunately for the youth of Utah, he died just a few years later.

Reva's first experience with sex discrimination arose when she ran for president of the school against one of the outstanding students, Marc Clark. The contest was tough—Reva assumed she was the first girl in Utah courageous enough to run for that high school office. The word "first" meant incentive, stimulus, ambition, and it carried a big stick in Reva's world. She witnessed fervent support in her campaign; even the townspeople got into the act with unprecedented interest and enthusiasm.

Then Principal Whittaker, a kindly man but of the "old school," called a meeting of the candidates and leading students explaining in halting tones that it just wouldn't do to have a girl president. It would be just too peculiar, boys and girls! Reva elbow-poked her girl friend, "This is it!"

The principal then outlined his suggestion as a compromise—Donald Vance (a third party) as president and Reva as vice-president. Whatever happened to Marc Clark in this wide sweep of the system Reva can't remember. Anyway, there was no arguing with an administrator who was staunch in his double-standard beliefs, so his suggestion/decision became final. Reva wasn't all that dejected because she felt confident of her influence among the students—eventually she would run the affairs of the student body, anyway!

Hijinks are always an inseparable part of student life, whether they are streaking, stuffing phone booths, panty raiding, or other antics less flamboyant but more mischievous. The American Fork High School seniors arranged a party, sans chaperones (now a word from the archives), one night in the domestic science rooms. As it was ending the boys claimed they knew where there was a supply of chickens and would fetch them if the girls would cook them. One of the spokesmen lived near the high school and claimed the chickens belonged to his father. When they returned with fowl of tremendous size, the girls' suspicions were aroused; Reva and the others quizzed the boys, giving them a vote of doubt. The boys stuck to their story, however.

But it was decided not to cook the chickens in school—in fact, not to cook them anywhere! After the party-goers debated all over town what to do with them, the chickens were ditched under a bridge, and mum was the big word! Next day the mayor of the town lodged a furious complaint that his prize chickens had disappeared. Seeing spills of blood at the school entrance and on the floor of the hall, the principal called a hasty conference of his top students for a grill session but no one squealed. When the heat was off, it was a boy who told and Reva says, "When anyone says a woman can't keep a secret, that's eyewash. My experience proves the opposite!"

In her senior year, Reva supplied the high tone of the American Fork High School debating team. In the competition between her school and Lehi High, the subject: "Should the United States Have a Strong Military Set-up?" had Reva arguing the negative side. Her instructor made the comment before the event that if Reva got angry she would be victorious. And the debater, topped by shining red hair, obliged in about the middle of the contest, which prompted the teacher to exclaim to his wife, "We have now won the debate!" Reva's efforts clinched the silver loving cup for A. F. High.

THE BECK family always considered American Fork more distinguished than most small towns in the country. A matter of pride, perhaps, but it does look up at the august Mt. Timpanogos (Sleeping Maiden), 11,750 feet high in the famed Wasatch Mountains of Utah. Its grandeur has inspired artists since before Pioneer days.

On I-15 from Salt Lake City, past the Point of the Mountain, are Lehi, north of which are the rugged Alpine Canyon and Box Elder Peak, then continuing south, American Fork, Pleasant Grove, Orem, Provo, Springville, and Spanish Fork, all running more or less parallel to Utah Lake and all firmly rooted in Mormon might and strength. Until just a few years ago these towns had a uniquely similar appearance; however, the building boom and the expansion of Brigham Young University have resulted in a rather drastic alteration of the contour of the countryside.

American Fork, named after a fork in the local river, was settled by Mormons and reflects the energy of those folk who were responsible for the first indomitable industries that sprang up on the Wasatch Front—sugar beet factories, woolen mills, mines, banks, and department stores.

One of the outstanding scenic drives in America is reputed to be on the American Fork canyon "loop." The smooth highway of today is quite different from the original road, but Reva's father, Christian Beck, took credit for assisting to design the forerunner of this majestically beautiful route. As the way winds upward, aspens send up their golden torches on a lush mountainside of oak brush and fir rouged by the crimson mountain maple. The granite cliffs of the craggy canyons brand this area The Rockies just as birches stamp the mien of New England.

Living in a hotel may have given Reva a head start in her awareness of the intricacies of human nature. The large dining room with six at a table was a most appropriate setting for story swapping. Many times a redheaded youngster was on hand, listening with wide ears while loquacious salesmen and rough, tough prospectors gave verbal form to their exploits between bites of apple pie.

The thought of mining prospectors, a genre generally removed from the current computer culture, links Reva with the good old days. Many of the older prospectors were permanent guests at her mother's hotel. Old man Hawkins and old man Osburn, stalwarts of the mountains, were "big, strong, honest, moral, and profane!" And they spoke their minds! Old man Osburn joshed Reva one day on seeing her with a wide ribbon around her hair tied in a large bow above the forehead, "My God, do you have a headache?"

No one knew why intelligent Mr. Hines preferred to be a hermit most of the year; he made the Grant Hotel his home when the heavy snows drove him out of the hills. And a bachelor guest, Mr. Dan, on his way to the local San Pedro station to catch a train would always swing Reva in the air, set her down gently, and present her with a whopping twenty-five cents, leaving behind an adoring girl. (After all, a night's lodging cost only 50 cents.)

At times the employes rather than the guests provided the intrigue. A pleasant competent cook was found to be stirring up more than soup and biscuits. Chris reported to his wife that town gossip described the nefarious visits with men of all ages in her hotel bedroom at night.

Well, scandal was certainly to be avoided, but the Becks could not fire their cook because of gossip—they needed proof. Her room was situated at the head of a flight of outside stairs, and, sure enough, by surreptitious observation one dark night of her clientele traipsing up and down those stairs, Chris decided the cook they were so fond of was expendable. But it wasn't without their regret and considerable embarrassment for the fifty-year-old femme fatale. As Saki said in *Reginald,* "The cook was a good cook, as cooks go: and as cooks go she went."

Another cook in the hotel's history, Mr. Parker, whose extracurricular life was not as involved as that of the lady cook of the night, was memorable for turning out the fancy cakes for Reva's birthdays; and Sena, one of the maids who was Reva's nurse when Mother Zilpha traveled to California, left behind kind memories.

The strenuous profanity—and in the early rural surroundings of physically straining work and the never-ending duel with nature there was no short supply—never became pedestrian for young Reva. Although she loved those mountain men and took for granted their speech patterns, she found difficulty in condoning it elsewhere; as a young person, she stayed conservative.

On being informed that a modern novel is shot through dozens of times with the word "fuck," the old-fashioned Judge winces. Not only does she move away from obscene words and jokes, she dislikes seeing a girl flaunt the absolute line of the breast in a scant-cut, form-fitting dress. In her youth, the "ruffle front" was a standard, especially for the flat-chested woman.

Although an early snapshot of her in one of those unbecoming flaw-revealing, low thigh–length wool bathing suits—undoubtedly clammy when wet—shows a most respectable figure with well-rounded proportions, Reva considered herself small busted and so a ruffle front in street dress became the perfect camouflage. Nowadays she hoots at the exaggerations considered "fashion" then.

Years have mellowed her stance on profanity, too, and long ago she accepted the fact that well-meaning intelligent people may utter vulgar and foul language for no apparent reason. She grew tolerant in judging others while holding herself detached. The one indiscretion she allowed herself was the occasional use of the classic "damn" and "hell"; these remain her most potent words in a tense atmosphere. Used with the right timing, she says, these words are guaranteed to relax any uptight individual uncertain in mixed company conversational manners.

Her liberal view on those two four-letter words evolved over the years, however, since she mentally condemned any contemporary who used them. But her attitude boomeranged. Once mistaken for being ten years older because of her dignified and precise demeanor, Reva reacted like any other sixteen-year-old—with indignation. She did not want to be twenty-six, yet!

THE YEAR before Reva graduated from high school, she and her future sister-in-law, Hazel, daughter of former Governor of Utah John C. Cutler, asked permission of their parents to take a summer trip to Yellowstone National Park. Reva was older than the high school student of today because of the later starting age in elementary school and because the family had moved to Salt Lake City one year, which had upset the grade classification. The girls considered themselves mature enough to be on their own.

Both girls' parents shared an opinion that money spent on lavish clothes or whims was foolery while expenditures on books or trips for their educational advantage were worthwhile. Also heartily approved was attendance at theatre plays and musical events, and frequently the Becks would board the Interurban (or "Bamberger" train) for Salt Lake City and an afternoon or evening of culture. Hazel's folks, living in Salt Lake City, always held a box at the Salt Lake Theatre.

So the girls' wish was granted and Reva and Hazel, whom Reva referred to as her beautiful friend, were allowed to tour the park in a horse-drawn stagecoach, the last year of stagecoaches before the incipience of the automobile bus for tourist travel. It was also one of the last seasons when all the beautiful hotels were in operation. Since the auto buses "whizzed" through the park in three days, a few of those hotels were forced to shutter their windows and doors for lack of patronage.

Deluxe accommodations and sumptuous food made each overnight stay in the world's most famous national park a glorious holiday, and the dress-up dances to a live orchestra every evening were just what the teen-agers ordered. On their return, the vivacious travelers agreed that a more pleasurable vacation did not exist.

Mother Zilpha

EARLY IN THE 1900S, sparsely sprinkled among the saturated populace of Latter Day Saints were the Protestants. It wasn't an easy life being a non-believer in a predominately one-church community, but Reva's mother was an example of the complimentary association with the church one woman could have—even standing alone. Her intelligence and sincerity impressed the townspeople who accepted her in the Church's activities. The Mormons, with a reputation for hospitality and kindness, were in turn respected by Zilpha Beck. The Chris Becks paid their assessments to the Church when the Second Ward chapel and the tabernacle were built, regarding the buildings as civic improvements.

The goodwill on both sides was appreciated. Zilpha's daughter was always treated graciously and requested to present her dramatic readings at many missionary farewells and homecomings. Included on picnics and camping trips, Reva keeps a poignant memory of the Church's generosity during an impressionable period of her life. Fun-loving Reva, having escaped from her childhood cocoon of anxieties, was pulled into the nucleus of many groups.

Her innovative mind never shut down. Once on a week's outing in

PHOTOS: *Zilpha Chipman Beck and Christian Mateus Beck.*

American Fork Canyon with a number of girls of the Mutual Improvement Association, Reva and a coconspirator planned to overturn the tedium. So one night when all the vacationers were silent in their long line of beds on the screened porch, the two jokesters sprang out of bed shouting, "A rat!"

Shrieks, screams, bedlam! Benightied girls leaped around on that porch as though it were a red-hot stove top. After a few noisy moments, someone noticed two of their members lying comfortably in bed laughing a lot and the others suddenly realized that tonight the joke was on them. Chuckling, they crawled into bed again and were soon asleep. But one wonders whether Reva's lifelong aversion to the rodent family is penance.

Zilpha Beck was a member of the first order of pragmatists; her child-rearing principles were unique and workable. As a child, Reva remembers being peeved at her mother one day, so with a pair of scissors she snipped off a hunk of her own hair above the forehead, quite sure it would cause consternation. But her mother played the entire scene like a dowager duchess, totally ignoring the flaunted ragged tresses; a daughter's simmering temper had to cool down all by itself and a hot head had to grow more hair.

As a high school girl subject to the whims and fancies of teenagers, Reva wistfully remarked to her mother one spring day as she looked out the hotel window and saw three of her friends walking by, "Ruby, Reba, and Dorothy each have on a new silk dress. I don't have one and yet we can afford it more than they can!"

Her mother responded, "Well, I believe in dressing up the mind." This remark, which was to linger all her life, pacified Reva who had been assured she would be going away to college while her friends would not. Mother Zilpha, surely an early advocate of the principles of women's liberation, operated a tight ship regarding her children and attendance at college. No question about it—all four were scheduled for complete educations! When friends, in the early part of the century, expressed puzzlement at sending a daughter to an institution of higher learning, Zilpha would reply, "You bet I am! Too many women have to make their own way and rear children who are not prepared to do so." Zilpha, being the dominant member of the Beck duo, took the initiative in child-rearing principles.

Although they would announce, "My children are not going to work for the other guy," the Chris Becks as employers and landlords let their sympathy run with the employe and the one who had to rent. Fairness and equal opportunity were key words in their family; they forever championed labor's rights.

The Equal Rights Amendment would have set well with Zilpha. In her estimation there was no separate man's work or woman's work; it was everybody's work. Many times, for instance, her sons were put to the task of mopping the hotel floors when the maids were too weary, or Reva was appointed to change the faucet washers.

Rap sessions at the dinner table were to be counted on and every family member became involved. Chris and Zilpha, well informed on the news of the day, praised Teddy Roosevelt for his courageous and progressive legislation and, over the years, Senators Norris of Nebraska, Johnson of California, Borah of Idaho, La Follette of Wisconsin, and, on the local scene, Governors Cutler and Bamberger. And those who had failed to carry out a public trust were noisily denounced—"elevated scrub" were two well-polished words in Zilpha's vocabulary. Subjects of numerous discussions, public lands and power would absorb as much as three hours at the dinner table.

In matters of discipline the offspring received their share but they were never hush-hushed, so they felt safe in saying whatever was on their minds. Reva was present when her mother lay in bed recuperating from an illness; brother Horace came in to talk and included a dirty story he had picked up on the corner. A neighbor visiting Mrs. Beck at the time expressed shock that a mother would permit her son such an indulgence, and Zilpha replied, "How else would I know what the young people are talking about up on the corner if my sons didn't feel free to tell me?"

Zilpha also encouraged her brood to attend the church of their choice for the moral values and self-control stressed. And at the dinner discussions Reva's ideas rated as high as the boys'. Consequently, they grew up with respect for each other, a healthy regard for women's abilities, and a tolerant view of churches. Having grown up in that atmosphere, Reva has declared in public life, "Show me a man who has a smart and intelligent wife or sister or mother and I'll show you a man who believes in the ability of women. Generally speaking, men who refuse to recognize a qualified woman on their staff or as their opponent or in public office suffer from an inferiority complex. Show me an intelligent man and I'll show you a fair-minded one."

Reva's father was one who respected an intelligent and enterprising woman and he always conferred with his wife whenever business changes were in the offing. Although occasional chuckholes pitted the smooth road of their marriage, the union was firmly based on mutual admiration.

To KEEP in step with progress, Chris Beck made necessary changes in the opera house by installing new seats for the first motion picture theatre in town. Shortly thereafter, a townsman wanting a piece of the profitable action set up a similar but smaller operation. He just happened to be a livery stable competitor.

Reva had been enrolled as a student at Westminster College in Salt Lake City just three days when she received the crushing news that the opera house had burned to the ground! With eyes filled to overflowing she learned that at three in the morning a man had screamed outside the Grant Hotel, "Mr. Beck, the opera house is on fire!" The Becks awakened to brilliant orange and red flashes piercing the black sky. The heavens were lightning bright. Chris and Zilpha threw on their clothes and dashed to the site just down the road from the hotel where furious flames were lashing from the roof over the stage—the huge stock of scenery was plainly enriched fodder for the ravenous blaze.

The owners could do nothing but stand by helplessly with aching hearts. The friend who had alerted them reported that he was passing the building and smelled smoke. After investigating, he found the back door ajar. The fire was pushing toward the ceiling of the stage and he smelled kerosene! As Zilpha watched the fiery demolition of the beloved structure, the man she suspected of arson returned to the scene of the crime and spoke to her.

"You did a good job!" she cried. He merely turned and walked away.

The heavy bare walls—all that was left after the holocaust—became part of a large garage and later were converted into store space. It had been more an institution than a building, Reva says, "seasoned with innumerable sweet memories." Gone forever is a tradition now only tucked away in affectionate sentimental remembrance.

Westminster College figures prominently in Reva's life—it was there that her career goal veered from one direction, acting, to another, public service. She, who had been blessed with an ability to recite from memory material she had read only once or twice, found that in attempting to learn her part in the school play she not only was unable to accomplish this unusual feat but she was unable to memorize—period!

A professor at the University of California later explained this as not uncommon when young minds are overloaded with intensive mental activity and concentration; Reva had amassed eighty-one credits, or the equivalent of three years of study, in two years. At last her love of learning had been her undoing. At least in a sense. In another respect, an observer might say that her profound ability, exhibited lifelong, to ad-lib—a staple for a statesman and politician—was compensation.

In the fall of 1974, Westminster began its 100th year and its centennial celebration. The institution had been established to provide high school and junior college education for Protestant young people in the Utah Territory, but today the four-year college is interdenominational. A recent newspaper article carried plaudits from the Judge—she has long advocated the college's present policy:

Westminster's innovative alternative degree program evaluates a person's total life experience and awards credit for specific, documented learning experiences acquired throughout the individual's lifetime. It recognizes off-campus learning and growth and, supplemented with personalized on-campus classes, makes possible the attainment of a college degree.

During her first year at Westminster, which was housed in just two buildings—Ferry Hall and Converse Hall—Reva won the Fourth Annual Prohibition Oratorical Contest (worth $15) sponsored by the Third Presbyterian Church with her oration, "Temperance in Utah," perhaps a presentiment of her history-making program in the field of alcoholism. Publicity of her award showed paradoxically a photo of a sweet, wide-eyed, beribboned Reva accompanying a report of the prize oration, which was packed full of fire and pathos to the last paragraph:

As we scan the pages of history, it is shown where empires have passed away, nations have been forgotten, and great cities have been swept into oblivion. Reform upon reform has been established but yet intemperance goes on, the deadliest scourge that has ever darkened the pathway of man. The kingdom of alcohol has had control of the world to a certain degree since the time of Noah. Every generation and stake of civilization has known the sting of such a pestilence, and it has been left to us of the twentieth century to stand firm and united in the effort to propagate the greatest moral issue of the ages. . . .

But the evils of intemperance do not stop with the moderate drinker. If we should paint the black pictures of the thousands of drink-cursed homes in our cities we would be called radical. In truth we glance at one that is typical. See—the stormy night, the wan, worn-out mother nestling her dear ones close to her, who are tugging at her faded dress for bread—no home but a hovel—no clothes but rags—no warmth but in the cold stove. All at once the mother sits up frightened, she hears an unsteady shamble, a bang at the door; the husband—the father—staggers in. He is drunk. What inspiration is there for that family to live on when their very support has been wasted and shattered by that demon called alcohol. . . .

But what is the state of Utah doing for the unfortunate baby tugging at the withered breast of its broken-hearted mother whose husband has been coaxed to nurse an appetite for alcohol dispensed by virtue and under the protection of the laws of Utah? . . .

When the prohibition petition was presented to the legislature in 1913, it was absolutely ignored, although the majority of the people were speaking through the sacred right of petition. However, in 1915, the legislature succeeded in passing a prohibition bill by an overwhelming majority; but through some boss-ridden fluke in the Utah statutes, the governor was able to defeat the sovereign will of the people. And when the women of Utah sought to be heard, the same

bi-partisan persons turned the deaf ear of an adder to the appeal of
the destitute women and children. . . .

The liquor clique of this state is a composition of ignorance,
selfishness, avarice and stupidity to be equalled only by the same
composition to be found in the hills of Kentucky, converting God's
golden grain into hell's legal tender. So, if you want to be a hearty
supporter of everyone and everything that is corrupt, and of the poor
houses, asylums and prisons, patronize the breweries, distilleries and
saloons by allowing them to live. It remains for those who seek a
higher degree of civilization, a better humanity, and a stronger love
for God to put shoulder to shoulder, break the shackles of bondage,
and stop the onslaught of alcoholism.

A recent reading of the over-sixty-year-old oration set off explosive
hoots of laughter from the Judge. "I'll tell you, Carrie Nation had nothing
on me!"

Little did the world—or Reva—suspect that the future proponent of
Alcoholics Anonymous had been the unwitting victim of alcohol in her
own past when, as a teenager, she had regularly gulped down her spoons-
ful of Peruna for anemia. The patent medicine, a brownish liquid, was
found to be a goodly percent proof!

In June 1917 Reva graduated from the junior college with which she
associated a few traumatic memories but also many touching ones of
forming special friendships and achieving top grades. In August she entrained for the University of California at Berkeley, an institution long
revered by her mother. Zilpha Beck had envisioned one of her children
becoming a UC alumnus ever since she had visited with her Uncle Joe
Filcher in California.

Clarence had degrees from Brigham Young University and the
University of Utah. Horace, enamored of the stage, had become a song
and dance man on Broadway for a short time—perhaps the only male
from American Fork to make good on Broadway. He had also been a
player on the Ellison-White Chautauqua system. After returning to Salt
Lake, he took his law degree at the "U." Filcher, the youngest, was later
slated to study at Westminster and the "U." So it was Reva's destiny to
fulfill her mother's dream.

Reva stayed the first night in Berkeley at the Shattuck Hotel, the
Hilton of its day. That evening, suffering from a severe cold, she
remembers applying for medication at the hotel drugstore. As she was
waiting by the counter, a distinguished-looking man inquired whether she
would be a student at the university. Hearing that she would, he kindly
expressed the hope for her happiness there.

Even though groggy from the effects of the cold, Reva, greatly impressed by his hospitality, kept an eye out for the gentleman who was

stamped in her memory. During the orientation days that followed, she discovered the gracious stranger was none other than the president of the university, Benjamin Ide Wheeler. One Saturday afternoon on campus, as she approached the Campanile, she was stopped by President Wheeler, whom she recalled as handsome as he sat on his sleek black horse. Their lengthy conversation overwhelmed Reva who was conscious of the compliment this erudite educator/administrator was paying a mere student.

Soon after arriving in Berkeley she applied at the registrar's tables, which were set under the trees on the university grounds, and found that a clerk had slashed her three-year credit accumulation to a sophomore rating. At the moment, Reva had the slight consolation that most of the transfer students' credits were being cut—even those from Smith College—and she didn't mind too much not being rated a senior. But to be demoted to a sophomore was shattering! That night, in a strange city with no friends, she struggled with pent-up emotions. The thought of three more years when plans for her life were bursting to be tried, let alone the difficulty of the extra expense, was bearing down on her like a rockslide. The sympathetic manager of Chapelhurst, a women's dorm where Reva had moved from the hotel, encouraged her to call the registrar at home.

After raking up the nerve to phone him, she explained her predicament in despairing tones, and he suggested that she meet him in his office the following morning at eight o'clock. In the morning the queue of students waiting to see the registrar extended from his office three flights down and to the entrance of the building. When Dr. Wood saw Reva through the glass-paneled door, he motioned her in and asked his secretary to inform the waiting line that because of his indisposition, the students should return the next day. In his ill health, he decided to see only Reva.

She then showed him the catalog of Westminster College, of which he had never heard. She pled her cause with great effect, giving hint of her forensic expertise of the future, and Dr. Wood became one of the many to look upon Reva Beck as a talent out of the ordinary. He made her a provisional junior. She knew she would prove his faith in her, making the grade with her customary ease; since then Westminster students have had no problem matriculating at UC.

A professor who impressed Reva with the clarity of her high school teacher, Morgan, was Charles Mills Gayley, an authority on Shakespeare. Even though his class drew hundreds of students, the warmth and sympathy of his personality embraced every student before him. A tall man with large, expressive brown eyes, it was said that he bought so many United States bonds that he couldn't afford new clothes, appearing day after day in the same shoddy green suit.

"On my membership certificate, 'The Mayflower Descendants of

America,' the signature of Charles Mills Gayley is there as an officer in the California organization," Reva said. "When I practiced law in Salt Lake City, I often looked up at the framed certificate which brought back fond memories of a great man at the University of California.

"One never knows just how much the contact with inspirational human beings means to a young person," Reva affirms. "I have always felt that these particular men set valuable examples in my life—that my work and decisions may have followed unconsciously the light their image shed on my life as a young person. How can one measure the value of that touch of warmth and sympathetic gentle intellectuality that doubtlessly trickled down to every student on the campus at that time? It isn't the facts one learns in school that are important, but the interpretation of those facts by a spirit who understands their worth." One who in a few years hence would be regarded as a distinguished teacher was summing up the influential effects of her favorite educators.

The period spent at the University of California was memorable, too, for a severe affliction; Reva was not left out in the national flu epidemic, which was responsible for widespread devastation of life and comfort. Reva's bout was especially enervating, perhaps because her health status during her youth always fell short of being hale and hearty. The heart condition was not pampered but contemplated in her daily routine; anemia was a hindrance to sustained physical activity; and a susceptibility to colds and chest infections would occasionally cause her much distress.

During her illness at UC, dormmates demonstrated much devotion, caring for her night and day. Eileen Bowling and Kathryn Collins were singled out as special friends with whom Reva has corresponded from Woodrow Wilson days to the present. And although she had seen another college friend only once since 1919, she exchanged Christmas cards every year with Grace McMinn, the girl who didn't bother to wear a mask when she nursed Reva fifty-nine years ago!

After the summer break at home, the well-dressed senior was waved off to UC again by several relatives at the Union Pacific depot in Salt Lake. A snapshot of the day shows her wearing a jacket cut to midthigh length, a matching walking skirt ten inches above ground topped by a silk waist accented with a chain and pendant, a wide crowned velvet hat, and pointy shoes.

In evidence were sailors and doughboys in transit; the Armistice was three months in the future.

Resuming her studies and establishing a good record for her final year, Reva returned to Utah from the prestigious university with her sheepskin denoting a B.A. and infinite hopes in the summer of 1919.

Teacher—Then Student

HAVING BEEN ADVISED by her oldest brother to put on a few years before tackling the profession of law, which would lead her into the process of legislation, Reva decided to teach high school after she obtained her undergraduate degree. Offered contracts without solicitation at American Fork High and Westminster, she chose the former for its proximity to home. And the hometown girl, supported by an enthusiastic principal, soon felt exhilaration in teaching side by side with her former instructors. A year of teaching classes in English, gym, and public speaking and directing school and community plays passed pleasantly and quickly—in her public life, that is.

In her personal life she was weathering some turmoil. Late in the summer of 1921 a marriage of one year between Reva and Harold G. Cutler went amiss. A brother of her sister-in-law Hazel, Harold was a tall, attractive young man Reva had met while of high school age, but although both were of admirable character, even a casual observer could note that

PHOTO: *High school teacher, Ogden, Utah.*

their temperaments and personalities were too divergent to create lasting happiness.

Harold, back from the grueling sacrifices on the battlefront, demanded a home-type wife, but Reva, having applied herself with diligence to become uncommonly educated, did not fancy herself spending her days whipping up soufflés or doing needlepoint. In this case, opposites attracted but split up in a year, with Reva seeking a divorce.

So, back to a career! Signing a contract with a $250 raise in salary, she then positioned herself in a high school in Delta, a small town on the railroad in western Utah. Loving the students who were short on the luxuries of life but long on zeal and aptitude, she was unable to communicate with the rather uneducated principal who even had trouble speaking the English language properly. So in a year she moved on to Ogden Junior High and then to Ogden Senior High School (Ogden is Utah's second largest city, located on the Wasatch Front, thirty-five miles north of Salt Lake City).

Fifty years ago, as now, education classes were required for a teaching certificate. Reva has her own stylized opinions on the efficacy of those classes; she is adamant that the time she wasted on them would have been more wisely spent on exciting subjects of which she was deprived.

"I remember once the professor asked what a teacher would do if, while her class were in session, a band playing lively music marched by the schoolhouse. I was called on. Frankly, I had found the textbooks in the course so unstimulating and so uninteresting that I hadn't read them thoroughly. But to answer the question, I reasoned, 'I would dismiss the class to go to the windows to listen and when the band marched on, I'd reconvene the class.' The professor exclaimed, 'That's right!' My, my, it certainly took a lot of brains to think of that one. Ever since those classes, I have had a prejudice against education courses."

Her pet peeve remains the unbalanced importance placed on the requirement of a certificate or degree. "There is so much room for improvement in the teaching field. Sure, I'm for degrees, to an extent—after all, I have two—but to say that a degree supercedes knowledge and ability where there is an abundance of each is unfair. A degree should be considered but it should not be the sole determining factor in the selection of teachers."

During Reva's teaching career at Ogden High, she was appointed supervisor of the Dramatic Arts Department as a result of a superlative record. In her second year in Ogden her enterprising methods and competitive spirit had boosted her debating team to the top spot; she had directed the successful presentation of *Clarence* at the Orpheum theatre in "Broadway" time (no time lost on amateurish prompting); and she had spurred the oratorical contest to fresh heights. Principal Albert Merrill recognized a conscientious whirlwind when he saw one and recommended her for a double raise in salary—which she received!

Dr. Garff B. Wilson, now University of California at Berkeley drama professor, an authority on the American theatre, and author of *Three Hundred Years of American Drama and Theatre,* sums up his feelings:

> For the first few days of the new term, I and other students of similar interests watched, measured, and evaluated our new teacher, Miss Beck. Then we capitulated—completely. She cast a spell over us. She became the most magnetic, stimulating influence in our lives. She was friendly, forceful, and clear-headed—with a fine sense of humor and a resonant, vibrant voice. Her classroom became the gathering place of everyone interested in Oral Expression—the term, in those days, for speech and drama. We took classes from her, we tried out for the debating team, for the oratorical contest, and for the annual school play. We could not keep away from her room. Every morning before classes started we would dash in to have a word with her. Every afternoon, when classes were over, we would gather to talk, to discuss, to ask questions, to get advice. And we would stay on and on and on until Miss Beck, completely exhausted, would call it a day, or until our parents, irate and puzzled, would telephone the school and order us to come home for dinner.
>
> Reva Beck challenged our minds. She also revolutionized the "oral expression" activities. Before her arrival, these activities had been moderately dull and fairly unsuccessful. The year book for my sophomore year records that the debating team did not win a single contest; competition in oratory was not mentioned; the school play rated two photographs but no comments. The year Reva Beck took charge, things changed dramatically. The year book records that the negative debating team, i.e., the team which took the negative side of propositions, won all of its contests. The affirmative team, of which I was a member, did the same. In oratory, eight of Miss Beck's students qualified for places in a competition sponsored by the Sons of the American Revolution, and all three winners were coached by her. The major oratorical contest of the year, a competition between three high schools of the area, was won by another student coached by Miss Beck—myself. I'll never forget the theme of her coaching: "Sound natural," she said. "Keep it true. Be sincere."

Garff Wilson, whose cherubic face belied the intense dedication that resulted in his selection as valedictorian of his graduating class, applied himself as a thespian, also. He had previously appeared in a few amateur plays, mostly church-sponsored, but they were nothing, he insists, compared to the experience Reva provided. He remembers:

> The cast was selected after a series of lively tryouts. Then we settled down to weeks of daily, intensive rehearsals. What a thrill they were!

We had no stage in our high school so we rehearsed in Miss Beck's room. Now the lucky members of the cast got to monopolize Miss Beck. As soon as our regular classes were over, we trooped to her room and worked like beavers under her demanding direction. We were the envy of the school. Now we had a reason to stay after school every night in Miss Beck's room—and a reason which even our puzzled parents understood.

George M. Cohan's melodrama, "Seven Keys to Baldpate" was the most memorable event in Garff's senior year. Miss Beck was reported as a slave driver, requiring the play's participants to memorize all their lines during the first week. "You can't concentrate on meaning and emotion if you're fumbling for words," she hammered home to the would-be John and Ethel Barrymores.

Miss Beck, while pulling and stretching the play into shape, permitted no slack in class attendance, and so the assiduous coach and players kept long hours. As a result, the performance, staged again at the Orpheum, was reviewed enthusiastically. Minister Dr. Edward Carver, who had witnessed the production on Broadway, claimed the local one was its equal! The Ogden newspaper noted that the cast surpassed expectations and handled their parts admirably. "Amateurs find difficulty in holding their characters throughout a play, yet these boys and girls succeeded in overcoming this difficulty remarkably well. They lived their characters, and carried their audience away into the mystery-shrouded inn." A letter received by Miss Beck and the cast from a co-worker conferred kudos, "Each one of the cast was almost professional. Undoubtedly this cast has set a standard difficult to excel."

And comment from the school was extravagant. "The fine thing about the play is that high school youngsters can be so skillfully trained as to attempt such difficult roles and succeed so well. Every member of the cast is entitled to high praise and commendation as also the instructor. The play reflects credit upon all participants and the school itself. The opinion of Ogden High School must have been raised at least a notch in the mind of anyone who witnessed that most splendid production."

Young Garff Wilson, who portrayed the author in the play and was on stage most of the time, is today, as an eminent UC educator, contemplating the presentation of the same drama with a group of Berkeley actors. And so "Seven Keys to Baldpate" will enjoy at least a half-century commemorative as far as Dr. Wilson's participation is concerned.

The professor waxed lovingly of his former teacher, with whom he still corresponds. Dr. Wilson speaks of the magic of the performance and the magic of Reva Beck's influence. "Since those days—so long ago—I have spent a lifetime writing about the theatre and teaching speech and drama in all its phases to university students. In the process of directing a play, or teaching a class, or delivering a speech, I am conscious of how often I echo ideas gained decades earlier from Reva Beck; how often I use methods which she taught me; how often I communicate attitude and points of view first encountered in her classes.''

"I feel sure that Garff has always thought my B.A. degree was in public speaking and dramatic art," divulged the ex-teacher, reminiscing fondly about a prize pupil.

"Well, I had only six hours in speech in college and they weren't good courses at all. What I thought and the way I taught originated with me. Someday I'll rake up courage to tell Garff because he has always claimed I was his inspiration. How I loved those teaching days!''

In 1925 Reva Beck, glowing from the accolades of the play's reception, sent some flattering clippings to her on-again off-again beau, then building a career in marketing teaching at the University of Colorado at Boulder, and Bert Duncan rushed his assurance, "I have always had unlimited confidence in your ability to 'make good' at anything you really wanted to. . . ."

Although her aspiration was to eventually read law, this job was no stopgap; Reva threw herself into it full force. Teaching was here and now, the bird in the hand, a vocation she respected enough to pursue indefatigably. It was her opportunity to touch the lives of young people and to plant guideposts. Having experienced a brief, unhappy marriage, she particularly welcomed the challenge this job was offering. It was certainly no stopgap—rather, a fulfillment, which precipitated her decision that teaching would be her first choice for a last job in her life.

Miss Beck's assertive students in debate and oratory made a grand slam in the competition at the University of Utah, much to the amazement of Dr. Maud May Babcock, head of the Speech Department at the "U." As far as Reva knew, every high school in Utah, except Ogden Senior High, employed one of Dr. Babcock's graduates to teach the art of oral expression. Reva's students, proving to be the most outstanding, provoked Dr. Babcock to inquire about the Miss Beck who had emerged the sleeper coach of the year—she had never heard of her.

Reva was delighted when she learned of the inquiry because the esteemed speech educator *had* heard of her—just forgotten! Years before, in her high school days, an experience involving Dr. Babcock hung heavy on her mind. But she chose not to let it suppress her desire to excel in a subject close to her heart.

"I had won the American Fork High School declamation contest and then the district contest. The selection I gave was 'Belshazzar's Dream,' a rather profound and certainly serious poem. The state competition was held in May at the 'U' with Dr. Babcock as judge. The principal of my school, Shedreck Jones, my mother, and a brother accompanied me to the auditorium in the horseshoe of the University of Utah in Salt Lake City.

"After I gave my reading, I looked down at the principal and my mother for assurance, which they reflected in their confident smiles. I knew I had performed as well as the other times. As each contestant finished, I became more confident—their presentations seemed so simple.

"When the judge gave her decision, she named as winner the girl who recited ' John Alden's Courtship,' the one I least feared! The only part of the reading that could show off a person's flair for expression was the tag line, 'Why don't you speak for yourself, John?' Well, I could see Mr. Jones was burned up! He and a group of adults I didn't know surrounded Dr. Babcock and wanted to know why I didn't win. As I remember, she said that 'Belshazzar's Dream' was a most difficult poem, altogether too difficult for a high school girl to recite, whereupon my principal jumped in with 'But if a high school girl presents it well, why shouldn't she be chosen?' He really was upset!

"Later Mr. Jones learned that 'Belshazzar's Dream' was the selection Dr. Babcock was using for her graduates that year. He decided that was the reason she wouldn't permit a mere high school student a chance to win with it."

The dominant personality of Maud May Babcock was most influential in drama in the West. She was undisputed in her teaching methods and in the standing of her department at the University of Utah. How fortunate that she was just curious about Miss Beck and did not feel obliged to investigate her credits for teaching speech.

It was a well-kept secret until comparatively recently that Reva presumed to impart the principles of the expression arts with little academic background, consisting of only two semester courses, but with a wealth of experience. She is very sure that department heads of college speech—those who are stolidly set on hiring degree people because letters after the name are more meaningful than a compelling speaking skill and the ability to clarify it—will not rejoice in this part of her history.

The principal at American Fork High School had been acquainted with her drama background and public speaking experience so did not question her teaching qualification; neither did any of her other employers in the speech field. Reva knew they were the exceptions, however, which takes us back to the diploma enigma.

"One reason some superintendents and principals stick so rigidly to requiring a diploma or degree is that they themselves could not get along without it. They know how to follow routine, don't care to go beyond it, so are comfortable with a degree and put their full faith and credit in it.

"Don't misunderstand me," Reva interjects, "there are brilliant people with degrees, of course, including superintendents and principals. My point is that the degree *alone* should not be the measuring stick of one's capability. And this goes especially for teaching. Teachers are so important that they should be chosen with as much care as one chooses a doctor or a lawyer. It's too bad we haven't made teaching a noble profession. What can be more precious than the development of all the fine potentialities that a young person possesses?"

To attempt changes for ethical uplift was in line with the development of potential. For instance, newspaper reading was an activity of Reva's English classes. Once, a gory murder had been much publicized and the reports described long lines of curiosity seekers waiting to view the woman's body in a funeral home. The next day Reva asked for a show of hands on how many in her class had stood in that line—apparently the majority. Whereupon she took the time to cast shame on a base human trait of vulgarizing someone's tragedy. When her discourse was completed, it was evident that not one student countenanced what he or she had done.

The 3:30 rush for freedom from Miss Beck's classes was unheard of! Quite the contrary—students, both boys and girls, stuck to her room like glue, student Garff Wilson maintained, causing Reva to assert that her most effective teaching was done après bell.

"The kids confided in me," she said, "and sometimes their confidences were shocking. Knowing my mother would never act shocked, I didn't either for fear they would clam up and then I wouldn't know what they were thinking. As a result, I was aware of all the little secrets that existed within a group of teenage people—who had a crush on whom and who reciprocated, who broke whose heart, and the whispered confessions. Believe me, I had a lot of consoling to do. But I never broke a confidence. Youngsters need heart-to-heart talks; they need to know that the teacher loves them and has their welfare always in mind.

"The boys would reveal the darndest things. A group of them had taken a jaunt in an old car one summer, and I remember their telling me one afternoon what had happened on that trip—harebrained and scary adventures! Finally, I said, 'Do your mothers know all this?' And they exclaimed, 'Naw, we wouldn't dare tell them.'

"I shall never forget the day my students asked, 'Miss Beck, may we call you Reva after school hours? You're more than our teacher; you're our friend.' Well, I wasn't quite sure I should let them because it could breed disrespect in certain situations. But by the way they asked me, I knew they meant it. So when the classes were dismissed each day, I was Reva."

That was at least fifty years ago, but Reva has steadfastly corresponded with many of her Ogden High friends and still hears from a few who are now past sixty-five.

"Those boys and girls I knew so well are now scattered all over the country. Most of them have been successful in their undertakings. Several have died. Several were so outstanding. One was Bud Walker, a splendid young man who often escorted me home after my night teaching classes, who was killed in World War II."

Another student to whom Miss Beck was devoted, Winifred McConnell, died young in 1932 and Reva carried her obituary in her wallet for many years. Winifred—intelligent, beautiful, and a talented pianist—touched deeply the life of her teacher and the tragedy of her early death was never quite forgotten.

Unabashed infatuation or admiration is reflected in notes to the beloved teacher. One from a girl student reads:

Dear Miss Beck,
    To be really writing to you, who has awed me so much that I hardly dared speak to, gives me a thrill.
    Everything seems so vague and queer that I suppose I shall not be able to say just what I would like to.
    All my friends have told me how much they love, admire, and respect you. For this reason my greatest desire has always been to know you as they do. I procrastinated, because I was really frightened or awed (I don't know what it was that I felt). Now this year has gone by and I do not have your friendship. I feel the loss, but in a distant way I think that I know you a little and carry on conversations with you in my mind.
    This all perhaps sounds silly, but it is the way things are.
    I wish you all the success and happiness in the world.
                                        Your admiring friend,
                                        LOIS FOWLER

Another of Reva's favorites sent her salutations in blue pencil on a yellow piece of paper: "Dearest Reva, I haven't reached that stage of affluence which permits me to enjoy the luxuries of either Christmas cards or calling cards. In lieu of them I'll use this. This is to let you know I still love Reva. EMERSON."

Others with whom she has chatted on paper over the years include Frank Rose, now a judge with the appellant court in California; Dr. Wilson, of course; Marjorie Anderson Blair; Dorothy Higginbotham; Hal Armstrong; Kate Healey; Jean Warner; Evelyn Wood, of Reading Dynamics (speed reading) fame; Midge McKay, niece of the late president of the LDS Church, David O. McKay, all of whom attest to the long-term effect of her teaching.

To go the extra mile in teacher/student interaction, Reva accepted invitations from her class to go horseback riding and ice skating. Those excursions turned out to be adventures; goaded by ebullient and spirited young people, she was forced to shuck her sports inhibitions caused by inactivity.

To reinforce the mounting enthusiasm for debate, she organized a girls' debating club named "Congress," just another of her extracurricular activities from which an embarrassing situation occurred. Since her preoccupation in late afternoon classroom sessions and teaching an evening class expended great energy, she found it took supreme will power to get to school at 8:30, the required half hour before the starting class (Reva can be definitely categorized as a "night" person). On most mornings she arrived just before the bell.

A grumbly colleague threw up the fact to the principal one day in faculty meeting. "How come she's so privileged?" Reva felt like shrinking through the floor, but the principal answered, "When any of you teachers does what Miss Beck does, you also may report at nine in the morning!"

In her third year at Ogden High, direction of the "Classicalia" pageant was added to Reva's work load. It developed into the largest pageant ever staged in Utah up to that time. Presented in the huge public dance hall, Berthana, Reva had planned the entire extravaganza, from directing the performers to designing the queen's throne and the costumes. A raging blizzard marks the event in Reva's memory; it was bitterly cold for March, which is important, she chuckles, when reviewing the consequences.

She decided that adding natives to the procession would make it really authentic, so she called to her room ten personable boys and presented her idea to them—black cork covering the body, orange breechclout, and each carrying a palm branch.

"My God, Miss Beck, you sure aren't going to ask us to do that!"

"You mean just a thing around the hips?"

"How do you put cork over hair on the chest?"

"I've got knock-knees, Miss Beck."

"My mother told me never to undress in front of people!"

Miss Beck sat poker serious, her eyes peering from behind owl glasses, her smooth red hair becomingly styled in soft bangs, her well-shaped hands folded on the desk top.

"Besides, we have dates that night, Miss Beck."

She looked from one to the other—with perception.

Pause. Clearing of the throat. Another pause. Scuffing of feet.

"Well," said one with deliberation, "if you ask us, we'll do it!"

But the sacrifice was considerable! Earlier, Reva had instructed them, because they had dates afterward, to change clothes and apply makeup (and later wash up) at the high school a few blocks away, which had the only suitable quarters. Then they were to enter the Berthana from the fire escape.

On the night of the pageant, when the dance hall was filled, a path from the restroom through the crowd to the queen's throne was made ready for the performers. Everyone lined up but the natives! Not one was to be found! The call went out—find the natives, quick! Reva almost panicked; her already pale complexion turned white as a frantic search followed.

Finally a student rushed up, reporting breathlessly that the errant ones were still on the fire escape because the door was locked! So all were discovered—shivering and doing a warm-up dance on the outside steps while the frigid, snowy wind tore at their practically nude and black-smudged bodies.

"Believe me, that was a test of their friendship," Reva chortled. "When they were rescued, what a sorry lot! But being wonderful kids, they picked up their palm branches and went on with the show."

As though the sleet scene were not the true test of devotion, a by-standing prankster loudly whispered to slim-hipped Larry Trousdale that his breechclout was slipping! Hands full of palm branch, poor Larry locked his knees together and scissored over to the queen's throne with obvious agony. Oh, the never-to-be-forgotten Classicalia!

IN JUNE 1923 Reva suffered the loss of her beloved father. Just the year before he had robustly hoisted Reva's trunk on his shoulder at the train depot, and now at the age of sixty-seven a prostate problem and developing complications claimed his life. Caring for him during his last illness, Reva had time to reflect on his full life. Chris Beck had been seven years old when he left Denmark with his parents and brothers. The captain of the ship that brought them to this country took an immense liking to the little boy and begged the parents to let Chris stay with him. "They didn't, of course," Reva said, "but he must have displayed characteristics he exhibited all his life—dependability, ambition, a desire to make others happy, a great love for morality and decency. Yes, I'm proud of my Danish blood and of my father!"

Weighted by the handicap of little schooling—on the frontier, education was not always given the significance it deserved—Chris nevertheless labored hard and long with a high sense of justice, native intelligence, and courage!

As the young marshal of Alpine he laid down rules that were never disobeyed, impressing on the citizenry, for instance, the importance of prohibiting cattle from straying in the streams supplying culinary water.

His manner predisposed the disinclination of the townspeople to break those orders.

A run-in on a business transaction was apt to bring out his Danish stubbornness. Once Chris had just finished a threshing job (at one time he managed a company that owned a threshing machine) and was about to take out his rightful payment in grain, as was the custom, when the crop owner resisted the amount Chris was claiming and even threatened him. Chris, confident of his compensation de jure, proceeded to load the toll on his wagon and head for the gate. Determined to carry out his bluff, the owner got to the gate first and padlocked it. When Chris reached it he climbed off the wagon, grabbed a sledge hammer, and smashed the padlock. He then drove out with the load, leaving the fuming man to think again about the advantages of a swindle.

Chris was requested time and again on a summer's eve to accompany the lawman of American Fork to the railroad tracks jungle for the unsavory mission of directing hobos to parts other than American Fork. Chris never refused and he never carried a gun.

His funeral, held in American Fork's LDS Tabernacle, was crowded with mourners. The local paper reported: "The deceased was one of the staunch men of this city, respected for his sterling worth and high business qualifications. He was an enterprising citizen, alive to the needs of the city, and worked to develop and build her resources. In the death of Mr. Beck the county loses a road builder of unusual merit. It was largely through his efforts that the road in American Fork Canyon leading from Mutual Dell, Community Flat, went through."

Reva's Uncle John Beck once fascinated his listeners by relating a hairy experience involving Chris. At his cabin near a mine in American Fork Canyon, Chris was talking to a group of teamsters when an intoxicated malcontent drew his pistol and pointed it at Chris's stomach, "I'm going to kill you, Chris Beck!" And Reva's gutsy father fixed his blue eyes on him and snapped, "Go ahead!" But Chris lived a long time after that.

And there was to be still more despair during this sorrowful period! "The day before my father died," Reva says, "the maid rushed into my bedroom early in the morning exclaiming, 'Come quickly! Your mother has had an accident!'" Zilpha Beck had been showing the maid where she wanted her to clean in the kitchen. As she moved some soda pop bottles, one fell and exploded, flinging up a piece of glass which cut the pupil of her left eye.

Once more Reva assumed the role of nurse and painstakingly ministered to her mother through a three-week ordeal of lying quietly on her back with both eyes bandaged. Reva's duty was to apply a wet compress every twenty minutes. Zilpha was put to bed in her son's and daughter-in-law's house in Salt Lake City to be close to her doctor. So there she lay, immobilized for treatment, victimized by a freak accident, and forced to burrow deep into the hurt of the loss of her husband. And all with the spectre of blindness hovering near. The day of the funeral was endured by the minutes.

"What time is it, Reva?"

"Five past one, Mama."

And at ten minutes past one came the same question. And during the oration of the funeral in American Fork.

"Tell me the time, Reva." And through the music and the procession, the plaintive voice in Salt Lake City kept asking, "The time, Reva." And through the moments of interment.

"It must be three-thirty, isn't it, Reva?"

"Yes, Mama." And at four o'clock Zilpha Beck's voice fell silent. It hurt so to cry.

In the bedroom Zilpha occupied were twin beds so her daughter could attend her constantly. Three weeks passed before Reva stepped out the front door. Meantime, Hazel, Reva's sister-in-law, prepared the meals and all the other necessary chores besides caring for her own family. Reva said, "Hazel performed yeoman service in doing everything she could to make the ordeal pleasant."

The doctor marveled at Zilpha's self-control; she never panicked during the excruciating trial of her patience. In spite of her willpower and Reva's dedicated attention, Zilpha Beck's left eye eventually had to be removed and she wore a glass one for the duration of her life. Even with the artificial eye, she remains in the family's image as an exceptionally attractive woman with a pleasant facial expression.

HOW OFTEN one hears that the mature person sacrifices the satisfactions of the present to look ahead to the larger goals of the future. A fellow teacher once asked Reva just how she managed to save the wherewithal to finance a nine-country tour of Europe in 1926 and an upcoming three-year law course on her teacher's salary.

"I'm always saving for an operation!" she told the surprised colleague.

The year before Reva's extensive tour of Europe, Chanel, whose fashion career was just beginning, would have raised both eyebrows at Reva's wardrobe, which consisted of two black silk dresses—one she wore while the other was at the cleaners. Of heavy material, they were simply tailored and draped well on her tall frame. She enhanced the somberness with chunky jewelry. But even a neat-fitting dress could not compensate for the monotony of seeing their teacher in black day after day, and the girls pled on the last day of school for her to please come back in the fall with color in her wardrobe.

"I took out my desire to buy new things by going window-shopping at night when the stores were closed," she disclosed. "Many of the teachers took only short summer trips—but they always took a trip. I didn't because I knew that when I did, I would really do it up big and take a full summer off. So for seven summers I would return to American Fork and become the chambermaid in the hotel—but for no wages. I didn't have to be a maid. I honestly don't think mother ever asked me to do anything; I saw what had to be done and did it. Besides, I loved being home with my mother and father. I didn't miss tritting around the country. I'd say if a person wants to save money, she shouldn't spend a little here and there but put up roadblocks to every desire to buy. Yes, it's amazing what after-hours window-shopping and wearing two black silk dresses can do for one's pocketbook."

In retrospect, the beautiful trip appears a lifetime highlight, filled with edification and adventure. But the strenuous sight-seeing all but impaired her health permanently. In Italy, complications from a severe cold were so distressing that "I knew I was going to die! I prayed for one thing and that was that I be permitted to live until I could put one foot on American soil." Prayers answered, she returned to Utah weaker in body but infinitely grateful.

In 1926 an Ogden teacher friend and amateur palmist, Evelyn Dobbs, predicted from Reva's hand that she would travel more than she ever dreamed and would be in tremendous crowds. Reva greeted this news with a "huh" because having just returned from the grand trip, she was up to "gazoot" in schedules and tours! As for crowds, she could not comprehend from whence they would come. Then Miss Dobbs made a final prediction, "You will write a book before you die!"

And so in the spring of 1950, twenty-four years later, an associate editor of G. P. Putnam's Sons Publishing Company of Boston was dispatched to Washington when Reva was then a member of Congress to ask her to write a book for them—the complete history of her life. Of all the women of Congress, present and former, why was she selected? Reva wondered. The woman editor replied that the congresswoman's background was the broadest of any woman in politics in the United States. She urged Reva to get started on her book, with October 1 as a deadline.

Evelyn Dobbs' prognostication came to Reva's mind, "But I was dreadfully tired and loaded with work," she says. "While I was flattered and felt I had a story to tell, I knew I could not take the time out to do it—it would be neglecting the things for which I was elected, although many legislators took the privilege. So I turned down the proposition."

She added, "The associate editor kept after me for over a year, but I was still so busy and so tired. I regretted it afterward. But my life has been full since that time and it seems I have much more to add to the chronicle." She did pen her memoirs in later life, but as a student of the occult might say—the element of choice permitted Reva to defy a turn of her destiny.

AT OGDEN HIGH, opposition moved in on innovation; change was objectionable for some. Reva's teaching methods were questioned by a couple of members of the Daughters of the American Revolution because she gave her oratorical students a free hand in choosing their subject matter. If a young person believed in a stand or precept strong enough to shout about it, Reva believed he or she should be allowed this privilege—controversial or not! (One student's stand was against religion, outrageous in a religion-based state.) Principal Merrill invited the dissenters to attend any of Reva's classes at any time, proclaiming, "Her students win so it must be a good method!" Reva has long chanted the praises of the fair, broadminded Albert Merrill—his distinguished image remains clear-cut today as the prototype of the ideal school principal. Bolstering that impression was an incident that lingers in her thoughts—when Reva suggested an idea to him one day that would entail some additional work on her part, he flatly refused, declaring, "You have enough to do. I will not sign a death certificate!"

Reva's double raises (even one was considered a special honor) had continued to be granted each year. But in the spring when the contracts were issued for the coming fourth year, only one raise was conspicuous by the other's absence. She knew she had expended the effort of at least two teachers; she was positive she had brought new glory to Ogden High in the oral expression field; and she hoped she had endeared herself to innumerable students. The omission was understandably perplexing.

In a conversation with Superintendent Karl Hopkins she wondered about his reasoning in denying the double raise (she had become used to this honor). He admitted her work was of the same caliber but still he felt he could not authorize two raises. He then pointed to a stack of letters and remarked with a wry smile, "There are hundreds of people who are making application to teach here. We are not at a loss to find good teachers."

The red hair was curling all by itself. His choice of words, that tone in his voice! She was furious! Pointing to the stack of letters, the ambitious young schoolmarm announced, "You take one! I won't be back next year!"

She suddenly knew this would be the year she would read law.

REVA'S MOTHER, having grown accustomed to the teaching successes of her daughter, expressed disappointment over Reva's decision, stressing the paucity of outstanding teachers. But Reva assured her she had served seven years of missionary work—she had literally given her all! Then she reminded her mother of her own counsel, "If you want to do good, go where the laws are made." Of course Mrs. Beck was conscious of her daughter's desire to study law with one goal in mind—to be a legislator. She quickly acceded to Reva's wishes with her blessings.

Reva reminisces, "That was a good turn Superintendent Hopkins did me. I might have been waiting until now to read law if he hadn't said what he did. As is often the case, the topside of upset is advantage.

"I'm not too proud of it," she confessed, "but many years later at a program in Utah when I was the speaker, Superintendent Hopkins was seated in the audience and I introduced him as a man who had done me a tremendous favor. He really beamed. And then I proceeded to relate the event that had hastened my study of law—much to his discomfiture, I believe."

Law school at the University of Utah proved a shiny but edgy new world—the transition from teaching to being taught was fraught with new tensions. Seven years since taking instruction. New people, new frontiers! And again, the internal struggle against taking the back seat on a new scene, which had clung to her since childhood.

"So often I have heard people describe me as an aggressive woman; this has always amused me," Reva discloses. Drawing within herself, the adjustment came fairly slowly, especially when Dean William H. Leary had a habit of proclaiming to the freshman class that if the field of law seemed difficult at first, it would become vastly more difficult as the course proceeded! Actually, Reva found it the reverse; perhaps the dean's zealous preoccupation with weeding out the weak was overdone.

"You simply scare me to death," she told him when he asked her why she appeared so fussed on being called upon. He assured her that he didn't intend to frighten her, that he knew she was knowledgeable in her studies, and that she had potential. From then on Reva began to relax. "By the end of the first year I had my feet on the ground and my head in the books." And she added, "I loved what I was doing although law school was hard work!"

Only one other woman law student joined the ex-schoolteacher in that 1927 man's world, and Reva was the one of the two to graduate. Among those practicing law in Salt Lake in the so-called roaring twenties, Reva knew of only two women. The change in numbers was not too marked between 1928 and 1872 when the first women—Phoebe W. Couzins and Georgie Snow—were admitted to the bar in the Territory of Utah.

Having been so recently immersed in the tutelage of young people, Reva felt the need of tapering off, so during her second law year she taught a freshman English class in the afternoon to fifty "U" students— altogether too many, she emphasizes. Deciding the class was overly large, the department head, Dr. Sherman B. Neff, asked her to request ten students to volunteer to be transferred. She complied with his request the next day but there were no takers.

"I told them I would certainly take no offense, that they would be benefiting me and themselves if ten people would leave my class. Still no volunteers. After this was reported to Dr. Neff, he personally visited the class and assured the students that it was a necessity. Still no action, whereupon he pointed out who must leave. Way down deep I glowed! Does anyone wonder why I'd like to wind up my life teaching?"

It would be a moment to treasure when the going got bumpy.

Her decision to make a scholastic record in law school tended to slip slightly in her second year in the presence of a tall, handsome law student who always seemed to keep Reva in his gaze. She eagerly listened to hear his voice in the name call— Joseph P. Bosone—of Italian extraction, and fascinating! Soon he asked if she would mind if he studied with her. Indeed she wouldn't mind!

Law classes then took on a golden glow. Not only was it a different other world but now a constant companion to share it with filled those nonstudious moments. Reva and Joe became inseparable—in the law library, at dinner, on dates to the picture show. They occupied separate boarding houses but often took their meals at the same home as their law professors.

Fascination on both sides soon ripened into love between two opposites—an industrious redheaded Danish/English idealist with no organized religious affiliation and a sports- and leisure-loving dark-haired Italian of strong Catholic beliefs.

Joe's proposal of marriage left Reva in an abyss, however. Aboveboard and motive-straight, she informed him that she would not take a pledge to rear their children as Catholics, as was his desire. Certainly they could become Catholics if they chose but she would not bind them. With heavy sadness she suggested that perhaps he should choose a Catholic sweetheart. They parted!

"We didn't see each other for a month," she said, a month that was measured longer than in seconds, hours, and days! "Then one Sunday Joe called. 'I've decided I'd rather have you—even with your convictions.' "

That summer Joe invited Reva to spend a few days at the family home in Helper, Utah, a small but thriving community in the center of the state, one of the country's richest in coal deposits. In fact, coal extrusions are part of the scenery just around the city's corner.

The Bosones, Italian immigrants, had retired and were living without financial stress on their savings and investments in a roomy house on Main Street. Warm and kindly, they, with Joe's brother, Fred, looked forward to pleasing their son's "intended"—the dinner that first evening was like an event! Efficient Mama Bosone had prepared a delectable veal roast stuffed with garlic and rosemary, mounds of fried bell peppers, the usual pasta, and a tantalizing ice cream dessert. Reva was then and there converted to Italian cooking.

That night in an upstairs bedroom of the Bosone home the young visitor blissfully contemplated the romantic life before her as she brushed her gleaming red hair and slept contentedly and soundly except for the occasional interruptions of strident train whistles when heavily loaded coal cars were nudged up the hill with a special engine called the "helper." But those train whistles, instead of unpleasant intrusions, set a mood that remains sealed in nostalgia.

In the days following, as she met Joe's friends, Reva knew she had never seen more beautiful people. Italy and the Italians had stood out prominently in her memories of the big European tour, and now it was thrilling that they would soon become her friends, too. But the engaged couple also passed on the streets of Helper those who weren't classified as friends and Joe would point them out as "Mano-nero," or Black Handers, members of a mafia group who had burned down a business building belonging to his parents when he was in high school.

The summer, full of dreams and plans, gave way to law school enrollment time once again for the two students, and on October 8, 1929, they decided to be married. Although the union was not kept secret, no public announcement was made until Reva was admitted to the Utah State Bar the following March; she decided at that time her professional name would be her maiden name—Reva Zilpha Beck. However, when the couple established offices in Helper in 1931, her Italian mother-in-law, of whom Reva was fond, took exception to the unorthodox maiden name idea, not understanding why any wife would want to retain her own name, especially when practicing in her husband's hometown.

"Mrs. Bosone just could not quite see the independence of American women," Reva explained. So because of this sentimental protest, the lawyer changed her name to the one she carries today.

According to a newspaper clipping, Reva was the eleventh woman admitted to the practice of law in Utah and the fourth woman to be graduated from the University of Utah Law School since June 1926 (old law school records yield little information on women's first efforts). Joe needed another year to complete his credits, so her oldest brother, now an established attorney, took her into the legal fold. Cognizant of the fact that a recent law graduate knows substantive law but little of the adjective law or the procedure, Reva was anxious to get the feel of her new profession.

In June, after Joe finished his semester and enrolled in summer school, she abandoned office work while awaiting the birth of her baby, due in the fall. By July Reva was ailing; her appetite had slipped, resulting in a significant weight loss, so her mother came to care for her. The basement quarters were small so Joe returned to his hometown, Helper, for a few weeks to make room.

The night before Labor Day the occupants above the Bosone apartment were whooping up a party. In the early morning hours, Reva stood on the bed and vigorously banged the ceiling with a broom, which apparently initiated labor pains. At 3:30 A.M. her husband was hurriedly called. Then a friend living across the street, who wanted the privilege, whisked the expectant mother, Mrs. Beck, and brother Filcher, who had been immediately summoned, to the hospital where Dr. Joe Phipps, beloved family physician, was soon on hand.

He and Joe soothed her brow during a hot night and a long difficult labor (apropos of the day) culminating in the birth just before midnight of a daughter, to be named after Reva's mother, Zilpha, and her mother-in-law, Teresa. Had she been a male, the monicker attached would have been Horace Filcher, a fact her daughter has repeatedly groaned over when she mulls the chance that she might have been born a boy and tagged with that for life!

After the birth, the lady barrister turned into a most solicitous, nervous, and adoring mother—in fact, the maternal instinct was poking through her efficient demeanor like a new chick pecking out its shell. The joy of parenthood has been a lasting one, too.

"There isn't a thing in this world I wouldn't give up for the privilege of being a mother. I am a career woman, but I would give up everything— and that's a lot—to be a mother if I had to make a choice!"

Notwithstanding the parental joy in the Bosone household, there was a widespread state of dissatisfaction in the land. Hard times were as common as the flies on the screen door! Joe was scheduled for graduation in the spring but his wife was already a full-fledged lawyer; the young Bosones agreed that in January (1931) Reva should open an office in Helper, Utah. Mama Bosone would care for the baby in the day while Reva practiced.

The new attorney-at-law set up her office in a bank building within walking distance of the Bosone home on Main Street. Her greatest concern was the possibility that the men of the community—mostly Greeks and Italians—would hesitate to seek legal advice from a woman, but that anxiety was relieved when they soon sought her out. Curiosity turned to admiration as they watched her expend the same high-voltage energy on their cases as she had on a classroom of students. Reva, in an entirely new locale, again became emotionally moved by the warmth of their acceptance of her and grew to love these hardworking people.

Law Office Open House

IN SPITE OF HER RESEARCH, determination, and a strong belief that justice would prevail, Lawyer Bosone lost her first case. Tried before a justice of the peace, the case had her defending a Japanese man accused of assault and battery. The judge made a quick decision of guilty. Reva felt so strongly that her client was innocent that she argued with the judge about his decision. Joe, supporting her in the courtroom contest, was in complete agreement with his wife. But the judge bullied by threatening to hold Reva in contempt, to which she exclaimed, "Go ahead!" He decided against it. A more experienced barrister, Reva later reasoned, would have asked for a jury because she learned that JPs, appointed by county attorneys, had a record of convicting defendants, if possible.

Her first jury case, however, was a different story. She was asked to defend two boys in a sex violation and being eager to take all kinds of cases, she accepted this one. (In a generalization, one might say that a case of attempted rape was responsible for the intrepid lady's rise to fame.) Inherited frontier family courage was displayed because in 1931 she understood that Utah lawyers were losing all sex cases, especially those of rape!

After investigating the facts, Reva and Joe, who drove home weekends from law school to assist his wife, were convinced that the two girls were not innocent. For instance, one of the boys had his arm in a sling at the time the offense was supposed to have occurred. Belief in her client has always been imperative; if it was lacking, there would be no commitment. "To argue a case knowing that my defendant is guilty," she insists, "would make me like 'sounding brass and tinkling cymbals!'"

Reva was advised to ask help of one of the experienced lawyers of Price, a larger town a few miles away, since the Carbon County Bar was highly reputed, but the Bosones figured that if Reva won, the established lawyer would receive the credit and if she lost, she would get all the blame. Winning would be tough—that was obvious! But if she triumphed in her first case in a district court, it could be a definite building block for her reputation. Too, it would be a challenge in experience since only one law school class in moot court involving trial practice constituted her background to date.

So a nervous neophyte lady lawyer confronting her first jury in the rich coalfield country of Utah was generating uncommon interest in the community and environs. Reva steadfastly pursued the facts and the law, keeping in mind the fact that the district attorney had a record of winning his cases (guilty verdict) for two years, which was indeed a record for any attorney! This time, however, the DA showed some trepidation for he offered to reduce the charge if Reva would plead the boys guilty to a lesser offense. No dice!

Joe, when home on weekends, assisted in extensive preparations. She knew that to be thoroughly prepared was her first advantage; a trait vouched for by colleagues in all walks of her life is thoroughness.

Joe arranged to take a leave from school to lend support to his wife during the trial—he, checking the evidence, she, studying the law. As the proceedings got under way in Price, Judge George Christensen proved an invaluable friend, giving 'the young lawyers every break. When he thought Reva should object to evidence, he would look her way and, of course, she would gratefully take the hint. Making comprehensive notes on weak spots of witness cross-examination and inconsistent statements of the girls making the charge, Reva built up a strong defense. On the second trial day, one could hear on the streets that odds were high on the Bosones winning their plea.

On the afternoon of the third day, the arguments were presented before an all-male jury, Reva's summation following the district attorney's. She chose to direct her statements to a stout, rough-featured man in the front row who appeared to be in sympathy with her (the tougher the exterior, the softer the heart was her frequent conclusion). Sensing that if she won him over perhaps he would convince the other jury members, she pled with all the compassion, sincerity, and logic she could muster.

Three hours later, drained of words and emotions, she wearily sat down at the lawyers' table beside Joe, who whispered his favorite nickname, "Honna, you were wonderful!" The perfect encouragement! Whatever were Joe's faults that later separated the couple, jealousy was not one of them. He was always heavy on the praise for his able wife.

Reva and Joe then returned to Helper to await the verdict. She was satisfied that she had argued to the best of her ability but they were naturally anxious for a quick verdict, knowing that the longer a jury is closeted, the more attorneys have to worry about. At 11 P.M. an alert reached them that the jury was ready to report. Rushing back to Price, Reva and Joe ran up the courthouse stairs and breathlessly watched the jurors file in.

When the foreman read, "*Not* guilty," Reva was at long last speechless! And overjoyed! District Attorney Fred Keller offered his congratulations. "You broke my record!" It was a sweet victory, to be sure—and exhilarating—after the intensive groundwork and argument. All the

Bosones stayed up late that night, analyzing and rehashing. What a time for jubilation! And one of the happiest times in the Bosone marriage.

Picture, if you will, the cool, poised attorney sitting behind her desk listening with discernment but detachment to the flustered prostitute explaining her embarrassing predicament. Now reverse the picture and you have Reva's first encounter with a lady of the night in Helper.

With no little apprehension, the young attorney, far from street-smart, awaited the madam after a phone call had arranged an appointment for counsel. Soon an attractive blonde of perhaps twenty-six, plastered with makeup and covered with a thick veneer of cynicism, entered the office, crossed the room, sat down, and casually lit a cigarette before uttering a word. Then with nonchalance, "I run a house down the street and I'm having trouble with my landlord." (Prostitution was legal in 1931 in Price and Helper.)

As the client explained her case, Reva became intrigued with the details of a life that was the antithesis of her own. She expressed interest, understanding, and that R. Bosone virtue—sympathy—all of which must have been effective. After a solution for her landlord problems had been worked out the young madam, on the second meeting with the counsel, showed quite a different personality—little makeup on her face, a relaxed demeanor, and, one could say, charming manners.

What had influenced her choice of vocation? Reva wondered out loud. One of a family of three girls, the client replied that she had left home in a nearby state to wait tables on the West Coast. Meeting many men, she admitted to taking advantage of the easy-money propositions. She then tried Honolulu, but because that city considered women of that bent open targets, she fled into the plantations and fields where she would accommodate many Japanese men in one day. A grim life but profitable! Fortified with a wad of bills, she then sailed first class to the United States in order to feign a bit of self-respect. "I wanted a little luxury," she revealed, "and to know how it felt to take the role of a decent young woman." Reva was astonished to learn that her way of making a living was a family affair—the woman's two sisters were occupied in the same way.

Another experience that sticks in Reva's memory started with a call from an "important" madam in town requesting that a contract be drawn. The law in those years prohibited prostitutes from appearing on the streets. Since the woman was a madam (and not just one of the girls), she could have considered herself exempt from this law. But in order to set a good example, she told Lawyer Bosone, she preferred not to appear on the streets either; would counsel bring the contract to her?

Reva delivered the completed document. "I don't really know what I expected to see," she said, reserved but inquisitive, "but the house was very orderly—the parlor, the stairs, her office were all beautiful, and it was quiet. We discussed the contract and then I left. Well, I have to say I have been in a house of prostitution. What hay my political enemies could have made of that!"

When Joe graduated in June 1931 he opened an office in Price, but two offices for a couple of beginning lawyers proved overly ambitious in the great depression, hence consolidation—Bosone & Bosone.

The family of three needed a place of their own. The elder Bosones offered Reva and their son one of their comfortable rental homes, but since they were to pay no rent, Reva didn't have the presumption to accept this generosity. She takes full blame for their settling in the almost squatter's quarters behind the Bosone home where three cramped rooms, one of which was unusable in winter because of lack of heat, was a far cry from a country manor.

"The kitchen had crude shelves, a small sink, and an old stove," Reva remembers. "We ate in the kitchen, naturally. In the other usable room we had a dresser, a pullout bed, and two chairs. Not much! But I was so in love and happy with my baby and law practice that I didn't pay too much attention to these meager surroundings, that is, until I stayed up evenings making baby clothes by hand—no sewing machine—and the cold wind under the kitchen door all but froze my feet. Finally, I propped them on a box.

"After dinner, Joe would take his favorite magazine and go up to his folks' comfortable living room where he would spend the evening. I couldn't go to the Bosones' because the baby couldn't be left alone. To practice law all day and sew half the night in those conditions was too much, and by June I was suffering from a terrible cold I couldn't shake.

"Each year I was in Helper I had to go home to mother with my baby to recuperate for a month from a persistent cold. My physical weakness has always been colds, so when one grabbed me and I didn't have the time to take care of it, it would finally knock me out."

Later in the couple's stay in Helper they moved into a newly remodeled apartment in the Bosone home, which at least satisfied the basic creature comforts.

Reva gets a bit philosophical recalling those early ventures. "There isn't any doubt about it—to mix a career and marriage and children is difficult. With a conscientious woman not one of those is neglected, certainly not the children. It is a matter of being ambitious. A woman doesn't have to leave anything out. The real question is—can her health hold up? This, of course, depends upon whether or not her husband cooperates—carries his share of all the work and responsibility."

Her views on the career/marriage/children combination were expressed in an interview on talk station KSXX in Salt Lake City during one of her visits in 1974. She insisted that it can work if each does his/her part.

Bootstrap Syndrome

"WHEN I WAS A KID I thought only poor people were Democrats!" and Reva grins. Her father and mother embraced the Republican party, but not in a narrow partisan manner—they attended all political rallies in order to be fair, they said, in their estimation of each candidate. They were interested in all classes of people being represented objectively and so did not stick strictly to a party line; i.e., they supported Woodrow Wilson and pledged allegiance to Theodore Roosevelt when he broke from the Republican side.

Freckle-faced Reva was a spectator at many of those rallies. At the age of nine she remembers sitting in the front row and being intrigued by the pointing finger of one of her favorites, Utah's great orator, Senator William H. King.

The Christian Becks, after taking in those meetings, would then involve their offspring in political discussions at the dinner table. Reva

PHOTO: *Reva Beck Bosone and brothers Horace, Filcher, and Clarence.*

65

would get the answers at home and then level them at her peers in grade school the next day. One disadvantage in having all those answers was her propensity for talking. Being ordered to stay after school for talking out of turn was almost routine.

"One afternoon the teacher made me write the 'Star Spangled Banner' five times," she recalled. "I thought she was going to read it, so I took the pains of writing it in the tiniest script possible. What a joke on me!"

A lifelong quote from Reva is, "I am a product of the dining room table." That large square oak table in the lace-curtained dining room of the private apartment in the hotel was more than a place to serve meals; it was a vehicle for a forum—a focal point for a family that thrived on the friendly argument.

"Forcing a person to work under those conditions in a mine is inhuman!"

"Of course we all know that, but nothing will change if the laws aren't changed!"

"Pass the peaches, please."

"Who's strong enough to attempt that?"

"Strong enough to pass the peaches?"

"No, dummy, to crusade for the law change."

"Well, for the nation, Teddy Roosevelt was."

"Now there was a great reformer."

"I wish he'd run again."

"What do you think were his best reforms, Papa?" Reva turned from her brothers' conversation to address her father who was lighting up his after-dinner cigar. This was the opportune time to bone up for the running argument at school with friend, Bert Duncan.

Pulling at the cigar and puffing a few times he answered, "For one, Roosevelt's eight-hour day legislation! And he lowered the boom on anti-trust violators," Chris said, checking off each point with his fingernail on the white tablecloth. "And he sure didn't like corruption of politics by big business. Oh, and the Pure Food and Drug Act and the Reclamation Act were passed when he was in the White House."

"Don't forget the Elkins Law," interjected Mama, "that forbade rebates to certain corporations. And Roosevelt stood up against the spoils system!"

"Didn't he win the Nobel peace prize?" Reva asked.

"That's very knowledgeable of you, Reva." Mama was smiling.

Reva smiled back and then looked down. "Ah, shoot a pickle! C'mon, I'll wash dishes, Mama, and you can wipe."

REVA'S DECISION to become a Democrat dates back to the spring of 1932. "I told my two brothers of my decision. They were prominent in the Republican party in Salt Lake City—in the inner circle of the inner circle, so to speak. Clarence advised me to follow my convictions, but Horace was nonplussed. 'What will my political friends say when I admit I can't influence my sister?'

"Perhaps life would have been easier for me had I become a Republican," she continued, "but I couldn't do it and be honest. I didn't wish to be different from my brothers just to be different. But to be true to myself there was only one thing to do—be a Democrat!"

A story that lay on her mind, occasionally churning and turning, was told by her parents concerning the Finn workers in the copper mine at Bingham, a few miles west of Salt Lake City in the Oquirrh Mountains. It was rumored that the superintendent had a habit of throwing a rock where he wanted the Finns to dig. After the workday, some of them would come out feet first! Gruesome to a tender and impressionable mind, this exposé was powerful enough to influence her to side with labor.

Enter now the first but significant beginnings of a distinghished legislator's career. Reva's decision to run for the state legislature was supported wholeheartedly by Oliver Clay of Price—one of Utah's dynamic lawyers and a well-wisher of the Bosones—and the county chairman, who was a superintendent of a large coal mine. Reva and Joe and enthusiastic Democrats of Carbon County then dug in, contacting the delegates and preparing the way for the nomination. These were initial experiences and no exertion was too grueling or too exhausting—the result, an easy victory at the county convention.

In campaigning for representative of the Utah House that summer and fall, the tall redhead, sometimes with her two-year-old daughter in tow, knocked on doors up one side of the street and down the other in towns all over Carbon County, even in the mining camps of National, Wattis, and Kenilworth, sometimes on mountainsides, sometimes in gulches, distributing leaflets and cards.

"I'm Reva Beck Bosone and I practice law in Helper. I'm a candidate for the legislature and your support would be appreciated." Her name was as familiar to the folks she contacted as radio's "Amos 'n Andy" or "Myrt 'n Marge."

"Oh yes, you're the woman who won that attempt at rape case."

"That was some case for a woman to take! Isn't law a man's field?"

"Why did you as a woman want to be a lawyer?"

Reva's response was consistent, quoting her mother, "If you want to do good, go where the laws are made." As Edmund Burke said, "Bad laws are the worst sort of tyranny." Often a retired father was the only one at home and Reva learned later that these aging patriarchs were some of her most ardent supporters. At times like this, recaptured from childhood was an impression of having her small hand grasped by the powerful one of Uncle Squire and being led in the cakewalk around the parlor of the hotel while her mother accompanied on the piano. At the age of three Reva knew the exhilaration of whirling to music, sensed the endless variety of movement to rhythm. This first experience set the mold for her predilection for dancing, but—importantly—it established her affection for those aged men sitting in the parlor whose smiling, approving faces she could see all-round.

Further in her young candidacy, besides speeches in each town, there were appearances at the big rallies where state candidates supplied the clout, all of which proved tiring but not difficult. With unemployed thousands in breadlines, the public was panting to hear about ways to improve the national economy. And issues and records were the only subjects Reva discussed, never personal diatribe. Sincerity and the ability to project it were always in her favor and she expected it in others.

Impossible to forget was her invitation to meet and campaign with bigwig state politicos in Vernal, a pastoral town in eastern Utah. At a rally one of those candidates exuded warmth with, "I want to get close to you fine people," impressing his less experienced colleague with an exemplary democratic attitude. The next morning the same person quipped in private, "Isn't this a hell of a place!" which gave Reva her first eye-opener in practical politics.

Three women figure prominently in those first chapters of her fledgling political life: Mrs. Carolyn Wolfe, state chairwoman of the Democratic party, Mrs. May Greenwood, and Mrs. Elise Musser (three women way above the cut of certain women to be confronted later in Reva's life) who offered inestimable help and cooperation not available from any other source.

"Election night in 1932 was exciting!" Reva said. "The voters felt that if there could be a change in government, there might be relief from the depression. Very early in the evening the voting trend was set—set for the Democratic party. The sweep was clean; every Democratic candidate was elected, and I was told that I led the county ticket!" And she had moved from the flatland up on the first rung.

When Reva became a legislator, time became precious—to be divided judiciously among the various elements of her life. She hired a faithful helper who cleaned, looked after Zilpha at certain times, and did the simple cooking. But the baking and canning chores fell to Reva. Two hundred and fifty bottles of canned fruit were added to the shelves each year because she budgeted her busy schedule to fit in the work, and goodies to last for a week were made on one set-aside morning.

On one of these mornings in Helper, just after her election, her active youngster was happily playing with a castaway purse in the living room. Her mother had locked the front door and left the key in it, knowing the lock was too high for two-year-old Zilpha to reach, so she concentrated her attention in the kitchen. Every few minutes Reva would check on her. Then on one of her peeks into the living room, she couldn't find her. Evidently Zilpha had pushed a small box against the door, stood on it, and turned the key to make her getaway.

Well, all composure vanished! Reva frantically inspected the yard, then called Grandma and Grandpa Bosone to hysterically report the missing person. Literally, she all but fell apart, demonstrating an extreme to an otherwise stable personality.

After thirty distraught minutes the search ended when they learned a man on Main Street had seen the tike down by the bank near the lawyers' office. The elder Bosone investigated and soon, "Here came sweet old Grandpa with Zilpha in his arms. She wore her white summer hat, long wooly underwear, and was hugging my big old black purse. Oh, what a funny looking darling! How thrilled I was to see her!" The reason for her excursion? She had walked down to the bank to see her daddy. One to learn by experience, Reva never again underestimated her daughter's ingenuity.

Grandpa Bosone and Zilpha were a twosome quite often—each adored the other. The wide-eyed little girl tended to lighten the cares of the elder Bosone, who tended to show off a few of his Italian traditions. One of these was a liberal use of garlic in cooking while the other folk were out of the house. When Reva and Joe would return from the office in the evening, Zilpha would greet them with a power all her own.

Madame Legislator

"You knew she knew she knew"

A move for the couple to Salt Lake City when the 1933 legislature convened in January became a permanent one. Practicing law in Helper had been invaluable and highly interesting but not conducive to gaining the widest experience or to building a savings account. The three Bosones with their helper moved into a three-room apartment; Reva's brother

PHOTO: *"Floor leader House of Utah Representatives stops to powder her nose."* Salt Lake Telegram, *1935*

Filcher and his wife Virginia occupied the other apartment on the same floor of a large house. Later a rather aged dwelling on McClelland Street was purchased which housed the Joe Bosone and Filcher Beck families for several years. The tight togetherness worked well and no particular rancor or disagreement was ever heard to divide them.

Reva and Joe again opened offices—Bosone and Bosone—in the same building in which her two lawyer brothers were already practicing law. The Felt Building, a five-story structure between Third and Fourth South on Main Street, has somehow escaped the sweep of modernity (down with the old and embellished, up with the new and stark). In walking down those long halls, one's heels still clickety-clack on the original ceramic tile floors of a building now placed on the National Register of Historic Places.

At the first caucus of elected Democrats in Salt Lake City, Reva became acquainted with the other women of the House—Edna Ericksen, Cornelia Lund, Mildred Rich, and Minnie Harris. Most of them looked on the honor of being elected a representative as the crowning glory in her life. Reva, being the youngest, viewed the prestige as just a springboard. But she rejoiced to see several of the members climb to even higher glory in official state capacities.

Mrs. Ericksen, wife of the late University of Utah Professor E. E. Ericksen and for more than forty years a friend of the Judge, has never lost the image of that first session.

"She was an awesome creature to me." Edna Ericksen was speaking of the lively legislator from Carbon County. "She could walk in on the floor of the legislature and go right to work. I was always embarrassed when I was to speak, but Reva used to say, 'This is my business,' meaning her profession as a lawyer. I watched her for a pattern and she never disappointed me. You knew she knew she knew! She just had a positiveness that made me know she was a strong person." And then an adjunct, "And that beautiful complexion!"

Going back over four decades, she continued, "One day little Zilpha [whose features came from her Italian father's side] walked in on the floor with her mother. I took to her right off. You know, I can see her today. She had such a beaming face and long, dark brown braids. She wore a short brown and beige plaid dress, gathered at the waist. And she looked so different from Reva!"

Mrs. Ericksen, now in her eighties with impaired health, commented that as far as she was aware, Reva never gave a "gallery" speech. "Always working for a cause on behalf of people, she was just and fair and honest!"

Even though Mrs. Ericksen has not corresponded with Reva recently, her feelings about her have not diminished. "She is one of those friends whom you may not see or touch often but you know she's there. It gives a sense of security."

The former legislator reminisced further, "Reva was not afraid to say no when it was right to say no. Oh, when she was on the bench, there were some people who swore to high heaven against her—she was such a forthright person! But most had great admiration for her."

One of a group of intimates who stood constant through days of bouquet throwing to days of slime slinging and back to bouquets, Edna Ericksen is a prime example of woman support without which Reva would possibly not have reached her highest peaks.

Reva knew long before the legislative session that in the event of her election she would introduce a labor law for the protection of women and children in industry; wages and working conditions were reprehensible! So with her usual passion for succeeding, she settled in at the state law library in the capitol to dig into the laws of other states in preparation for writing a new statute. When it was drawn, she realized that it might be held unconstitutional by opponents, so reasoned that an amendment to the Utah State Constitution might be a safeguard. Where could she get a trusted professional opinion?

Her first thought pointed to Judge Daniel N. Straup of the Utah Supreme Court who had instructed her in moot court classes at law school and had remained a kindly confidant. Although he believed her bill was constitutional, he counseled, "Why not plug both ends and introduce your constitutional amendment?" This visit with Judge Straup gave her the strength and encouragement to push her cause. Learning as she went, she loaded her briefcase with facts and proof and was able to get the bill out of the Labor Committee.

"But I just could not understand why no saleslady or working woman showed up to testify. Later I understood they didn't dare because it would have meant their jobs!"

The word spread that the fight would be on the floor, where the farmers and Republicans would try to defeat it. The opponents took the attitude that the Senate would defeat it so they might as well vote for it—which actually eased its House passage.

Opinion was opposed to minimum wages and hours for women and children in a time of oppressive conditions and the absence of meaningful labor legislation was mind boggling, but it was obvious that legislators negative to Reva's bill would be in there swinging. So the unquenchable sponsor made numerous personal contacts where she deemed them crucial and despite the vocal antagonists, her proposal passed the Senate. Also, passed in both bodies of the legislature was her amendment on working conditions for children which the voters later overwhelmingly adopted.

"The wage and hour statute was one of the best things I ever did for labor," Reva says. "Now a good many leading women want protective laws for women repealed. I realize equal rights for women are stymied by protective laws so I have decided that these groups of women are right."

On the last day of the session Reva discarded her law references and facts on the bill. "Such naiveté!" she declared. "Three weeks after the session, my friend, Margaret McQuilkin, who worked closely with the governor, phoned to say my bill was going to be vetoed! That was truly difficult for me to understand until I realized the opponents had not let up—they had reached the state attorney general, who was going to advise the governor that the bill was unconstitutional."

Frustrated but not defeated, she and Joe, who supported her in this gigantic effort, started all over again to find the law. After spending three days of frenzied search in the law library they contacted Grover Giles, chief deputy in the attorney general's office.

"I put the cases in front of him while Joe and I stood on either side of him to point out the law. He read much of it. I shall never forget his looking up and saying, 'Reva, how is it that you are the only one interested in this bill? Where are those people whose lives it touches?' " And she explained with all the verve of an evangelist, "Well, if people like me, who don't have to answer to anyone, can't protect these people who do, who can? You must know they would lose their jobs!"

That unexpected Golden Rule explanation prompted Grover Giles to advise Governor Henry H. Blood to sign the bill, and the Minimum Wage and Hour Law for Women and Children created the Women's Division of the Utah State Industrial Commission.

A superb motivator, Reva had the capacity to organize for positive persuasion. One of her finest efforts in this behalf has to be her roundup, after four weeks of in-session observation, of sixteen legislators whose views were similar on all legislation. She felt that if they could be organized into a solid block, it could be the determining factor in pushing through social legislation and defeating that of vested interests.

When the idea first occurred to Reva, she contacted Ray Adams to discuss the possibility; they agreed on a selection of names of astute members to be included, names like Irving Arnovitz, a leading lawyer, and Walt Granger, who later advanced to United States Congressman. They would meet in secrecy after the day's session to review and digest the good and bad points of each bill coming up on the floor the following day. After a decision was reached, this "progressive bloc" would then be an important influence in the fate of Utah statutes. A loyal tie was also effected; fifteen men always supported Reva in future political activities.

"As a young child and for a good part of my adult life I wanted to take a ride in a caboose! But this gal changed her mind," Reva confided. The train limit bill had been a "regular" in the Utah legislature for twenty years but had never been out of committee. This year Reva had barely enough time to get located in her chair in the House when she was approached by representatives of the railroad trainmen to introduce their bill. She reserved her answer until she had investigated the Interstate Commerce Commission reports on safety.

Every night after the session until early morning for two weeks Reva primed herself on the safety aspects of railroading and the hazards of long long trains. She remembers, "Those railroaders, I think, got a real kick out of a woman studying such records and they worked hard to get all the facts I wanted." When she was positive the bill was convincing and endeavored to correct a serious situation, she introduced H.B. 37, which provided that trains should be limited to seventy freight cars and fourteen passenger coaches. Reva's plea, based on the appeal for protection of the lives of railroad workers, was "that on trains having over seventy cars there were more than five times as many accidents as those having under seventy cars."

"The Fight of the Session Was on the Bosone Bill," headlined one of the evening newspapers after the bill was debated in the House that afternoon.

Added to the legislators' problems were the crowds. "Up to that year of 1933, there had never been such a record of lobbyists," she says. "You couldn't move in the halls surrounding the House. The gallery was jammed. The railroads had sent their company unions and the trainmen were out in full force."

The tremendous responsibility Reva assumed when she was elected to the legislature is sensed in her philosophy about lobbyists. "I believe in lobbyists. In the Utah House of Representatives in 1933 and 1935 and when I was in the United States Congress there was a strong move to curtail the activities of lobbyists. I went along with this idea only so far. Certainly they should not be permitted on the legislative floors and should not impede the members in their passage to and from the floors, and in Congress they should be registered. But other than those limitations, there shouldn't be any.

"If a legislator of the state or the nation is a weakling who succumbs to the lush crooning of certain lobbyists, blame the constituency, which should have been more interested in sending a qualified candidate. A man or woman who studies the measures with an impartial attitude and then has the ability to analyze the situation and the character to stand by his or her conviction has absolutely no fear of a lobbyist. He may be informed by him but he weighs what he hears. No, it is an insult to a good legislator's qualifications and character to say he can't withstand the pressure of lobbyists. Nincompoops are easy prey and unfortunately we have some in all legislative bodies. They are elected only because the constituents are uninterested in the great government under which they live. After all, the grass roots element controls; what is done in high places reflects the grass roots thinking and character."

That afternoon, armed with answers and retorts, she stood durable as a redwood, with no recollection of sitting down for three hours. When the news of a fight was noised around, many state senators came to observe. Dan Shields, a prominent lawyer and legislator, commented in the early 1930s, "I was never for a woman serving in the legislature until I saw that Bosone gal!" He continued to observe her in action, give her support, and shout her praises for years to come.

The bill's opposition spouted lower freight rates, saying, "But how can we continue this plea if we increase the costs of railroad operation?" Another complainant of the bill said it would probably be declared unconstitutional and claimed it put too much of a burden on the railroads when they already pay a high percent of the state's taxes. And still another referred to it as vicious and radical—the railroads deserve a square deal!

Reva Bosone then dipped into her briefcase to rally. Those "poor railroads" had a book value of $132 million in 1922 and $156 million in 1932, and net profits of $38 million in 1930 for railroads (from Moody's *Financial Index*) did not add up to poverty!

In the middle of the debate Reva was called outside. Unknown to her, brother Filcher had been a gallery observer; he reported that the attorney for the railroad, sitting on the back spectator row on the floor, kept handing an anxious legislator notes and he in turn would shoot a question to Reva. Rankled by the audacity, Reva returned to the session, asked for the floor, and opened up the sluice gates on the perpetration of the railroad attorney and the member of the House. The outraged gallery burst into an uproar and was subdued only by the speaker's orders. Shortly thereafter, the spotlighted attorney and his group tippytoed off the floor, and with the member's information box closed, he remained quiet.

The arguments on the floor continued, however, vehement at times. From the trade publication, *The Railroad Trainman,* "Charges of intimidation and of lobbying were hurled by Mrs. Bosone at her colleagues and at representatives of railroad companies present in the audience. One Member was openly rebuked for quoting statistics not yet available from the interstate commerce reports which Mrs. Bosone charged had been secured from a lobbyist, sitting on the floor in violation of house rules."

Reva invoked the rule of "call of the House" and all members were forced to go on record on this piece of legislation. Some of them explained their motivation when voting. Representative Chris Greenhagen, considered the father of the old-age pension law, was reported as saying, "Opponents of the bill have threatened that if I voted for the bill, I would be killed politically forever. So to show how little I care for their threats, I vote yes." Representative Frank Edman of Salem proved stalwart when he declared, "Until I can be shown that railroad companies care as much for human life as they do for car wheels, I shall continue to vote yes on this bill." And the gallery demonstrated approval by repeated applause.

Nonetheless, Reva was defeated by a 34-to-20 vote. But knowing the history of the bill precluded any great disappointment; after a two-decade attempt, it had been brought out of committee and onto the floor of the House where it lost by only fourteen votes! Reva had steered it further in the 20th Assembly than it had progressed in twenty years.

And appreciation was not withheld. In her quest for the office of city commissioner that autumn the Brotherhood of Locomotive Firemen and Enginemen and six other related associations gave her their unreserved endorsement.

The same fate befell the chain store tax bill on which she put her shoulder to the wheel as forcefully as she had on the controversial train measure—defeated but not overwhelmed. Attorney Darrel Lane led the parley for the opposition and sparks from the debate lighted the House that day! Proof of the resistance of the time was evidenced in an editorial:

> Emulating Moses, the great lawgiver, Representatives Bosone and Hoyt in the state legislature have already started out to write a second Book of Exodus. If they should by any chance be permitted to finish their work, it will tell the story of the wanderings of a band of Zion's children out of their chosen land into other fields where the tax gatherer, perchance, has some idea as to what is meant by the slogan, "Live and let live."

She also fought for a wage payment bill because "in Carbon County I saw husky, healthy miners weighted down to peonage by coal companies that did not pay their men for seven and eight months at a time. It was there I saw the vicious economic system which forced the miners to do their business in the company store, buy at high prices, use their credit because the company had not paid the wages, and remain in debt and in peonage from year to year. The bill, amply supplied with teeth to take care of not only the Carbon County situation but other situations in various parts of the state, failed, fought by powerful lobbyists."

In the vortex of struggle, compromise, and victory of this session, Reva supported the small claims court bill and the anti-injunction bill which struck at company unions and outlawed the Yellow Dog Contract. She stood for a reduction in the legal interest rates, for a moratorium on home foreclosures, for an extension of redemption time after foreclosures, for unemployment insurance, against deficiency judgments, for shorter hours on public works. For weeks the nonstop legislator sparred with the Republicans on the sales tax in an endeavor to force big business to stand its share of the relief bill. Some of these bills were passed and others were put to sleep by the Senate.

Mrs. Bosone has a few maxims on introducing legislation. "At no time in my legislative experience have I been concerned whether or not bills were popular. If I believed in them I didn't care what others thought. I have to admit that is a poor attitude provided one wants to be elected or reelected. The nice guy who votes the popular way, who stays out of legislative controversy, remains in office for years and years. He doesn't have to spend time and energy in a campaign defending his vote. But poop on that kind of citizen! I have no respect for him. I have always striven to be the public servant that people compliment but fail so often to support.

"The satisfaction of being true to one's convictions is in being able to walk down Main Street and look each person in the eye!"

The soul having been elevated, the body and mind nonetheless felt the punishment of eighteen-hour days in hammering through social legislation. After the 1933 session a zombie went through its paces in the Bosone & Bosone offices; for a week or two Reva was a total loss and Joe threatened to bill the state for his wife's nonproductivity. After regaining her old energy, she wondered why she wasn't satisfied just to introduce legislation to name the state flower!

Clients

THE BRAND NEW LAW OFFICE needed recognition, so out went the announcements into a world of mortgage foreclosures, bank closings, vast unemployment, no relief programs, and unbelievably tight money! When President Franklin D. Roosevelt declared the bank holiday (for which Reva believed he was justified), her fortune consisted of fifty cents!

In Utah alone in one year, fourteen banks with deposits of $10 million, the savings of thousands of Utahns, had failed. After one of Reva's cousins withdrew her money from one bank and was rushing to deposit it in another she thought was safe, it closed!

Other gloomy statistics that bear out the hard-times stigma of the early 1930s include 882 bankruptcies in federal court in Utah during 1932–1933 and 635 home mortgage foreclosures in Salt Lake County during the same period.

And to rub salt in the wound of depression, the summer of '34 was the most devastating that some folk could remember for heat and lack of rain. Water was rationed! Two baths a week was the maximum. Lawns stayed mostly thirsty. And everyone just hoped for anything better!

The Bosones had clients—but mostly clients with no money. "My sympathy has always lost me money and an awful lot of energy. A compensation case I remember well came in which whipped up a lot of that sympathy. No lawyer would take this particular client's case because the law was against him. He was in our office every day for around three years! The poor guy had no place to go and he knew we were working on his case.

"Well, Joe took it to the Supreme Court of Utah where he won it. A tough case and one that created new law. It was written up in one of the country's law reviews; the Industrial Commission paid compensation to our client and the statutory fee to us.

"But from that day on we never saw the client again! We were told he was living up his money in houses of prostitution."

Recurrent soft touches—the Bosones took case after case that wound up as free; overridden by merciful hearts, they were giving them away in those days. Their general practice ran the mill from writing wills to tackling murder cases. Experiences that stand in review include the day a former judge, now deceased, came to Reva's office accompanied by a man from a neighboring state. Joe was out of town at the time.

The man had been charged with molesting a young girl and he felt he could not return to his state under the scandalous circumstances. So Reva was asked to take an affidavit stating that the man was innocent to the girl currently in reform school and influence her to sign it. In this event, Reva would receive $1,000 as a fee.

Money was scarce but she knew no amount of treasure would have induced her to commit such an unconscionable act. Even if she believed the man to be innocent, she knew it was for the court to decide. When Joe returned, Reva, who seldom played a practical joke, decided to try one out on her husband. She explained the reason for the visit with the judge and the indicted man and then told him she had taken the case.

"My God, you didn't!" he yelled, throwing his hands in the air. "I can't believe it. You call the judge immediately—we need money but not that bad!" Reva thought she knew what his reaction would be but she wanted to hear it in this manner.

In the practice of law, obviously, pressures on the value system can be enervating unless one has certain moral standards. Recent political developments have proved that the ever present temptations involving power and money can be difficult to resist.

Reva's accumulation of "firsts" was further augmented; she became the first woman in Utah to serve as a lawyer in a murder trial. Her brother Horace had requested Reva and Joe to assist him on a case involving a young man from American Fork who had been charged with murder. In great anguish he begged Horace to take his case. All three attorneys felt empathy because of their acquaintance with and knowledge of the defendant and his family.

"Our client was one of the best kids in our hometown," remembers Reva. "Smart, too. I was always fond of him. His mother was a person of high moral fiber—a wonderful woman devoted to her children. The father, however, long gone from his family, was referred to as a bootlegger in a Salt Lake City bawdy house. Up to the time our defendant, at the age of sixteen, was allowed to visit with his father, he had a clean record. I'm sure his mother didn't know about the father's circumstances when she let her son go to his father."

Horace Beck and the Bosones admitted that their man was guilty of planning burglary with an ex-convict friend, but of strangling a little old lady and burning her home—never. The defendant testified that he and the ex-convict, who knew there was money stashed on the premises, planned to burglarize the old lady's house in her absence. Prior to that, however, the defendant in casing the house saw the intended victim in the front yard; she reminded him of his mother so he suddenly had a change of heart. That evening he met his friend and backed out of the agreement, all of which enraged the more experienced criminal, and a violent argument ensued.

Horace argued in the trial that the friend, not their client, had the motive to kill. The ex-convict had rented a room from the woman and he admitted hating her. In the outcome, the ex-con was found guilty and Beck's client was sentenced on a lesser offense and placed in the county jail. Later, in the state penitentiary, the friend confessed to the murder. Horace appealed the case to the Supreme Court of Utah and within two years the court ruled with the attorney, setting aside the decision of the lower court and dismissing the case.

"My brother had done an outstanding job," Reva says, "for which he received a small fee. Joe and I received nothing. We have never seen or heard from the defendant since!" During this trial, which was filled with emotion, most of the friends and relatives of the defendant's mother appeared to have abandoned her, so to be of comfort and consolation, Reva's mother drove up from American Fork to sit with her in the courtroom.

"We had done what we thought was right and humane," Reva said, "but due to the personal aspects of the case, we three suffered some embarrassing publicity."

"I Move to Reconsider"

REVA ATTRIBUTES her loss of the City Commission race to bad judgment on her part, listening too intently to enthusiastic supporters who enticed her to run although she was quite aware that her status as a newcomer in town would work against her. Her disappointment was keen, but she has since felt that those campaigns resulting in losses were like the sculptor's layers of clay—building her up for future successes.

She ran twice more in later years, piling up a better record each time, and won the nomination in the third contest—but not the post.

In order to run for the commission office the first time, Reva had resigned from the legislature as a representative of Carbon County. So to serve as a representative in the session of 1935, it was necessary for her to wage another campaign, this time from her residence in Salt Lake County.

On the morning of the county convention, Reva's domestic helper offered to take Zilpha to the hall and distribute campaign cards. The candidate was grateful for the offer since extra money to spend in this election was simply not available. Arriving at the hall at noon, Reva was glad to see her card on every vacant chair which hopefully would be filled soon. She spied her helper trudging up one side of the auditorium passing out the information to those present and four-year-old Zilpha, resembling a tiny Margaret O'Brien with a dash of Italian, pitter-pattering down the other side pleading as she looked up into each delegate's face, "Won't you *please* vote for my mother?"

"Well," Reva laughs, "delegates came up to me later saying they couldn't turn down a sweet little girl who had asked them to vote for her mother." Then she added, "What Zilpha said and did was her own idea, I want to say!"

Reva worried a lot, as usual (lawmakers' jobs were coveted), and contemplated losing; she maintains it's easier to take defeat that way. But friends assured her that her record in the legislature would nominate her. The friends were accurate, the strongest support originating with women and labor.

That fall she found the campaign mechanics much more rugged in the main Utah city. Again, time and a vast store of energy were required to promote her cause effectively in the many cottage meetings, numbering five a night, to reach the grass roots constituency. She followed a strict line, always admonishing her volunteers: "You must never attack my opponent on anything but his record. You are not to slur the character or private life of my opponent. If you do, I will go on radio and denounce what you have said and denounce you permanently." The point was well taken.

Early on election night in November 1934 the Democrats celebrated another general victory. And again, the burden of responsibility of representing a county, now the largest one, tended to slope Mrs. Bosone's square shoulders. Not one to take any job lightly, she says, "A woman I knew, planning to throw her hat in the ring, said she thought it would be such *fun* to be a representative!

"Nothing should motivate any candidate for an office except service. If there's enjoyment, it comes from making new and lasting friends and in the realization that one is able to make a serious contribution."

AFTER a blustery snowstorm, the skies in the Great Salt Lake area generally brighten rather than hold on to their storm clouds. In January, during the legislative session, winter days can be enchanting, especially on Utah's Capitol Hill. Of handsomely turned granite on the outside and superbly crafted marble on the inside, Utah's statehouse (on a real hill) stands as impressive a building as can be found in the United States. Designed by the renowned architect, Richard L. Kletting, and financed by Harriman inheritance tax monies from the Union Pacific Railroad, it was completed in 1916.

Walking from the interior rotunda through the stately copper doors to the portico, below which are numerous wide granite steps, one could easily have a feeling of omnipotence. The eye travels straight south down State Street to Point of the Mountain, twenty miles away. It then takes in the roughed-up white frosting of the Oquirrh Mountains to the southwest and skims the bright sliver of Great Salt Lake to the west. In the southeast, however, is the most dramatic view; it sweeps from crest to crest in the jagged Wasatches: Red Butte, Mill-A, Mt. Olympus, Twin Peaks, Lone Peak—all snowed to baseline. And between the capitol and this natural grandeur is a vast array of man-made accommodations in a large valley—in the summer flounced by thousands of trees and in the winter tucked in by a white powder topping.

A man-made creation that never fails to inspire Reva is the ten-foot-high statue of Massasoit, sachem of the Wampanoag Indians of eastern Massachusetts, at first positioned under the capitol dome. Sculpted by Cyrus Edwin Dallin—the illustrious sculptor of Indians and designer of the Pioneer Monument in Salt Lake City and a native of Springville,

Utah—this heroic replica in bronze stands as though ready to conciliate, peace pipe cradled in his arm. It would prompt the lady legislator to cere-moniously pay homage each day as she entered the capitol to attend the session in her traditional well-pressed wool suit, pinning on the fresh rose presented the women legislators.

"I love the character of Massasoit. I loved him when I was a child and first read about him," she said. "In recent years his statue has been moved to the front grounds of the capitol. This infuriates me because the excuse given was that since Massasoit was from Massachusetts he was out of place in the Utah capitol! First of all, he was an original American who lived before Utah was ever heard of; and secondly, this sculpture is a tribute to a great native son.

"I surmise that one of the statues that took Massasoit's place would have shriveled in his shadow. A record of profits—ruthlessly chalked up by a former industrialist who is so honored in a bronze statue now in the capitol rotunda—could never replace the reverence for this land as prac-ticed by this marvelous race of people. Yes, I love Massasoit!"

A LAWYER FRIEND in the legislature, Ed Richards, managed a capsule campaign for Reva in her quest of the Speaker of the House seat in 1935. Walter Granger, one of the members of the sixteen-man bloc, beat her out by only a few votes, whereupon he helped her fight for the floor leader-ship of the majority party against Grant Macfarlane, a leading lawyer in town. She won, but with congeniality. (To keep her opponent's friendship was almost an obsession with Reva.)

Regarding that bout, she discloses, "Many honors have come to me, but none has thrilled me more than being the first woman in the history of the State of Utah to be elected floor leader of the majority party. All the women members supported me and most of the men."

Mrs. Albert Jensen, representative from Salt Lake County during that period, commented then, "For Utah women, at least, Mrs. Bosone's election was a triumph almost as great as the appointment of Frances L. Perkins, a member of the national cabinet." Mrs. D. C. Gibson of Helper said, "It means a new deal in politics for Utah women." (This did not prove necessarily true, however.)

The next step toward Reva's goal was her appointment to the Rev-enue and Taxation Committee, formerly an all-men domain, certainly an impressive start in her second term. One of the first considerations was the natural gas tax bill. A bill with a gas tax plank had been introduced in the 1933 session, so Reva was confident that the author of that bill, along with the legislator who was most articulate in its behalf, would push the current bill through the Senate.

It passed the House, and Reva, who meantime had been made chair-woman of the Sifting Committee (equivalent to the powerful Rules Committee in the United States Congress), was anxious to see this bill come out of the Senate. The inequity of the tax system had been pinching her sense of justice—why was the gas company so favored when the coal mine industry, so vital to Utah, was heavily taxed? Representing Carbon County had made her painfully aware of the discrepancies.

Pressures on her to drop the bill were heavy but she knew and the opposition found that she was simply unable to compromise her principles. The two senators, grandly enthusiastic in the previous session, meanwhile had cooled their support while stringing Reva along. "I learned a lot about politics from that experience, which was a shocker! A few years later one of those two state senators aspired to the national Congress. First pop he saw me, and first pop I said, 'You'll have to go back to the state senate and keep your nose clean before I can ever be for you again.' He never ran again. I have always believed that since he wanted to go further in politics, he has lamented his session in the state senate."

These early encounters convinced her that the legislature is the place to test the individual's political attitude and character. "No person should ever become governor or a member of the United States Congress without first having served in the state legislature. A candidate can appear to be the most patriotic, intelligent citizen around; when he gets into the legislature, where he cannot equivocate, his mettle is really tried. Without having this knowledge, the constituency is sitting in the dark when it elects candidates."

One person who would say amen to those sentiments is the man who was floor leader of the United States House of Representatives when Reva served as a member of Congress. John McCormack once advised several other members planning to try to influence a change in the Utahn's thinking on a bill to desist. He said he was quite sure that if she believed in certain legislation, no amount of persuasion could change her vote.

Her theory held that even though she knew the facts of political life which state that the expedient legislator stands a much better chance to be reelected, she preferred her mother's guideline: "Do right and fear not."

Reva's tribulations in the House with the Child Labor Amendment to the national Constitution even now incite incredulity. Her close friend, Mrs. Burton W. (Elise) Musser, who later was selected by Cordell Hull to represent the United States at the Lima Peace Conference, had introduced the amendment in the Utah Senate where it passed easily, encouraging Reva, who took for granted it would zip through the House where she was its sponsor. Once more, the lesson she learned dearly explained the reason it had passed the Senate—the opponents were sure the farm bloc of the House would kill it.

So again, where there was Reva there were crowds, interest, tension, controversy, and fascinating debate. The galleries were again overflowing. And Reva became aware of being followed—everywhere. The eye of the press was upon her. And it was out to get her—in print. Good press is what she was; her very nature stimulated headlines. And a talented reporter of legislature affairs for the *Salt Lake Tribune,* Bernard L. (Barney) Flanagan, was sufficiently impressed with Floor Leader Bosone that almost twenty years later he joined her congressional staff in Washington, D.C. And now, more than twenty years after that, the three of them—Barney, his wife Lila, and Reva—get together to look back with humor and amnesty on jubilant, disastrous, and triumphant times that accompany political and writing careers.

For several days Reva had been soliciting support from the sixty members of the House and at last she was sure of thirty-one votes— enough to win ratification. In debate, as in other showdowns, she was a battler all the way.

"Sometimes I wonder why I had to make the job so all-fired difficult!" She was insistent, however, that this measure was particularly necessary for welfare reform and she extended herself accordingly.

Again, illegal lobbying was muddying the legislative waters. This time it was a minister lobbyist who was relaying information to a sympathetic representative in an attempt to force a defeat. How could any citizen, let alone a minister, she wondered, fight a bill concerned with safe working conditions for children? Later she was clued that the spiritual adviser was issued his instructions by a benefactor of his church who lived in the East.

Reva was keeping score as the vote was called when she heard Wilbur Maw, a farmer who had promised otherwise, answer "no." Up she jumped as though propelled by rockets! What a crisis! Every vote was indispensable! She bounded over to him, rasping, "My God, Wilbur, what is the matter with you?" slightly dazing the mind changer.

When she saw the bill was going to be defeated by one vote, she quickly got the floor and asked to change her vote to "no" (to move to reconsider, one had to vote with the winning side). Evening newspaper headlines proclaimed her change of vote and her request for a reconsideration of the amendment the following day. The story described her dash to Maw's seat and conjectured about her dramatic exclamation to him.

The next day Wilbur Maw lived up to his original promise and his vote enabled the bill to pass the Utah legislature. Reva was the recipient of congratulatory wires from Mrs. Eleanor Roosevelt and Mrs. Frances

Perkins of the United States Cabinet, the latter reading: "I have just heard of yesterday's actions by the House on the Child Labor Amendment and I wish to congratulate you on your part in obtaining ratification." However, the amendment was never passed by three-quarters of the states so it failed to be added to the United States Constitution.

Three years later, however, the Fair Labor Standards Act came to the rescue of exploited children with the same stipulations as incorporated in the Child Labor Amendment.

In this 1935 session Reva again introduced the Train Car Limit bill, which passed the House but not both bodies. Not even in 1937 did it make its way clear through the legislature. She, with Representatives Macfarlane, Holdaway, and Edman, sponsored the Metropolitan Water Act providing for incorporation, government, and management of metropolitan water districts, which passed. Another bill that became law in 1935, raising Reva's ire, prohibited the sale of liquor by the drink. According to a news report, "The vote overrode pleas of the floor leader Madame Representative Reva Beck Bosone who denounced the bill as an answer to the bootlegger's prayer."

Since the influential Sifting Committee considered all bills that had not been passed within the last two or three weeks of the session, the pressure on Chairwoman Bosone was extreme. She had been elated to be appointed to this position by Speaker Granger since it had been a male-dominated job and here was a singular opportunity to demonstrate that a woman could function in this capacity capably and independently!

"The selection of legislation by this committee was a terrific responsibility. Time was limited. I knew some of the good bills would die in committee. Since I had no strings attached to me and never have had, I was interested only in that legislation that would, in my opinion, do the most good for the greatest number of people.

"It was hectic," said the chairwoman. "I could scarcely sit at my desk without being called into the hall. To move was to be badgered. The telephone in my home rang practically constantly. But none of this irritated me because I believe people should feel free to contact a public servant. What may be a small matter in the mind of the official may be very important in the mind of a constituent. Who is to judge? But there is one thing about accepting this kind of procedure—it is physically difficult on the legislator!"

Tricks of the lobbyists' trade were familiar to Reva, but the only one in her experience involving money was played by a woman in Utah who proposed to pay her $100 to introduce and support a bill important to a business group. Reva had known this knowledgeable woman in various Democratic organizations. But assuming that she was ignorant of the meaning of the proposition, Reva explained that she was committing an indictable act for which the punishment was severe.

Apparently this caution did not penetrate because Reva subsequently learned that the woman tried her pitch on another legislator, who likewise refused her. Then the two legislators, with something in common other than their elected status, waited with curiosity to see if anyone would accept. Someone did—and the member turned out to be a reelected man of good reputation, a public servant who in future elections, however, received two fewer votes!

As a congresswoman, Reva participated in debate on the bill for the investigation of Washington lobbyists. Arguing against a probe, she maintained that if members cannot withstand the lobbyists, they should not be in Congress. "How are we going to reach the lobbyist who gets himself elected to a legislative body? What are we going to do with that one? The most vicious of all lobbyists is the person who represents selfish interests and gets himself elected. That occurs, as you know, in state legislatures and in the Congress of the United States."

Speaking at a Women's Legislative Council meeting in Salt Lake City in the winter of 1936, Reva minced no adjectives in charging that purely selfish reasons motivated lawmakers when introducing 50 percent of the legislation passed in Utah! Insidious lobbying by big business interests and public utilities was directing the course of state legislation. "A bill was introduced in the last legislature to make contracts entered into by fourteen-year-old children valid with the aim of producing more revenue for a large Salt Lake City concern. Luckily the bill was killed by the Senate Sifting Committee. What our state needs are more unselfish people who will fight for the good of the state rather than the good of private interests.

"This organization should choose a few bills for the public good and devote its full energy to lobbying at the first of the session, before the final rush, and make its lobbying as effective as that of the paid interests."

The floor leader's record was embellished by yet another accomplishment in the special summer session of the 1935 legislature when Ray Adams asked her, in his absence, to carry the ball for his State Unemployment Insurance Act. Once more she ran the full length of the field and made the goal. That statute later set up the Utah Department of Employment Security, which has operated for the benefit of the citizens of Utah ever since.

After the two sessions had adjourned the former state legislator was seated at the snack bar in the City and County Building when someone asked her a favor involving a drive to another city at her own expense.

Reva replied that she could not afford it, whereupon an acquaintance, overhearing the remark, said, "If you hadn't been such a damn fool in the last session you could have toured Europe!" A tour of Europe, she professes, would never clear a bad conscience for her!

THE RELATIONSHIP between Reva and her mother formed a bond that sustained each woman lifelong. When Zilpha Beck died, that bond was as much in evidence in Reva's life as before.

"A few years ago a political friend in Utah said critically that I never made a speech without referring to my mother. She was right. There isn't a situation about which I may speak that I wouldn't be reminded of what mother would say."

Perhaps the extent of the void experienced by Reva and her three brothers when their mother died that early spring of 1935 could be noted in their avoidance of voicing their thoughts about her for as long as ten years after. A stranger would have thought they had forgotten. Just the opposite. In order to avoid emotional reactions they just never spoke of her; it was a mutual understanding. Each confessed to holding her memory dear.

In spite of the family's arguments that Zilpha Beck, who was intensely interested in her daughter's career, wanted Reva to continue her legislative contributions, Reva regrets not abandoning her work to be a constant comfort to her mother during the lingering illness resulting from cancer. She did visit her at all hours, however, and continually checked on her. Reva's deep affection for the woman she cherished above all others left her vulnerable in the loss and in a state of misery for months.

"I thought if I could only touch her how relieved I'd be," she despaired. Finally a dream in which her mother appeared and insisted that she take her arm mollified the terrible longing and is graphic in her mind today.

The funeral, held in the Second Ward Chapel of American Fork, was a lasting tribute to Mrs. Beck's courage in preaching her convictions and her character in carrying them through. The legislature had sent a committee delegation to attend the funeral; two resolutions of respect were read—one from Governor and Mrs. Henry H. Blood and the other from the Italian-American Civic League. One of Reva's colleagues was heard to say, "Apparently a most unusual woman has passed away!"

When Reva stresses that her mother's kind but strong personality and insistent moral teachings molded the lives of the Beck children, one is reminded of Garson Kanin's remarks in *Tracy and Hepburn:* "Kate greatly admired her mother, an uncommon relationship in any generation. A result of admiration is often emulation and Kate has gone through life emulating, or attempting to emulate, her mother and her father."

Says Reva, "No bouquet has ever been handed to me that I haven't thought of mother. My friends have long since learned that when I'm handed a bouquet, I weep. I weep because the bouquet is really for her, not for me; if I'm anything at all it is because I'm a product of my mother!"

MOST of the year of 1935 had been strenuous, sad, and fatiguing, but the coup de grâce was in the offing. In the fall, the state chairwoman of the Democratic party was due to be elected. Incumbent Ruth Penrose evidently was not enemy-free because several prominent women in the Democratic organization sought out Reva, asking her to run as the opposition. They were determined that the state needed a new chairwoman and if Reva did not accept, they would seek someone else. Reva wasn't well acquainted with Mrs. Penrose at the time but she reasoned that if these women with a single thought were so strong in their conviction, perhaps she should accept. So after she had announced her candidacy and was caught up in the campaign, she learned that those same women had changed their minds; they could see that Ruth Penrose looked unbeatable. And indeed she was!

Reva, meanwhile, had placed herself in what she describes as one of the cruelest situations of her life. At a crowded Democratic women's meeting in October at the Newhouse Hotel, she arrived late and slipped into the last row. Only those in back saw her. As she observed the proceedings, she saw herself verbally hanged in effigy! One woman after another tore into her with vengeance, each more vicious than the one before. Watching an absolutely crushing display of hatred, Reva sat stunned, unable to leave. As a gesture to finish her off, a tall, elderly woman censured with: "Who is this Bosone? She's never rung a doorbell. She's a lawyer. Well, send her back where she came from. We don't want her!"

Frustrated, Ruth Penrose arose and exclaimed, "Ladies, you've said enough! Mrs. Bosone has a perfect right to be a candidate." She followed up with a few remarks against the ugly comments. Since she was unaware that Mrs. Bosone sat somewhere in the audience, she impressed Reva deeply with this beneficence. When the meeting adjourned and Reva was seen leaving, an embarrassed silence prevailed; Reva does remember seeing many flushed faces. Without referring to the scene, she left the hotel quietly.

"Days later," Reva recalls, "a friend met me saying her conscience bothered her, that she should have defended me at that meeting, that she should have put her arms around me, that I seemed so all alone.

"Well, you'll never know how all alone I felt. I hurt way down deep. But a few years later those very same women did an about-face, and one in particular never failed to apologize every time she met me, 'How I could eat those mean words I said about you in that meeting!'

"Ruth Penrose, my defender at that meeting, became one of my most devoted friends. She managed my first congressional campaign and I must say, she is one of the kindest human beings I have ever known!"

IN THE SPRING of 1936, the idea of filling the vacancy of assistant city attorney occurred to her. So it would be a precedent! But Reva had been breaking barriers since her high school presidential aspirations. And about this time she had resigned herself to the fact that she was being made to shoulder the family financial responsibility and had better try to establish herself in a steady income position in these testy depression days.

Joe had decided that money could be made drilling oil wells in Montana but the venture proved a financial bust. He often devoted two or three days a week to his favorite sport of fishing and the hunting season in the fall always claimed his presence from the law office. Ultimately, the case load fell mainly upon Reva, who already carried her share of extras such as participating on the County Welfare Board, presenting a course in parliamentary law every year, and giving innumerable speeches, not to mention the ever-pressing duties of home and motherhood.

She consulted the city commissioners about the assistant city attorney job—prosecutor at the police station—much to their consternation!

"I wouldn't think of having my sister in such a spot!" declared one of them.

"That's no place for a woman!" said another.

"Do you know the type of people you'd be dealing with?"

No argument was effective enough to change their views. So finis to an idea that was a brave thought. After all, women were not even accepted by men lawyers for jury duty in 1936, a condition Reva altered after becoming a judge.

That summer in a visit with her distinguished friend, former Chief Justice of the Supreme Court of Utah Samuel R. Thurman, he grasped her hand and said, "Reva, I think you should run for a city judgeship this fall and then go on up to the Supreme Court." The jurist, in his late eighties, who was the authority on water law in the West, had always championed the cause of women. In the 1896 Territorial Convention held in Salt Lake City, he supported their efforts to win suffrage. According to

Judge Thurman, the renowned pioneer woman, Mrs. Eliza Snow, riding on horseback, covered the state gathering petitions which she stuffed in gunnysacks to deliver to the convention. Brigham H. Roberts, the great Mormon orator, was for denying women their vote. It is is said that Judge Thurman pointed his finger at all those sacks in the corner of the convention hall and argued, "How dare you refuse the women whose names are in those gunnysacks the right to vote?" Well, the Judge and his cohorts won, and not only did women get their suffrage but they were given jury service and other important considerations.

"The women of Utah should bow low to Eliza Snow and that great supporter of women's rights, Samuel R. Thurman," declares Reva.

Now the mature jurist was encouraging Reva in her ongoing career. "How about seeking one of the four nominations for the city judiciary?" he asked. And that question provoked an on-the-spot decision. "That's just what I'll do!" she announced.

Her Honor

SEVERAL AIDES-DE-CAMP thought her name would be accepted at the county convention by acclamation, but, hesitating to risk the possibility, Reva asked her former law teacher, Dean Leary, to nominate her for the judgeship. "Believe me," Reva emphasized, "I was thrilled he would do this because he valued his reputation." One must assume this is exaggerated modesty on Reva's part because Dean Leary had revealed his confidence in her ability when he answered an inquiry about her qualifications with these specifics: ". . . she has an ability to see legal points with a balanced judgment. . . . She is extremely conscientious and enthusiastic about anything she undertakes. . . ."

PHOTO: *On the bench in the 1940s.*

True to custom, Reva fretted about the possibility of losing, then won the nomination and the election by a most comfortable margin.

"The morning of December 1, 1936, I awakened with qualms and apprehension," she recalls. "With any new position in my life I have been sure of only one thing—I wanted to do a good job. The responsibility that came with being one of the few women judges in the United States—approximately twenty-five, I believe—and the first one in Utah, weighed heavily on me. I had prepared for the job by studying the procedure and had received valuable advice from professional people, but I was nervous nonetheless."

Breaking in the job took some doing—everybody was minding Judge Bosone's business. Unsolicited advice came from likely and unlikely sources, but certainly not from her husband or brothers. The very fact that it did not makes an experience ironic.

A not uncommon theory then supposed that a woman in a man's job received her know-how from a man. In those early days, her husband and brothers were continually confronted by those who were curious about why she held as she did under certain facts in court. Knowing Reva's convictions about living her own life, they always answered, "I don't know the facts; she doesn't discuss her cases with me. There must be some good reason why she held as she did."

Joe, who was always proud of his wife's accomplishments, said he was about the last to know what was going on in his wife's court.

But a secret they had conspired to keep from her finally surfaced one day when Joe mentioned in passing, "Reva, do you know you have been investigated?"

The Judge looked bewildered. Then she remembered the time she had caught the men lawyers in a sotto voce conference, excluding her, and was handed a lame excuse.

"Well, we tried not to let you know," Joe continued, "but I can tell you now you were found to be entirely innocent."

"Innocent! OF WHAT?" the defendant bristled.

"Someone complained to the Bar Association that you always recommended either of your brothers on cases when you were asked about a lawyer."

"What a lie! I have never mentioned either Clarence or Horace. My reply has always been to consult the Yellow Pages. There are about four hundred lawyers listed and all but about seven are reputable."

"I know," Joe nodded, "and that's exactly what the Bar found out."

The Judge immediately phoned the executive secretary of the Utah State Bar who confirmed a complaint that the Bar felt compelled to investigate. He remarked that he thought the investigation was the only course. "Without it, the rumors would have persisted and some people may have believed them. Now you know and the Bar knows that you have been cleared." Case closed.

Reva postscripts: "I had reason to think then that I had an enemy in the Bar in Salt Lake City who would have done anything to discredit me."

Reva Beck Bosone is a public woman but also a very private one. Assuming the responsibility for child rearing was as important to her as introducing a state law—in fact, the upbringing of Zilpha took precedence. She was particularly watchful never to leave her daughter alone. When the maid was not at the Bosone residence, Zilpha would be in the company of her mother—wherever that was.

One time Reva explained to the tike, age three, that mother would have to attend a big meeting and sit with the speakers, that she would take Zilpha with her if she would remain quiet and never move from her chair in the front row (where mother could watch her constantly). In such case, mother would continue taking daughter to various functions.

Sitting wide-eyed and prim in a navy blue coat and a tam pulled down on one side over dark brown bangs, happy Zilpha passed the test with aplomb, prompting onlookers to wonder whether she had understood the complete text of the speaker. From that day, Reva was confident that Zilpha would not cause her problems. Not only was she not a problem, but little Zilpha was a source of amusement, becoming imbued with the spirit and atmosphere of the political meetings which was later evidenced in novel speech patterns such as: "I make a motion that we buy an ice cream cone . . . that we visit Aunt Norma (Horace's wife) . . . that we get a little puppy!" And then she would cinch it with Robert's Rules of Order in an audience of one. "Those in favor say aye and those opposed." The vernacular suited Mother Reva—maybe she had a budding legislative assistant!

ALL the little, and big, earthy offenses within the jurisdiction of the Police and Traffic Court wound up before the bench of Judge Bosone and found an equitable ear. She drew many supporters but some Salt Lakers could not resist tossing a few grains of salt on the righteous Judge. Humorist Swen Teresed reported that he succumbed to the temptation of easing through a yellow light on 13th East and tried to cut a deal with the Judge to rob the *Deseret News* morgue of the worst pictures of her if she would suspend the sentence! Recognizing a sinful bribe for what it was, she answered with a resounding NO, adding with a twinkle in her eye, "You're lucky to get off with $5." And Ham Park in his "Senator from Sandpit" column referred disrespectfully to "Leva Buck" Bosone. To which she said, "So?"

Police court handled a potpourri of criminal cases. Inconceivable misdemeanor violations tended to test the Judge's credulity of them. "It's pretty difficult to realize the extent to which some of those offenders went!" However, if she entertained the slightest doubt (always based on reason), she would find the defendant not guilty. After three months, A. Pratt Kessler, the able prosecuting attorney, gently challenged her findings.

"Judge, when a defendant comes before you, you put yourself on trial. You know you couldn't have done what he did, so you find him not guilty. But sometimes he *is* guilty—he really *has* done what the charge alleges." She thought that fair criticism and decided to listen more objectively; she soon became aware of a segment of the human race devoid of any obvious moral standards.

Nevertheless, before the courts used social workers, her compunction to dispense fair judgment had her requesting the police chief to assign a police officer to court each morning who would investigate the backgrounds of selected defendants. This information, plus the advice of psychiatrists and general practitioners, facilitated the process of sentencing justly—for the city and for the defendant.

Handling hundreds of cases of petty larceny and shoplifting, the Judge asserts that most of the offenders could have paid for the stolen goods. In fact, in her recollection, in only one case was the offense deemed a necessity—when a mother stole a bottle of cod liver oil for her child.

A respectable-appearing couple from a nearby town had acquired their Christmas gifts the easy-on-the-pocketbook way. Thinking big, they had even tucked an electric toaster in their shopping bag. The young wife of a district manager obtained an ample supply of Christmas gifts by the "lift" method, and her generosity to friends during the holiday season could be easily understood. Two parents, with the help of their children, had shoplifted for an entire day.

"I fairly ate the heads off the parents," the Judge declared. "Can any decent person imagine conspiring with his teenage son and daughter to steal? Well, those parents were jailed, believe me. I turned the kids loose."

These tendencies are often blamed on kleptomania by the public, says the Judge. "Of all the cases I handled, only one concerned kleptomania. An attractive, middle-aged woman pled guilty to stealing fishing reel and tackle, but she had never fished in her life. The list of her stolen goods was unusual, to say the least."

Arrests that tended to perk up the mundane entries on the court agenda were from the ancient profession, of which there was a sizable number. The prostitute on the stand was alluding to her profession as

work. The lady judge turned to her and asked, "Do you call that work?"
To which the worldly woman answered, "If you don't think so, Judge,
you better try it some time!"

Reva Bosone was accused many times of having asked that question
after she assumed the city judgeship; it was obviously calculated to un-
nerve the new "square" magistrate. Just a story, the Judge claims,
because prostitutes were always taken to her chambers and not to the
open court.

Shortly after Reva donned the robes, an officer walked around her
desk and whispered of a defendant, "She's only a prostitute."

"So what? A prostitute has rights in my court like anybody else." And
so she did. Why be so tough on the gal, she reasoned, when the other of
the two-to-tango team walks away? The Judge always looked around for
the partner. If the officer had bypassed him, the case was dismissed.
Believing in equal justice, Reva was recently incensed over an incident in
which a woman municipal judge in San Francisco was called on the carpet
(by a man judge in the Superior Court) for dismissing cases against
several prostitutes because the other person to the crime, the man, had
not been charged. "The idea of another court butting in!"

Unforgettable was an experience at the end of the day's court session.
Two officers brought to the bench a young woman charged with rolling
the colleague of a famous entertainer from Hollywood who had been in
the Salt Lake area to organize a benefit performance. This man wound up
with the defendant after getting word of her availability from a bellhop
the night before. After being taken for $100 instead of the usual, much
smaller, rate (everything was cheaper in those days), the paramour was so
enraged that he called a friend who worked for a newspaper, insisting he
wanted his money back; the friend in turn notified the police.

Judge Bosone listened intently to the incredible story.

"How much money do you have left?" she asked the young woman.

"Eighty dollars."

"Keep it! Any man who goes out with a prostitute should have sense
enough to know he may get rolled!"

The old Salt Lake City jail connected to the police station building
featured a flamboyant past with illicit ladies. In the 1920s when the
women were flushed out of the three downtown houses of prostitution
after police officers were issued orders to close them down during the
LDS Conference, they would be held a few days on the top floor for a VD
test and then given a floater (escort by police) out of town. But before
they were released, a few of these ladies of the night had been known to
tie sheets together and slide down the drainpipe between the police and
telephone buildings to make their getaway! No such lenient setup is
available in present accommodations in the maximum security high rise in
Salt Lake City.

Call girls were considered a few steps higher on the "easy virtue" ladder, and during World War II certain servicemen stationed at Camp Kearns (located ten miles outside the city) complained that they contracted VD in Salt Lake City. Judge Bosone, sensitive to this effrontery to her city's name, exerted every authority to eradicate such an impression.

The late former Sergeant Al Rogers, a tall, slim member of the police force from the early 1920s to the late 1950s, recalled that in talking things over with the Judge one day she suggested that he check out a nearby quality hotel on a situation that might be involved in the spread of the disease. So Rogers, head of the anti-vice squad, and two other policemen found, after going over the reservations list, a nest of five girls and five army captains in one room; one of the girls was a mere fifteen years old!

In the attempt to apprehend them and take the girls to jail and place the captains in the custody of the MPs, a scuffle ensued which left the hotel room awry. Rogers recalled the incident vividly because the next day the hotel manager angrily called the police department, making his own indictment that the arresting officers had been boozing, whereupon the indignant Rogers dispatched a strong letter informing him that not one member of that anti-vice squad imbibed. No further word was heard.

In the 1930s and '40s the word "commune" meant what one did with nature, and young people of both sexes living together and sharing their beds with different partners each night aroused shock that might not cause an eye to bat in the swinging 1960s and '70s. When a case in point came to the attention of the Judge, she tried to persuade them—this time, four boys and four girls in their late teens—to adopt a different approach to life that would be spiritually and mentally rewarding to themselves and to society. After extracting from them a promise to return to their respective homes, she kept her word not to call in the parents. Then she ordered a sympathetic police officer to keep them under surveillance while they were on probation. As far as it was possible to learn, an adjustment to the morality of the times was reached and no further aggravations were reported.

Two fourteen-year-old girls provided a succinct education for the Judge. She had no jurisdiction over juveniles, but the police officers believed that in unusual cases her compassionate manner with young girls could accomplish better results than immediately ordering the girls to the juvenile court. One of these offenders was a comely teenager who was being held a day or two in the city jail awaiting the court's schedule to investigate her background. But the Judge didn't get the opportunity to deal with her because the women prisoners in the girl's cellblock demanded her removal. Cause? Vile and obscene language!

The other incident concerned a pretty girl escorted to the Judge's chambers by a truck driver who had picked her up on the highway hitchhiking and was anxious to ensure her well-being. It could be mentioned here that never on the Judge's *criminal* court agenda was there an entry for a truck driver, casting a positive light on individuals of that vocation.

Judge Bosone questioned the young girl at length. A runaway, she concluded, with a non-caring father somewhere. Would the girl be interested in living in a comfortable home in Salt Lake City if the Judge could find one? She would, whereby arrangements were made with a prominent couple and their congenial children. The accommodations and atmosphere were close to ideal in this home, but it was soon learned that every night the young girl would slip downtown to solicit lovers.

Appalled on discovering her tricks, the couple nevertheless assumed an even greater responsibility by promising her a nursing education if she would resume conventional habits and finish high school. But eventually the benevolent couple called the Judge to report their charge missing. And missing she stayed, as far as could be determined. Heartbreak—for counsel, temporary guardians, the real father who showed up in court and proved he was no villain, and most of all for the girl herself, who would have to make many adjustments and compromises.

In those embattled years the Judge waged a few minibattles of her own. One of those chosen by a county committee to contact cafes and restaurants in town to allow black soldiers to be served meals, she took heart in the community's enlightened attitude when those establishments opened their doors to the soldiers.

She takes satisfaction, too, in knowing that in 1940 she carried a banner for another cause. Two young black women had been spectators in her courtroom in the City and County Building. Afterward they went upstairs to the snack bar for refreshments and were refused service. Court Clerk Fern Corless was a witness to this discrimination and reported it to the Judge, who then sternly faced the mayor, "I won't eat there until the policy is changed! They pay taxes and this is a public building," after which the policy change was accomplished.

Forgiveness is highly celebrated at Christmas, and of the city jail prisoners "who have offended themselves more than they have the city," twenty-eight nondangerous individuals were set free through the solicitude of Attorney F. Henri Henroid, who presented their case in well-turned verse, touching the just heart of Madame Judge:

> To the court, in her majesty, hear ye this plea
> For release on the morrow of those not so free—
> Subpoena contention and summon all strife,
> But pardon these errant one day of their life.
> And though I condone not their erring and vice

Such erring has happened not once and not twice,
But millions and billions have sinned just as these
From the walks of New York to the Antipodes.
Who among us would shrink opportunity here
To bring to these hearts a Happy New Year?
What a thrill! What a chance we have on this day
To banish all sorrow and drive it away!

(Poet Henroid recently served as chief justice of the Supreme Court of Utah, proving a gift for rhyme never hurts any career!)

To those prisoners standing before her with the varying expressions, Judge Bosone was granting a reprieve. She was reported to have said, "It is the hope of this court that you will begin the New Year right. Most of you have appeared before me at other times and asked for leniency on the grounds that you were either drunk or this was the first time you had been before this court, but I tell you now that it is the wish of this court that you never appear here again. Many of you have pled guilty—many have pled not guilty. But the greatest Christmas present that you can give to this court is never to appear here again!"

Even a glance at the police blotter might have shocked that sister of one of the commissioners who had discouraged Reva from pursuing the job of assistant city attorney. And yet pressure had been brought by those same men who formerly had shouted, "That's no place for a woman," for Judge Bosone to remain at the police court for three years! That long stretch gave her cause to appreciate the calmer atmosphere of the civil bench were she next moved. She was still mother confessor to troubled citizens from all over Utah, but the undeniable demands of the police court were lessened in her new assignment, something of a blessing in light of her coming personal ordeal.

REVA was always pleased that her husband's smooth good looks and likable personality were generally admired (Joe's sophistication made him especially attractive to women), but marital diversion was particularly abhorrent to her; Reva remembered cringing when a woman defendant, lover of a married man, chided in court, "Let the best woman win!"

The Bosone marriage, to the onlooker seemingly bombarded with influences that could cause dissonance, had to its advantage the "mutual admiration" cohesion. Joe's ability as a lawyer, as well as Reva's, was undisputed and each was liberal with a glowing word for the other when deserved. Their association as law partners created no friction—they just never argued over how a case was to be handled. Maintaining separate offices, they shared a reception room and a secretary. In those depression years both had to practice their skills just to bring in enough to make a livable home, but Reva was obviously the workhorse of the two.

A fair attitude prevailed in their private relationship as well as in their career lives. Scores of friends and colleagues from her legislature days would drop by the office with invitations to Reva for lunch. Joe was unperturbed—he knew they would dine in a public restaurant. There was never a problem—he knew his wife's ethics and morals were straight as a high wire.

After a week of intense work in the office, the couple would usually relax on Saturday night at the atmospheric Pinecrest Inn at the end of the road in Emigration Canyon where aromatic breezes fanned the thick forests. They would choose a small table on the side and always make two cocktails their limit for the evening. Friends gossiped that the Bosones danced every dance cheek to cheek, especially to Reva's favorite, "Stardust," now an evergreen in popular music but in the thirties a fresh, swingy tune. If it was played when they were apart on the dance floor, Joe had one objective—to find his wife and make that dance romantically theirs!

As professional pressures multiplied, Joe assumed a few home chores—he often prepared breakfast and enjoyed cheffing the meat course at dinner. He even provided nursing duties, catering to Reva's needs throughout a three-week illness; and on one occasion his worry over Reva's flighty heart action kept him awake all night.

When Reva was elected to the bench, of necessity they no longer practiced law together, but comforting to her were Joe's genuine expressions of interest in her success. (Contrary to one supposition, Joe never did try a case under his wife's jurisdiction.) But a friend of both asked later, "How would you feel if you were referred to as the Judge's husband?" In those days of women's unlib, the Bosone union started out successfully on the unique career basis as equals. Reva says not, but it is impossible not to imagine that as the honors were bestowed on her, Joe viewed himself as playing second string, much like the mates of movie queens.

In the summer of 1939 an attack of hay fever was so aggravating that Reva, with Zilpha, decided to spend three weeks in Long Beach, California, in an attempt to get relief from her allergy in the sea air. After her return she learned by accident of Joe's dates with another woman.

The first spike had been driven into the Bosone romance! Reva was shocked, having never considered the possibility, and then heartsick, having tried always to be the lover and companion Joe had married. She was further appalled to learn that this was not the first of his assignations.

Mindful of his loving acts with her, Reva could not comprehend that Joe did not care deeply for her. In a conversation with long-standing friend Oliver Clay, she heard him explain, in dissecting the situation, the gambit of husbands loving their wives but insisting on outside affairs.

Joe's vehement apologies and adamant promises to reform, sometimes on bended knee with tears in his eyes, assuaged her for the time being—Reva was a forgiving person. But there came a time when she viewed the situation of repeated infidelity as intolerable. Whenever she broached the subject of separation or divorce, however, young Zilpha would become recalcitrant.

Driving home one evening Reva and Zilpha spied a Ford like Joe's parked in front of a house that had been made into apartments. Zilpha cried, "Stop!" Since there were many Fords in town like Joe's, Reva was hesitant at first but decided to wait across the street for a while. Then she turned around and drove up behind the parked car. As she sat, engulfed in a sense of futility and despair over what she might see or what she should do, a young girl emerged from the house. Reva asked whose car was in front of hers and the youngster replied, "It's Joe's."

Reva decided to enter the apartment pointed out by the child and there saw her husband eating dinner with two women. Her erratic heart skipped a few beats at that moment; she walked out and informed Zilpha, waiting in the car, who promptly acquiesced, "Okay, Mother, you can get the divorce."

Neither of the couple wanted the separation. Reva was still very much in love with her husband and Joe balked at signing the divorce waiver. When she broke down and wept in front of Judge Herbert Schiller, he sympathetically encouraged her to cry it out.

"That midnight," Reva recalls, "I went outside and hand-sprinkled the front lawn. It seemed to calm my nerves. Joe drove up and came over and put his arms around me saying, 'You don't want to get a divorce. Why?' I told him he knew more about the reason than I did and he said that within six months everything would be all right.

"The night before the six-month interlocutory period ended, Joe called to ask if I would set aside the divorce. My heart wanted to accede but my reason said no because I wasn't convinced that the situation had righted itself. The divorce became final. I didn't ask for alimony or child support."

The tragedy of stepping apart is compounded by tendencies to trace in the memory those lovely intimacies, the triumphant moments of reaching a goal together, the daily rituals of give and take. Oliver Clay would report to Reva, "I saw Joe today, and all he did was talk about you!"

Four years later as she stepped from the bench one day Reva gasped to read the name of her former husband in the marriage license column of the newspaper. At that moment Judge William Burton, on his way from court to his car, offered her a ride to Main Street. She accepted, and once in the car she could no longer hold back those choking emotions and broke into anguished sobs.

"What in the world could make you feel like this?" asked Judge Burton, but there were no words to contain her answer. When the tears finally stopped, they continued on their way.

The break remained unhealed for approximately ten years but Reva never regretted her decision. From then on, there was complete emotional detachment, even disinterest, and time covered all ties and bonds, if not memories. But true to the charity of her nature, she maintained a friendly relationship, especially to keep Joe informed about their daughter. In July 1974, Joe died after a long illness during which his former wife visited him on her every return to Salt Lake City.

REVA'S CAMPAIGN for reelection to the city judiciary contained a wild rumor that if left to circulate could have "circulated her right out of the judiciary." A friend reported to the Judge a conversation she had overheard in the Newhouse Hotel, the popular election headquarters, where two men had accused the Judge of divorcing her husband to marry divorced Paul Peterson.

Judge Bosone was acquainted with Paul M. Peterson, representative from Park City, by whom she had sat five years earlier in the state legislature; she became a good friend not only of Paul, but also of his wife and family. Disgusted that she and Peterson could be wounded in that manner if the story were left to fester, Reva made a thorough check of district court records and discovered that another Paul Peterson (the address was different from her friend's) had been divorced. This libelous castigation on the part of her political opposition was particularly abhorrent to her.

Reva's brother, Filcher, was called and posted on the scandalmongers. Before she could chart what his tack would be, he rushed to the hotel, grabbed each rumor spreader, jamming him against the wall, and promised his guts all over same wall if he didn't retract the wanton tale! Filcher's powerful right shoulder was a potent deterrent to resistance. The lie faded away.

In this campaign, as in so many others, Reva mentally prepared for her political demise. Against all principles of positive thinking, she truly believed in her defeat, which leads one to think that her many optimistic friends and believers counterbalanced the effect and swept her into office each time—only, of course, after Reva herself had labored unstintingly before the election!

Since the cor ˙ ˸ection was a national one, the hubbub and excitement were more noticeable even though the Democrats appeared sure-fire winners. With Reva's respected status, she was used by the state committee in places where a candidate was floundering, and once more a Democratic victory and a woman's reelection to the city judiciary were sustained.

PERIODICALLY over the energetic years the problem heart flagged her attention with warnings, but she more or less ignored them and allowed even more "straw" on her back. One of those extracurriculars that helped to create the maelstrom called Reva Beck Bosone's life was her member-ship on the board of Utah's Research on Natural Resources Foundation, an arm of the state headed by two engineering deans at the University of Utah. She gains much satisfaction from recalling her services in this respect.

The board aimed to analyze experiments of pilot plants around the world studying and processing coal and its by-products. A laboratory was set up in the "U" Engineering School and after a few years a voluminous report was written on the board's activity, emphasizing the small pilot plants' probes. Reva understands that this report was requested worldwide and that in some schools it was being used extensively.

The group worked often, diligently, and gratis! They confronted many dead ends; most of the big Utah mines were owned by eastern in-terests and in those days their attitude was why bother with by-products? Low-sulphur, long-burning, high-quality Utah coal was plentiful. But the members of this board were conservationists who were convinced even in the 1930s that exploitation of coal beds was an extravagance that should not be indulged.

And there was Reva's participation in the Consumers' Welfare League as vice-president. L. E. Elggren kept the heartbeat strong in this organization and Reva is ready to confer all the credit on the hard-toiling Elggren.

Reva's prosecuting attorney in Police and Traffic Court, A. Pratt Kessler, of necessity worked hand in glove with the Judge. A close friendship, enduring for thirty-eight years, had its start in those practical times. Judge Bosone united Kessler and his wife in matrimony and Kessler has given his promise that he will pronounce the remarks at her graveside!

Of opposing views in political persuasion, Kessler claimed none-theless to have given her his vote and his support, even though, as chair-man of the State Republican Committee in 1950, his name was reportedly involved with authorizing a smear sheet prepared by the infamous poison pen of Walter E. Quigley, which insinuated Communist loyalty and questioned the honor of Reva Bosone and Senator Elbert Thomas, in particular.

As an active Republican, Kessler was cautioned during one heated congressional campaign not to be seen walking down Main Street with Reva Beck Bosone. "It becomes a life and death matter," he quipped recently of the partisanship of some campaigners. His retort to the member of his own party was that the Judge could walk down Main Street with him anytime!

"She bent over backwards to help the downtrodden," he said. "She possessed high ideals and integrity."

As Reva moved to the civil court, a grateful editorial paid a fitting tribute to her contributions: "The Telegram recommends to the judges who will succeed her on the police bench a careful study of the enforcement methods and policies she established which have proved such an important fact in discouraging that driving recklessness and carelessness which is the greatest cause of accident and death."

To know that others had taken notice of her efforts was satisfying. One such obliging attorney wrote wordily, "Your passing from this responsible position, which you have so ably and courageously filled for a long time, warrants friendly comment from those whose legal concepts prompt appreciation of credit and merit rising above and beyond political consideration, unalloyed by the contaminating influence that so often contributes to make of courts a farce in the minds of honest people and deserves favorable mention."

Her prosecuted public was free with the praise, too. A Christmas card from a defendant in a morals case reads: "Thank God for people like you to set people right. I'm feeling wonderful now. Thanks to you."

And from the state penitentiary "I wish to thank you for calling Warden Nebeker in my behalf. I cannot find the proper words to express my gratitude but assure you that anything you have done and may do for me will be deeply appreciated.

"All I can really say is that, though I am unable at present to show my real feelings, my release will find me an entirely different person than I have been heretofore.

"I believe I can safely say that you can be positive that I will not let you down in any belief you may have in me. My entire outlook on life has been changed.

"I swear that you will never have cause to regret any consideration or interest that you might have shown in my case."

IN the Criminal Division of the city court where Judge Bosone moved, the preliminary hearings in felony cases were held. Former associates are quick to assert that Reva had an intuitive ability for assembling around her an exceptionally competent crew. In the 1940s she called on Dr. Foster Curtis, psychiatrist and chief medical officer of the Veterans' Hospital, who never refused his free services although carrying a huge professional load. His answer to his astute jurist friend was always, "I'll be down sometime this afternoon." After examining the suspects, he would then report his opinions on the cases, a sizable number of which were sex offenses.

Consequently, the Judge was greatly assisted by this evidence (producing another first in court procedure) in passing judgment in such cases as the quiet, polite father who had raped his four-year-old daughter, tearing her body almost beyond repair; the refined husband who went on a rape binge and when apprehended was found to have acted peculiarly in recent months, like shoving out his foot to trip his young daughter; the complaining witness who had a handsome man arrested because he had knocked him down but who later admitted propositioning him; the Peeping Tom, the prototype of the next-door neighbor or the Sunday School teacher ("That's the reason they are so difficult to find—they are such nice guys!"); the exhibitionist, in the same class as the Peeping Tom—irritating to society, but usually harmless; the arsonist, much more dangerous, who relieved his sexual frustrations by watching the fires he set; the impotent man who polluted the air with invectives to women on the street (the Judge believes that some writers of obscene literature may have a like problem).

In her court she requested attorneys to excuse all spectators in sex cases. There was no reason not to be discreetly kind, she avers.

The role of judge was sometimes a pitiable one when it carried the responsibility of listening to cases of acquaintances and then sentencing them. Among the prisoners in court one morning was a young woman whom Reva knew, one whose relatives were well known for their contributions in the community. A man was called to the bench with her; they were charged with misconduct when both had been arrested the night before, having been found in a compromising position under a bush in a park. They pled guilty.

Torment surged through the Judge as she whirled her high-backed chair around to face the wall, tears smarting from beneath closed eyes. The courtroom crowded with offenders waited in curious silence. Finally, turning her chair back to face the defendants, she spoke barely audibly to the man standing in front of her—he should know that the woman's prominent family should not be forced to suffer such a disgrace! And the man seemed capable at that moment of being truly repentant. "Your Honor, I'm sorry," he submitted. Reva then placed them both on probation.

Nothing is known of the man's whereabouts, but the woman's respectability and charitability in later life contrasted with the indiscretion of a youthful escapade. She is now deceased.

Other perplexing cases that needed diagnostic attention included the overbearing woman who claimed she was sick and tired of having a woman passerby blow down her back as she walked down Main Street so she had beat up the bewildered complainant, who had never set eyes on the defendant. Dr. Curtis, after examining the defendant, reported that she constituted a real danger to the public, possessing homicidal tendencies, after which she was committed to the state mental sanitarium.

An assault and battery case demonstrating the sadism of a group of youths dispelled any sob sister notion about Judge Bosone that some might have held. Four young men over eighteen had stopped their car near a sidewalk and asked two girls to get in. When the girls refused, the boys climbed out of the car and pursued them, one of whom escaped. The other, having a sore foot, was caught. Nearby, a middle-aged man witnessing the caper hurried to the girl's aid. The man then became the victim and was beaten by the youths so brutally that bumps the size of eggs swelled on his face and shoulders!

"When the boys pled guilty I had them sit inside the bar and told them I would handle their case in my chambers after court. As they sat, their expressions were of amusement.

"In my chambers I looked across the desk and said, 'You boys don't have a little yellow streak running down your backs. They are a foot wide!' Their backs stiffened—I had hit a nerve. Well, by the time I got through with them, there was no longer amusement on their faces! They went to jail. And Officer Morrison kept track of them for a long time. To my knowledge, they never did repeat."

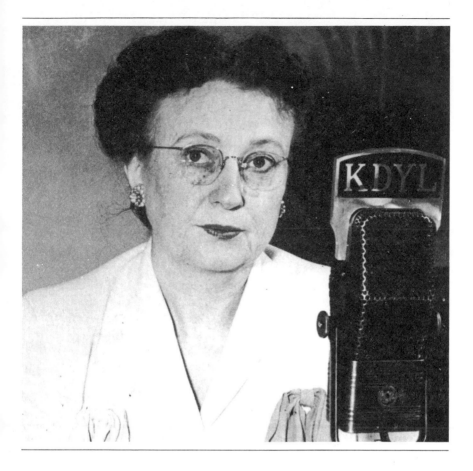

In the Spotlight

IN REVA'S THIRD TRY for the City Commission post, the feminists among her volunteers produced a campaign letter reading: "We've come a long way since the dark days of 1830, when women did not dare open a prayer meeting without the presence of some minister or elder. For, saist the men, if left to their own devices, there is no telling what those poor misguided females might pray for."

A few years later in the Lafayette Ballroom of the Hotel Utah the lights were dim as a spotlight played on the stage where the salient

PHOTO: *As a radio personality.*

features of a life of service were being dramatized. At the head table a napkin was held high to a face; it was fast becoming soaked with tears. The year—1943. The occasion—the ritual banquet of the Salt Lake City Council of Women's Hall of Fame, which was held every five years. The face behind the napkin was Reva Beck Bosone's, for she with six other outstanding women were being honored in Utah's most auspicious way. And no telling what prayers had been behind those achievements!

The cover page of the *Salt Lake Tribune*'s society section extolled: "Had their ideals been made into slogans and hoisted, each by its champion, there would have been a mingling of pennants reading something like this: 'Rehabilitation' . . . 'Social Justice' . . . 'Piety' . . . 'Literary Inspiration' . . . 'Leadership' . . . 'Cultural Progress' . . . 'National and Race Tolerance' . . .'" As the other women who were older responded, one could feel that this event was putting a period at the end of their lives. But in the Judge's remarks she informed the audience that the ceremony had given her the green light—the inspiration and the confidence to dedicate her future years to better service than she had already rendered. Rarely as emotionally touched, the Judge again held thoughts of her mother as her "bouquet" was bestowed.

In the fall of 1944 the Judge, exemplifying the woman of service, was asked to fill the role of WAC civilian chairman of the Ninth Service Command comprising nine western states. And in February 1945 she, with Captain Margaret Dean and others involved, flew to those nine states for a meeting with the governors and civic-minded women of each state to stimulate recruiting for the WAC program.

In April 1945—the notable month of the San Francisco inaugural of the United Nations—Reva, Mrs. Emily Smith Stewart, and Mrs. S. Grover Rich, a former state legislator, were chosen as official observers to the meeting. This official designation assured them tickets into the Civic Auditorium. But an extra honor was forthcoming for Reva.

"In the small conference of women who were planning to propose an equality clause in the charter for women, I had the opportunity to advise on the language. I was not one of those who sat at the table, but when it was learned that I was a lawyer the proposal was handed to me. It pleases me very much," said the Judge, "that I had the privilege of having a tiny part in that great occasion!"

In the hectic pace it was inevitable that something had to give. At last Reva was severely cautioned to trim a fat schedule to the bone for her health's sake. She knew her professional life could not be compromised (whatever she did was with finesse), so her extra activities were phased out—Phi Delta Delta, County Veterans' Welfare Board, Society of Mayflower Descendants, Alpha Iota, Soroptimist Club, the last two of which she became an honorary member. The only extra activity in which she indulged was the Women's Italian-American Civic League that she herself had spawned.

The slowdown meant more evening and weekend time at home and home meant the McClelland Street residence—old, well kept but unpretentious, looking very much like the school child's simple drawing of a house with the smoke curling from the chimney—with serviceable, built-for-comfort furniture, flowered rugs, potted plants, and a piano—*always* a piano, in tune.

Even with doctor's orders, it was well-nigh impossible for the Judge not to throw her soul into each and every involvement, which is the quintessence of her advice to women: "Meet what comes, head-on, and with interest!"

Reva claims to this day that she and house chores work well together—dusting, canning, and cleaning are happiness! In fact, she takes credit for creating a few of her most brilliant speeches while washing the dishes. One can hear her vibrant voice as she swishes the dishrag over the dinner crockery, "I prefer a government that will act as a referee rather than one claiming paternalistic control!"

Housedresses were the fashion for work at home in those days, even for judges. Marlene Dietrich and Katharine Hepburn were the women's pants advocates—and daring they were. Reva, wearing a cotton print, would accomplish on her home days the seemingly impossible. Splurging on work-saving appliances or gadgets was not up her alley; she was content to operate everything manually. Mowing the lawn (in a hat to protect her fair complexion) and darning socks were included in the weekly chores, and turning out a lemon pie on occasion was a specialty, although she delighted least in cooking of all the home-type tasks.

Her culinary efforts did not go unheralded, however. Grace Grether, former editor of the women's page of the *Salt Lake Tribune,* says that the Judge on election day evening could round up in one hour for a roomful of dinner guests a tasty roast enhanced with garlic and rosemary (her mother-in-law's recipe), salad, vegetables, and a very special dessert—a scrumptious lemon pie. The pie recipe is given here inasmuch as a flock of requests descended on the *Tribune* when her delectable dessert was described.

BESTEST LEMON PIE

4 eggs
2 lemons
2 tablespoons water
Walnut of butter
1½ cups sugar
Grate lemon rind, juice 2 lemons, add water, beat in egg yolks, add 1 cup sugar and butter and cook all in double boiler till thick, stirring

occasionally. Beat egg whites, add ½ cup of sugar, and fold the first mixture into the egg whites. Pour into baked crust. Chill. Top with whipped cream.

In the middle 1940s Emerson Smith of radio station KDYL invited the Judge to plan a five-minute program five days a week from her court chambers to air in the late afternoon, with which she obliged for a time. But five minutes was inadequate to "finish anything worth saying," so the station suggested a fifteen-minute segment on prime time, 5:45 P.M. every Thursday, to be called "Her Honor, the Judge." The format would include a discussion of her cases and philosophizing on them. Without preaching, she had an opportunity to enlighten a listening audience with a lesson in human conduct.

Her schedule was fattening up again, however, requiring her to scrape around for the extra hours on Wednesday night to write the radio script—gratis! But parents in the Salt Lake community made their teenagers a captive audience at dinner time for the Judge's weekly message, and even today she receives expressions of thanks from mothers for that program. The Judge was informed that KDYL received recognition for its civic involvement in the year's series in New York City. Although this and other extra commitments drained her physically, she now enjoys reminiscing about the benefits of them to the community which in turn accrue to her; she qualifies it as selfishness!

The premium program of the series was set at the Utah State Penitentiary. The Judge had been convinced that the temptation of keys left in parked cars caused car thefts, triggering in some cases a life of crime. She asked Officer Lee Rogers, head of the car theft department, to suggest an inmate who had begun a criminal career by stealing cars. Rogers was not hard put to think of one and gave the name to the Judge who would interview the convict before writing her script.

The warden permitted the use of his office for the examination. Tom (not his name) took a chair across the desk. Young—about twenty-six— with clean-cut features, the man had finished high school and gone one year to college, surprising, considering his junkets in two penitentiaries.

"What in your opinion turned you into a criminal?" was the Judge's first question.

"Well," he began, "I lived with my grandparents who made home brew on weekdays and drank it, and then on Sundays pretended to be good church members. I couldn't understand their deceit. It had such an influence on me that I began stealing cars!" And on and on.

When he had finished, the Judge leaned forward slowly. "That," she leveled at him, "is a bunch of eyewash. Now tell me the *truth!*"

Tom froze for a few seconds, then sat straight up and looked the woman jurist in the eyes. "I'm a mean son-of-a-bitch!" Knowing he couldn't fool this skirt, he laid a long and honest account of his criminal record on her. At the outset he revealed that when he would see an elderly man with a cane walking down the street, he would have a sudden impulse to hit the man over the head with his own cane!

His first offense was stealing a car. According to Tom, a key left in the ignition is a temptation to any youth who doesn't have access to a car, and he believed this one act aided and abetted his own downslide more than any other. Agreeing to write his story from which the Judge would form the questions and answers of her program, he nevertheless claimed he was in for a hard time from the other inmates. But he would take it.

On the day of the program, KDYL equipment was moved with much ado to the prison site, which fascinated the observing trustees who were decidedly on their best behavior. Tom performed like a pro and the Judge was elated with the outcome; obviously, there was rapport between the convict and the lady judge. Certainly the radio audience responded with enthusiasm to this precedent in programming.

The Judge kept track of this prisoner, who posted a good record but finally could not resist the temptation of escaping when the occasion made it expedient for him. Apprehended later in Chicago, he was returned to the Utah facility.

"Some people don't seem to be put together right in the first place," the Judge says equivocally, wanting desperately for the young man to shape up. "They have brains, are good-looking and attractive, respond sometimes to fairness, sometimes to good environment, but then slip into the role of a criminal. Tom was one of those."

But she was reminded of his message—important to the courts—that if a young person were not let off so easily the first time, he/she would not be as likely to make the same mistake the second time. In Tom's experience and in those he knew it was easy to get by with three or four offenses before a severe sentence was imposed.

Tom's first phony explanation to Judge Bosone happened to be typical. The Judge was informed later that when social welfare students met with prisoners about the reasons for their criminality, each convict had a melodramatic story to spin. The students and their professors were pushovers for the fabricated yarns and the storytellers laughed all the way back to their cells. Reva speculates on how many textbooks have included such stories as the truth.

A flashback in connection with the Utah State Penitentiary is extra bright for Reva. "The prisoners were giving a musical to which they invited the governor, state officials, and other VIPs. I was one of those invited. On this occasion, all of the guests were introduced and a handclap was given in response. When I was introduced the ovation was tremendous! Maybe an ovation by state penitentiary prisoners would not thrill the average citizen but it certainly did me, because many of those men had gone through my court and so by reputation I must have been known as a fair judge."

And then one day the men prisoners made her an honorary member of their Alcoholics Anonymous group—the Golden Key Chapter—which hit the sentimental Judge right where she lives!

Another program that contributed to Reva's reputation for nosing out the unusual but workable ideas for greater emotional impact was her segment on Mother's Day when she gathered together a woman high school teacher, a parent of adopted children, a single woman who cared for a widower's two children, and a father who was also a mother to his children. The four persons she selected represented the unselfish spirit of motherhood and carried it out in their daily lives. This show was also highly lauded.

The Judge, herself, qualified as a substitute parent. Friend Emily Stewart wired her congratulations one Father's Day, "You do a wonderful job."

Indeed, her irrepressible daughter proved the Judge's parental prowess. Reva, however, insists she has been ever blessed by having "a child who has never given me any problems, who was always obedient and understanding, who possesses a strong sense of humor." As an example (from a publication): "She [Zilpha] piped up from the back of the family car, 'Don't worry if you hit something, Mother. You're the judge, aren't you?'"

Zilpha, talented, versatile, and independent, never gave evidence of the need to compete with her illustrious mother. At the age of ten she turned her small hand to cake baking and it is safe to say that from that time Mother Reva never had to grease and flour another cake pan. At age twelve Zilpha was stitching up her own dresses and at fourteen she lovingly presented her mother with a handsome custom-made black evening gown.

Zilpha's poetry writing, pursued from grade school through teenage, was the appropriate step to her forté of song writing, which received special recognition from orchestra leader Les Brown. He voiced the opinion that at twenty-one years of age Zilpha was one of the best amateur song writers he had ever met.

As she grew older, she met many tests she set for herself, including one very auspicious "first," mentioned later.

ADJUDICATING from the bench and then describing the cases for prevention's sake gave the Judge some solid satisfaction. Latter-year satisfaction was derived from a letter sent by A. Sherman Christensen, senior United States district judge, written in 1972.

"I recall an appearance I made before you when you were Judge and as an inexperienced attorney I was trying to work out some problem on behalf of a family man who had jeopardized his employment by getting close to the line of legality. I felt that you were both a perceptive and technically correct Judge in your decision that he had not quite crossed the line and also a compassionate and understanding Judge by believing it important in that case to look carefully at where the line was."

And satisfaction of another kind was realized in 1946 when she was admitted to practice law before the Supreme Court of the United States.

The association of Dr. Phipps with the Beck and Bosone families was more than that of a medical consultant and his patients—it bordered on devotion. The tall, portly doctor, kind-featured and white-haired, always gave generously of his time and counsel, and Reva, in turn, always expressed sincere interest in his practice. As a result, his short visits in her home practically every Sunday morning were looked forward to—the judge and the doctor collecting each other's thoughts.

One morning before she stepped on the bench Reva received a call from the good doctor who reported that he had just operated on a sixteen-year-old youth. He had performed to the best of his ability but he felt that a higher power was needed to save the boy, now in critical condition, and asked that Reva offer prayers for the young patient for three days when she was able; he was making the same request of two other friends. Reva Beck Bosone and Joseph Phipps shared a strong belief in a Supreme Being and the power of prayer.

So for three days, when her attention was not required—when a witness was being sworn in, for instance—Reva would glide that black leather chair around to face the wall and plead for the boy's recovery. At the end of three days Dr. Phipps called to say, "The boy will live!" Both believed that faith had changed the course.

Spirits of the Judiciary

FREDDIE SOLIS was a favorite of the Judge. She saw a lot of him, not in the social order of things, but when he appeared before her on the bench time after time. He was among those who wouldn't "hurt a flea"—he didn't rob, rape, or rustle. He just guzzled, but it was hard for him not to get picked up when he overdid it—like all the time.

Then he disappeared from the scene for a comparatively extended period. One day Judge Bosone spied him on a city truck and inquired about his absence.

"I've been on vacation, Judge," he answered.

"Oh, where did you go, Freddie?"

"San Francisco, where I got drunk and spent sixty days in jail!"

And there was Ed Avery, who practically lived in the city jail. The Judge was particularly fond of Ed. One night he got up to take what he thought was Epsom salts but was really Drano. The doctor was quickly summoned by the jailer and he was saved by a stomach pump. A policeman commented the next day that Ed had really got his pipes cleaned out!

In those years the police station building, in which the court was also located, stood on First South and State streets and, as previously men-

PHOTO: *Salt Lake City judges, 1943.*

tioned, was connected to the city jail. Occasionally, when the alcoholics
would be too ashamed to face the Judge one more time, they would ask
jailer Jorgensen to request their sentences be sent down to them.

"I tried every way I could think of to keep those 'dehorners,' as they
were called, out of jail," she says. "If one of them could stay out longer
than he did before, I'd make it worth his while by suspending a number of
days."

One recidivist's proud reply after being queried on how long he had
been out of jail was, "One week!" The courtroom broke up because little
did the spectators realize this was a record for him. Occasionally the rub-
bing alcohol and cheap wine addicts would stay sober for as long as three
weeks when the Judge would arrange jobs with personal friends who
tried to help, but no method or gimmick was lasting. Often she would run
her car from one end of the valley to the other after a tiring day on the
bench in an effort to locate work for an unfortunate she had just sentenced.

Once a small group pled guilty to a drunk charge but asked the Judge
whether they could speak. Since Reva always permitted defendants to
say their piece, they informed her that the arresting officer had called
them sons-of-bitches and bastards.

"Did you do this?" the Judge asked, looking at the officer. He nodded.

"Case dismissed!"

On hearing the verdict, the defendants straightened up, lifted their
chins, and strutted out, casting a withering glance at the officer. "I will
never forget their expressions," she said. "The memory of those winos
walking out of court will always be with me. Oh yes, I knew they would be
back in two or three days or maybe the next day." And sure enough, they
were.

Former officer Tally Burbidge recalls that a court scenario might go
something like this:

> "Jacob, do you realize this is the sixth time you have appeared
> before me in as many months?" Judge Bosone leans forward in her
> chair to be closer to the man standing before her.
>
> She says in lowered voice, "Edna and the children are out of food
> again, and they need you to stoke the coal in the furnace at night.
> These are cold days, you know. And Christmas will soon be here. Do
> you really want your loved ones to go hungry and shiver while you
> spend time in jail?"
>
> "No, your honor," mumbles the disheveled defendant, eyes
> downcast.
>
> "What's the charge this time?" asks the Judge of the clerk who
> reads, "Intoxication, found lying on a city street."

A slight pause and then, "Three days. And Jacob, *please*," wringing the greatest pathos from the word, "you have a duty at home. Let this be our last meeting like this. Okay?"

"I'll try, your honor," he whispers.

The bailiff leads the man from the courtroom and he is replaced by another, different in appearance, but on a similar charge.

Later in the day the Judge phones the Elks Club, which has maintained a long-standing welfare program of towering repute. And Jacob's family is assured of a Christmas dinner and appropriate children's gifts.

The men prisoners were put to work at odd jobs at the courthouse—swabbing the courtroom floor, sweeping, polishing the Judge's chambers. An observer at the time remembers those chambers as constantly shining from grateful elbow grease. Captain Headman, chief of the Detective Bureau, enlisted their efforts in building the road from the state capitol to the police range on a hill behind the statehouse. Those roadbuilders affectionately called it "The Bosone Highway."

"Freddie passed away one fall when I was home campaigning for re-election to Congress," the Judge recalls. "One of the police officers said he should have called me because he was sure I would have attended the funeral. If I had known I certainly would have done just that."

Years later, her wine-drinking jail friends from days of old were always greeted enthusiastically on the street when the Judge returned to Salt Lake City. If she happened to walk along East Second South, she would be surrounded by friendly former defendants—the lady in the trim suit and coiffed hair and the often unkempt man, on occasion attempting to stay upright. And as they chatted amiably, she ignored the glaring glances from passersby—strangers who could not understand since they possibly had never been put to a severe life test.

A question that kept attacking her mind like a jackhammer was why men who are not criminals should be incarcerated. "I firmly believed them," she said, "when they pled each time they appeared that if I turned them loose they would not take another drop. I knew they meant what they said. But they just could not live up to it."

One morning as the Judge was about to commence the court's business, her eyes glanced over the crowded bull pen as they had so many times before. This time frustration built up to the boiling point. There *has* to be another way! There has to be a fair, humane, therapeutic method of treating these unfortunates who have no guideposts in their life!

And she did indeed come up with an idea. Reva Bosone in her varied career has often been a few leaps ahead of her time, and with her idea of a "drunk farm" she must have appeared radical to those who were the staid, uncreative public officials of the day. The moment she was convinced of the solution to the bull pen, she rushed to the City and County Building (and one can envision this well-dressed woman hotfooting down State Street, trailing little circles of exhaust as in the old-time cartoons) one noon hour while the commissioners were still in session to outline her plan which would attempt a renewal of the body and mind of the alcoholic in a rural atmosphere. Jail was obviously a destructive force on the drunk. But the farm principle embraced such a strong plan for rehabilitation that she went with high hopes.

"The gentlemen listened courteously," she recalled. "But an important churchman in the group argued that those men had no character. They needed willpower. Ad nauseum! I have never had patience with churchgoers who have no tolerance, no sympathy for the errant ways of man.

"One of the commissioners, however, who had been a star athlete in his day seemed to think the idea might be a good one. I was happy for this encouragement. But finally they all gave me a pat on the back with a 'You're a nice gal but . . .' routine."

Far from being dissuaded, the Judge explored the possibilities of a drunk farm with the enthusiasm of a bright student hell-bent for a scholarship. Farm sites, food costs, legal snarls, comparison costs to jail room and board—all came under her scrutiny. So preoccupied was she that one day as she was hurrying up Main Street, she looked down to discover an old garden shoe on one foot and a dress shoe on the other. The sight was so humorous that she laughed aloud all the way to her destination, conjecturing later that all who heard her must have passed judgment on the dotty Judge!

Forearmed with a portfolio of statistics, she returned to the commission; chivalry still reigned but chances for the new "radical" facility remained low. The Judge haunted their offices—all she got were lame excuses and courteous bows.

She enlisted the services of two civic-minded women, Mrs. Emma P. Evans and Mrs. Amy Brown Lyman who, after touring the jail, became strong converts to the drunk farm theory and who committed themselves to the unique cause. But with the commissioners still wary, their efforts seemed much like trying to dig a tunnel with a feather.

Despite the headlines in local papers when the idea was first presented and the fact that many papers in the nation had carried the story, the city officials did not become convinced of its potential, which was later fulfilled in other cities—at California's Saugus Rehabilitation Center, for one, which has received high praise for its treatment of alcoholism.

Still eager to find an effective remedy for the disease that debilitates so many otherwise productive persons, the Judge learned of a brand new organization in the nation called Alcoholics Anonymous. The philosophy appealed to her but she learned that a group could be organized only by an alcoholic.

A year later she spotted a small ad in a local paper announcing a meeting of alcoholics. On calling the number listed the Judge was excited to hear of an AA group, small, to be sure, but definitely in existence in Salt Lake City. From this small step emanated a rehabilitation program of which there was no precedent in the nation.

"The first order of business in the police court was to hear the pleas of the long line of drunks from the jail and sentence the guilty ones," the Judge said. "Most of these men had reached the bottom of the ladder, so to speak. They had no money and no friends. Because of this I felt an added responsibility to see that each one was treated fairly. I spent time on these cases—never rushed through them as I have seen done in other courts of the country. Manifestations of certain defendants' characters and facts about their backgrounds influenced me to have them remain after court had adjourned.

"At that time I asked the defendants to attend a meeting of Alcoholics Anonymous in the Newhouse Hotel. If they attended for three weeks they were to reappear in court to tell me their reactions, in which case I promised to suspend the jail sentence. They did not need to join AA."

With very few exceptions, the Judge's suggestion met with success— the defendants were definitely interested and had decided to continue the affiliation. The beginning of a sober life had intense meaning for them. The Judge had sanguine expectations!

Then several weeks later two of the original Alcoholics Anonymous leaders stalked into her chambers after court. "Are you trying to wreck our group, Judge Bosone? No once can be forced to join—that must be done by the free will of the alcoholic!" Reva, whose first consideration, the same as theirs, was for the sobriety of those addicts, fought to hold back her indignation. Hastening to outline in detailed terms what her procedure consisted of, she emphasized that if it had been misconstrued, it was due to no failing on her part!

Their reaction to her defense marked the beginning of her ennobling association with Alcoholics Anonymous in the early 1940s.

When Reva asked the two formerly irate gentlemen whether they would like to attend court each morning and use her chambers to inform the alcoholics she selected about their program, they were at once receptive and eager. Proof of their cooperation was shown by members of AA who continued to attend court as though on the payroll; Judge Bosone believes that the ritual of an AA member being in court each morning helped other courts to see the light.

During the court session, in an undertone she would ask each defendant charged with intoxication whether he or she suffered from a steady drinking problem. If the answer was yes, she would instruct him or her to follow the two men through the courtroom gate into the Judge's chambers. The curious, dubious, apprehensive expression on each face seemed to shout, "What now!" But when the individual had been briefed and asked by the Judge for an opinion of the program, almost always came the response, "That's for me—because I can't do anything about it myself."

"Needless to say," the Judge stressed, "many, many alcoholics never had another drink after they appeared in my court. To this day I receive cards and letters from families whose husband or father was made sober through that group of men and women that makes 'miracles' happen."

A case in point involved a distraught woman who sought counsel with the Judge in her chambers before court one morning. She choked out the story that in her desperation she was headed for a divorce lawyer's office that very morning, but the thought occurred to her to see Judge Bosone first. Her husband was at the moment in the bull pen about to plead guilty to a charge of intoxication. She insisted he was fundamentally decent but that he couldn't help drinking to a state of intoxication every night without exception, creating a family atmosphere so ruinous to herself and their two young sons that one of them in panic had asked his mother and brother to kneel with him in prayer that the next time he would see his daddy he would be sober and remain forever sober!

The Judge asked the woman to step to the door of the courtroom to point out her husband; his sentient expression impressed the Judge, now experienced in value estimations, as a possible responsive member of Alcoholics Anonymous. She turned to her distracted visitor and said expansively, "Your son's prayer is answered. His daddy will return sober and he will remain sober."

"That would be a miracle!" she gasped.

"Miracles do happen," the Judge answered, being grateful that she could give this encouragement.

The husband, acknowledging to the Judge his weakness to use any willpower to overcome his problem, received the message from the faithful AA court emissaries and became a devout member. Resuming his carpenter's trade, adding forty pounds to his tall, undernourished frame, paying off the home mortgage, and taking his family on a thirteen-year-delayed vacation, he literally proved the claims of the organization. It had wrought a miracle.

And there were the mavericks or rather the self-deceivers who were insistent that they could turn it off anytime! One such young man, articulate, attractive, defensive about his livelihood, claimed he was the best mechanic in Salt Lake City and that he certainly was no alcoholic.

"The very reason you are here shows you have no control over your drinking," countered the Judge, who literally begged him to attend a meeting of Alcoholics Anonymous. He refused, even as he repeatedly appeared before her. Several years later, when Judge Bosone on one of her visits to Utah was scheduled to address the oldest AA organization in the state, she was greeted by the same charming detractor. Introducing her that night he described to his colleagues and their guests the Judge's efforts to interest him in AA and his obstinacy. But having been cut down gradually to a nonentity by the bottle, he realized the Judge's advice was on target. It was because of her that he was present that night. And instead of being the best mechanic in town, he was now the head of the sales department of one of the largest companies in Utah.

Judge Bosone confirms that from her experience the dry alcoholics were those who had sunk from a foundation of a serviceable home life and/or job and had been able to count on resuming useful pursuits when rehabilitated. The dehorner, on the other hand, who had never enjoyed the accouterments of a more affluent society and who would not have the occasion to look forward to them, would be better fitted for treatment on a drunk farm.

The movie, *Somewhere I'll Find You,* with Clark Gable and Lana Turner was captivating Salt Lakers at the Center Theatre in October 1942, but clubwomen of the city had more humanitarian ideas one day as they were conducted on a tour of the city jail by Judge Bosone, who was seeking their support to improve the situation. The Judge, who had returned from a cross-country trek comparing jail conditions, declared, "It has been a disgrace for years for the City Commission to sit and allow such things to exist just because it is a jail." Not all were callous, however, and she praised Mayor Ab Jenkins (the former racing car driver) and Police Chief Reed E. Vetterli for their cooperation.

The prison and court system is supposed to be remedial, but a jail like Salt Lake City's tends toward "solidification of criminality," she protested. Overcrowded jail conditions could be remedied by the establishment of a new women's ward on the third floor of the public safety building annex and by construction of a drunk farm (one of her constant plugs), the Judge repeated to the women's groups assembled.

Dr. Curtis reiterated her plea, "Judge Bosone is trying to better curative conditions for inebriates jailed in this city and I definitely feel she is on the right track, particularly in the care of the chronic drunk who clutters up our jails and handicaps our war effort with the amount of time and space he demands from public officials and institutions. I think she is right in suggesting that drunks be given the benefits of an open-air, busy life in country conditions."

And Police Chief Vetterli concurred, "There is no question but that we have been a bit archaic in Salt Lake in these matters. In the past we have probably neglected to focus our attention on the rehabilitation of these cases and I feel that Judge Bosone is right. We agree there should be certain changes."

With these and others in accord, she was determined to humanize a condition that was being "winked at, that left people to seethe in horrible discomfort and insanitation. Imagine a jail without a delousing machine or a laundry!" she admonished.

"The wives, mothers, and sisters of these drunks plead with the police court judge to help their relatives, but they question the efficacy of the jail," Reva complained. "Anyone who has studied alcoholism knows it is a disease, and who would think of putting a diseased person in jail as a treatment? When a judge sees day after day dozens of men wasted by liquor, men who in many cases were able artisans at one time, he knows the tremendous extravagance in the loss of manpower."

When revenue from the city court was found to be almost $28,000 more in 1942 than in 1941, Judge Bosone and representatives of the women's clubs requested that $25,000 be set aside to acquire the farm and facilities. "After the farm gets going it should be able to pay its own way," she announced.

Despite the encouraging factors—even the inspection of a site in Murray (a small town in the valley)—the farm never received the necessary official boost. But never a quitter, she stayed hopeful for her project for years, making later pleas or inducing others to make them.

In 1949 the *Telegram* editorialized: "Such persistence must be admired—and we think it is time for Salt Lake City to do something more than admire it. We think it's time to give Representative Bosone's idea a trial." Many others did, too, among whom Tally Burbidge, a former officer on the force now retired, bemoans the city's short-sightedness to cope with the ever present issue of problem drunks. In the 1940s this nation numbered three million alcoholics and excessive drinkers. Today the report places the total closer to nine million!

In the 1946 session of the Utah State Legislature, a group of Alcoholics Anonymous leaders and civic-alerted men lobbied so effectively that a bill setting up the Utah State Board on Alcoholism, with an appropriation for the agency's operation, passed both houses. Under the State Welfare Department, it was structured to appoint its own director.

Every Utahn of long residency is familiar with the name of Thomas Kearns, one of the state's all-time wealthy citizens from mining concerns

in the legendary Park City, and his son, Thomas F. Kearns, who struggled furiously to overcome alcoholism. The younger Kearns became one
of the first members of the AA group in Utah, in practice a true missionary, elevating the board to the successful level it operated on for
years. From this board was formed the Utah Committee for Education on
Alcoholism with volunteer members.

Among the board members appointed by the governor were Kearns
and Seth Oberg, another enthusiastic AA leader. Familiar with Judge
Bosone's court procedures, they decided that Reva would make the ideal
executive director. But the Judge, alas, was not just languishing on the
couch! "It would take ten women to follow Reva around," Joe had been
fond of saying.

Perhaps a terse description of a typical Bosone day would place her
life in true perspective. Morning had her leaving a clean house and
presiding on the bench till noon. Munching a sandwich at her desk, she
was in the habit of signing complaints between bites. Then she was on the
bench again at 2:00 P.M. If by any reason no cases were scheduled in the
afternoon, she studied cases and interviewed defendants. Her day in
chambers usually ended around 7:30 P.M. More responsibility awaited her
at home with her young daughter and household tasks. And lastly, it
could be safely said that volunteer work and speeches (numbering approximately five a week) left her no extended thumb-twirling time.

Her answer to Kearns and Oberg was an unqualified no!

At this point the two perspicacious gentlemen organized their offense; for three months they called on the Judge two or three times a
week until Zilpha, who was creatively graphic in her estimations, dubbed
them the steamrollers. Defenses broken down by rational pleas and
elaborate compliments, Reva was finally convinced by them and by the
National Committee on Alcoholism that an Alcoholics Anonymous member, whom she had suggested, did not have the requirements for the di-
rectorship.

She agreed to serve under certain conditions: if Tom, Seth, and June
Kendall, a man from central Utah, would forego their anonymity to participate in the programs throughout the state, revealing their alcoholic
condition and relating their personal histories. Unheard of in the AA program! A tall order—but she was convinced this was the only procedure so
she demanded it. She got it!

What salary did she want? None. She had put forth a helping hand to
alcoholics for years for nothing—why charge now? But it was soon evident
that the job would occupy the lunch hour, time after 5:00 P.M., and many
nights. And any time left over!

"At the first board meeting I had a state program outlined. It was accepted. In fact, Tom, Seth, and the others went along with each proposal. They certainly did live up to their promise," she said in admiration. "And they did set a salary of $300 per month."

Being in a church town, her first impulse was to consult Apostle Joseph Merrill, who was in charge of temperance teaching, for church support. (She postulated that an appeal to the alcoholic's intelligence was the only effective way, and this philosophy was reinforced by vast experience in dealing with the compulsive drinker.) The plea, no matter how impassioned, fell on unwilling ears. Apostle Merrill apparently associated all drunks with a loss of character and willpower. The fact that temperance preaching had not worked did not alter his stand.

Even the morale of a redhead occasionally plumets, and Judge Bosone hurried to phone her loyal friend, Emily Smith Stewart, daughter of the president of the Latter Day Saints Church, George Albert Smith, to discuss the matter, ill-concealing her depressed and feisty mood. Mrs. Stewart, after offering words of balm, advised Reva to work from the church members *up*, not from the church heads *down*. When the congregations are impressed, the high echelon will be nudged. And so it came to pass.

"I wrote dozens of letters to community groups and high schools throughout the state suggesting that I bring a few members of AA and stage a program, a program they would never forget!" Reva assured. The response was encouraging but the initial turnout was spotty. At the first gathering in Logan, only a few showed up at the Tabernacle. Reva heard that folks were leary of being seen for fear of being labeled drunks. The participants gave their all, however, with the Judge speaking first as a nonalcoholic, presenting her conclusions from experiences on the police bench before which hundreds of inebriates had passed. Then the dry alcoholics were introduced, each holding the audience engrossed with a story of his ignominious battle with the bottle. Preaching was the first thou-shalt-not!

Then the scene changed; a few months later the Judge and company spoke to a packed auditorium when asked to make a repeat appearance in Logan—this time at Utah State Agricultural College (now Utah State University).

"A common experience," she recalls, "was a small meeting first, then a big one. As the word spread, townspeople lost their timidity; they filled up the hall because alcoholism touches directly or indirectly almost every home."

The program mushroomed, and about a year later Alcoholics Anonymous claimed 600 members as a result of that effort. In high school assemblies, 20,309 students from all over the state were exposed to the educational program. The following year eight states had requested information and thirteen states had passed legislation pertinent to alcoholism.

In the alteration of cities because of growth and deterioration factors, rummy locales may get switched or wiped out. Salt Lake City's "wino way" on Second South between Main and State streets was no exception. Today this area has reached a stratum of respectability not believed possible in the 1930s and 1940s. In former times, however, unless one was a judge, social worker, or police officer, one seldom set foot on the south side of East Second South. In the current expansion of concrete—laterally and vertically—the winos have scattered and it is difficult to pinpoint a comparably dense aggregation. An inhabitant of this environment was thought to be particularly suited to receive the advantages that a drunk farm would offer.

Those whom Judge Bosone had sit with her on the rostrum in the statewide Alcoholics Anonymous presentations had long histories of falling and rising. Mrs. Dorothy Green, an attractive young widow with two small children, was her showpiece. A member of the women's AA group, she became the Judge's contact for women alcoholics. Her unselfish activities contributed immeasurably to the program's success. As an AA national publication explained, "Brotherly love is the motivating power that has caused this group to grow and be sustained through its formative years," and Dorothy Green was the embodiment of this philosophy.

She never refused her services except to tell her story from the rostrum, insisting that speaking in front of people would be too frightening. But one evening in the Nephi, Utah, high school she startled the director by saying, " Judge, I'll speak, but I'm scared to death."

The Judge's memory of those remarks is sharp. "She described how she would be drunk for weeks. How her beautiful red hair would get matted with wine. How, when she would be riding on a bus and would see a beer sign, she would have to get off and seek the nearest tavern to get drunk.

"Then she described the peace of mind and great happiness that came with being a dry alcoholic. How Alcoholics Anonymous found her and delivered her from a tragic life.

"For her and all the others who gave counsel with an open heart to those in distress," says the Judge, "I trust there is a special place in heaven.

Consequently and gradually the Church and the community grew to accept the alcoholic for what he is—sick! Apostle Matthew Cowley was a strong instrument in converting the Church officials, and Apostle Merrill eventually mellowed in his views, even throwing a few bouquets the Judge's way. Representatives of the medical profession were slower to convince, allowing only two beds at the county hospital for inebriates; however, attitudes gradually changed there, too. And job opportunities for dry alcoholics opened up.

"I heard a man say once," the Judge said, "that if you want to get a job in Utah, say you're a member of Alcoholics Anonymous! With open arms the people came to understand the alcoholic—that is the way it should be."

Always an innovator, Judge Bosone beat her counterparts to the punch by organizing the first Alcoholism Institute ever held in Utah on June 16, 1946. Invitations were issued to industrialists of the state, school administrators, religious representatives, and judges and law enforcement officers, among others, to attend a session on alcoholism in the grand ballroom of the Hotel Utah. Three outstanding professional men from other areas had also been invited—a well-known lawyer from Los Angeles and a member of AA, a psychiatrist from the University of Washington, and the most eminent person in the field of education on alcoholism, Dr. Raymond McCarthy, executive director of the Yale Clinic.

Dr. McCarthy perceived the numerous seats in the ballroom before the affair began and commented, "You surely don't expect to have all those seats taken! If so, it will be the first time I have seen such interest in alcoholism by the citizenry."

As a matter of fact, there were no open spaces in the seating and the event was considered a singular success. Lucid explanations on the nature of alcoholism cleared up some muddy preconceived ideas. The audience was sparked that day to tackle the widespread problem.

"David Keith, another affluent business leader from Utah, and his wife had driven down from his lodge in West Yellowstone to attend the Institute," the Judge said. "I'll never forget Dave, sitting on the front row in his wheelchair. The whole program on alcoholism was the nearest thing to his heart. As a young man and until a few years before he died he had been an inebriate. Being sober had given him a new lease on life and he had made many plans. It was as though his life were just beginning. Handsome and generous, he was one of the most considerate men I have ever known. I've been sad just thinking about his life. You see, having been under the influence of liquor for so many years, he hadn't really lived. Then when he had the chance, he was gone! A few weeks after the Institute he died of cancer."

The Judge is extravagant in her praise of Keith and her beloved friend, Tom Kearns, for their offers of funds, office space, and service in the public's enlightenment on alcoholism. Dedication beyond the respectable bounds of duty pointed to strong character, even though flawed by intemperance.

As word of her ambitious program passed around the land, two other honors were bestowed on the diligent board director. In 1947 Mrs. LaFell Dickinson, national president of the General Federation of Women's Clubs, was so stimulated by Judge Bosone's message on alcoholism at the state convention of the Utah Federation of Women's Clubs that she prevailed upon the Judge to present the keynote address on the same subject at the national convention in June of that year in the grand ballroom of the Commodore Hotel in New York City. Affording a unique opportunity to create national interest in Utah's precocious treatment of alcoholism, Reva has felt lifelong gratitude to this gracious leader of the nation's clubwomen.

An amusing sidelight concerns an encounter of the two women later in Washington, D.C., when Reva was a congresswoman. Mrs. Dickinson confided, "Judge Bosone, when I saw your-diamond bracelet in New York City at the convention I asked my husband to buy me one like it." Reva smiles when she thinks of it. "If he had, he would have saved money because mine was costume jewelry, but very good costume jewelry!"

The *Ladies' Home Journal* featured an article on the work of the Utah State Board on Alcoholism in its April 1952 issue entitled, "Teen-Agers and Alcoholism, Utah School Program," edited by Margaret Hickey of the Public Affairs Department. Stating that alcoholism takes the fourth highest death toll among diseases in the United States, she credited Utah as a "pioneer in the field of education about alcohol—the first state both to reject in her high schools the old fashioned temperance speakers whose 'scare' approach only bored or amused most students, and to replace this with a special program telling teenagers something they *could* understand and accept; the *medical* facts about alcohol and what it can do to the person who drinks it, strengthened by the sound emotional appeal of the personal stories of members of Alcoholics Anonymous." And due credit is given the Judge further in the report.

Former Senator Frank E. Moss also hailed Reva for her antecedence in the field of alcoholism and heaped tribute on her 1930 and 1940 activities in that respect. Judiciary colleagues during that time, they have maintained a congenial friendship over the years. In 1951, during her tenure in Congress, Reva appeared before the Labor and Federal Security Subcommittee of the House Appropriations Committee, urging that funds be made available to pursue research on the causes and cure of alcoholism.

Knowing Utah's background of positive steps in this direction, Moss, when he was elected to the Senate, had more incentive to take definite measures. "After I came to the Senate," said Moss, "I guess I was the first one here in recent times to introduce a bill on the treatment and care of alcoholics, which eventually became law after some passage of time.

Senator Javits joined me after I had introduced the first bill, and when Senator Hughes came to the Senate he headed the subcommittee and became really the leading figure at that point. But the Hughes, Javits, Moss bill is the one that is now law as far as federal involvement in the care and treatment of alcoholics."

He continued, "I know Reva was always very proud of the fact that we finally got it written into law and got some appropriations to do something about it on the federal level—and also to determine fully, as the courts did long after Reva started work on it, that alcoholism is an illness and not a criminal offense, that people therefore should be entitled to treatment rather than incarceration."

When Reva was elected to Congress in 1948, two popular spiritus frumenti anecdotes followed her around at gatherings and in Washington columnists' most flippant prose.

A going-away gift from beloved AA members would always be one of her most sentimental items of memorabilia. At a party honoring her before she departed for the nation's capital, Tom Kearns presented her with a huge box. On opening it, she howled with delight to find a silver tray inscribed, "To Reva Beck Bosone, with 100 proof affection from the old soaks at home." The hometown friend suggested that she probe deeper. After exploring through more tissue, she discovered a silver cocktail shaker. She hasn't said, but one can imagine that the combination offering brought a mist to the eye! Despite the affection contained in the shaker gift, however, she was most adamant about serving in it nothing stronger than frigid aqua pura.

Mrs. Bosone's drink-serving customs were also quite evident when she encountered an attendant with a bucket of ice in her new office. According to a columnist, on being asked how much she wanted, first-term congressional member Bosone said thanks but she didn't need any ice today. Ice—ice? Who needs it? She ran after the man into the corridor.

"What is that ice for?" she is reported to have called.

"To put in things you want made cold—if you have any things you want cold," was his obliging reply.

Thinking that's what he meant, she announced, "Ice will not be required at any time in my office!"

Another member of the press qualified her actions. "Bosone doesn't object to liquor, she just doesn't serve it."

Three Times—She's In

IN JANUARY 1946 Judge Bosone returned to Police and Traffic Court as magistrate for the third time. For the speeder and the drinker this news must have induced a certain amount of trembling! The day after she resumed her place on the bench not one arrest card for "drunk" was made out although New Year's has a way of loading up the police court calendar with such charges. Traffic violations were minor, also.

Her creative determination to right a few wrongs in the system always won her a few and lost her a few. The *Salt Lake Telegram,* long a touter of the jurist's traffic reform, considered her a winner! Not so kind were other residents of the valley, one of whom sent a scathing indictment labeling her Bosone, Queen of the Gestapo. But the Judge was serene—she had nothing to fear but fear itself and she was doing right!

With many years of experience behind her lending a professional polish, she "quickly disposed of her calendar of fifteen cases," reported one newspaper, "which included eleven cases charging drunkenness, one trespassing, one violation of right-of-way, one reckless driving and two disorderly conduct cases."

Once when a man pled not guilty, the Judge asked, "If you can't remember to wear your shoes," looking at his stockinged feet, "don't you think maybe you should change your plea?" The man thought for a moment, then decided perhaps he wasn't all that sober. The Judge fined him $10.

An eighteen-year-old youth was brought in on a charge of cussing in front of women. A new fine—what to charge? She decided: "Fined fifty cents per word for each word of ten words!" And the young man found that if he had said, "Good heavens to Betsy," he could have kept $5 in his pocket.

Her courtroom was always a source of interest, but a situation that threatened the image of Madame Judge was beginning to cause anguish. One day she called a conference of the town's reporters, including King Durkee, Fred Hamlin, Jr., and Bill Adamson among others.

"Fellas," she said, "I know you love me and I love you, but I cannot allow you to run a story or photo on me *every* day! Readers will get sick and tired and I'll make all sorts of enemies. So lay off!!"

They slacked off. But one can understand their disappointment—

what could be juicier for the local page than pronouncements from the attractive red-haired judge? Van Porter, a young *Salt Lake Tribune* photographer who covered events in her courtroom, has professed undiminished respect for her from those pressured times to the present, based on that judicial style known as no-nonsense but fair.

The ending of the war and of gasoline and speed restrictions contributed to alarming irresponsibility on the streets and highways. The fatality toll was up 50 percent over the preceding year of 1945. From January 1 to February 22 thirty-nine deaths had shocked Utahns. February alone had claimed twenty-four lives in twenty-two days. The prediction that the toll for the year could add up to the worst in the state's history was sobering to the citizenry. So a potential death driver program to make "safer and sorrier" the drinking, reckless, hit-and-run, negligent motorist was inaugurated in February 1946.

The *Deseret News,* as well as the other two local papers, reported that after carrying on a one-woman campaign against traffic accidents in city court, Judge Reva Beck Bosone invited members of the press, radio, and city officers of Provo, Ogden, and Salt Lake City to attend a meeting to plan a crusade against the mounting death and accident toll in Utah.

Reva, spearheading this great endeavor for traffic teamwork, was very conscious of being a woman. Would these men who were leaders in their communities take her seriously? Undaunted, she invited them in a letter which read, "I believe that you are convinced now that the traffic hazard can only be reduced and eliminated by cooperation of enforcement, courts, and public sentiment."

To her gratification, all those invited, with the exception of two who sent excuses, appeared at the meeting. The media pronounced it an "ambush for death" and a way to eliminate the "chief agent of the grim reaper."

The following ultimatum on violations was agreed upon, with Judge Bosone being elected chairperson of the newly named Tri-City Traffic Safety Committee:

1. A minimum fine of $100 in addition to a three- to five-day jail sentence for drunken driving.
2. Minimum fine of $50 for reckless driving and hit-run convictions.
3. Fines of $35 for speeding or running a traffic light or stop sign.
4. Mandatory jail sentence for driving after operator's license has been revoked, and a stricter adherence to the revocation procedure.
5. Road blockades throughout the city to check mechanical condition of vehicles while their owners are driving them.

Pedestrians would be liable to the same general enforcement procedures as drivers and fines of $35 would be imposed on those guilty of walking against a red light. And a ten-point program for the three cities was recommended.

Far from being the intent to build up the city's revenue, as disgruntled offenders were wont to suggest, the plan was devised to decrease violations that lead to accidents. "It has been my experience," the Judge said, "that the revenue is cut down by heavier fines—most motorists are unwilling to take a chance when they face a stiffer penalty when caught."

Utterances resounded from elsewhere; she admits that she had been referred to in the East as "that woman judge in Utah," but she knew a drastic problem needed a drastic measure. "If the fines we are establishing are not high enough, we will raise them until they are—higher than the present maximum of $300 for drunken driving!"

The crusade succeeded—it just didn't last long enough. When the Judge was elected to Congress, the committee dissolved. An old friend in the Traffic Department in Salt Lake City told her many years later that what Utah needs now is another Tri-City Traffic Committee! In weighing the contributions of her life, Judge Bosone classifies the thrust of that committee as one of her finest hours on the bench.

"On My Record I Rest My Case"

THE UNITED STATES HOUSE OF REPRESENTATIVES had a special lure for those friends who were politically ambitious for the Judge. The other lure, of course, was the United States Senate. But the most logical idea was to run Reva for the House first. Each election year the Judge checkmated those enthusiasts, "Not now, but sometime." She was reminded again in the spring of 1948 by her supportive friend, former State Legislator Edna Ericksen, who was most insistent that the Judge get on the ticket. "Not yet," the Judge repeated.

But a rarely displayed but effective temper introduced a whole new ball game, and Salt Lake City's Mayor Earl J. Glade turned out to be the pitcher to walk the Judge to first base. Evidently an agitator persuaded the mayor to appoint an employe to snoop on the city judges. Were they really busy enough? When the judges found out, all four were aroused at the temerity of the mayor, an elected official the same as they. His depart-

PHOTO: *On the campaign train, American Fork, Utah, October 1948.*

131

ment did not govern the judiciary and he possessed no background or experience on which to base his concern.

One morning Reva was endeavoring to straighten out a few disjointed thoughts; she knew her schedule was usually ponderous and she believed her fellow judges to have the same. She found herself shutting the desk drawers with a little more force than usual. What a picky complaint of the mayor's! A bit much. In fact, much too much! It was the break for lunch. Why wait? Indeed! At 12:15 P.M. she sought the nearest phone and dialed Mrs. Ericksen. "This is it! I'll run for Congress!" After that, the press was informed.

"I can't take credit for those decisions," Reva exclaims, lumping all the big ones together. "Perhaps temper flips the direction, which may have come from divinity." She is definite in believing she was guided.

Edna Ericksen's flashback on hearing the Judge's decision was filled with exultation. "I gave a hip-hooray!" she recalls.

Again the Judge, who was no slouch at the job, was to wage her latest campaign on an ounce of time and money and a magnum of vitality. Volunteer workers supplied the vigor and drive impossible to find in the same proportion in a paid operation; her exemplary record in the state legislature always attracted volunteers. Edna Ericksen was made chairwoman of the women's committee in Salt Lake County and Ruth Penrose served as the Judge's campaign manager. Lucille Darton was deemed soothsayer. Other linebackers never to be forgotten in that first local skirmish for the congressional nomination included Dr. Waldemer P. Read of the Philosophy Department, University of Utah, who put her name in the running, and State Senator Sol Selvin, who seconded.

The opposition in the same party posted Ray Leavitt, chairman of the State Road Commission, and Willis Ritter, Reva's former law school teacher. Still handling on an average of one hundred complaints a day in court, Reva, of necessity, confined all campaign speech making to noons and evenings, creating a high-velocity life!

Reva and Ray emerged from the convention as the Democratic nominees. Thankfully, no personal attacks or biting innuendoes were part of Mr. Leavitt's campaign pitch, and as usual Reva argued only issues, so the confrontation did not leave any dangling grudges.

Early in the evening of the runoff primary in September Reva knew her campaign package was wrapped up and sold! She prepared to meet her Republican opponent, William A. Dawson, a lawyer and former state senator and national congressman, in November. Dawson had been elected to Congress in the Republican sweep of 1946. Confident that the Republicans would continue strong and that Dewey would smash the Truman effort, he kept his campaign soft sell, pushing the old saw that since Judge Bosone had done such a grand job on the bench it would be a shame for Utah to lose her.

But when her friends, phoning names from the white pages, heard most contacts confirm their intention to vote for the Judge, they knew the way the wind was blowing. Especially exhilarating was it for her supporters, considering the daring of this lady Democrat running on the Truman ticket which faced the intimidations of the Republican stronghold. Former Senator Moss believes great credit belongs to Reva for having the courage to "jump in and run for Congress when the prospects for the Democrats didn't look good at all earlier in the year."

Margaret Truman states in her book, *Harry S. Truman:* "Everyone in the world seemed to believe it [that her father was a "gone goose" (Clare Boothe Luce's expression)] except Harry S. Truman, my mother, me, a loyal little band of White House aides—and the people who came to meet our campaign train." Reva Beck Bosone didn't have to be convinced—she was among those who cheered and believed in a Truman victory. Early in the 1940s, when Senator Truman had investigated military contracts in Utah, the Judge was one of a welcoming committee who met and lunched with him at Camp Kearns. For all those years she had been aware of his ability and charm.

When the Truman campaign train arrived in Provo, Utah, the Judge enjoyed the honor of introducing the president to the huge crowds from the back of the Ferdinand Magellan, the presidential car. That momentous occasion was preempted by an even more prestigious one. When the train pulled away from the Provo station she inquired whether or not it would be stopping in her hometown, just a few miles down mainstream. It would not, she was informed, because the train was moving on a time schedule to Salt Lake City. The Judge, with tap roots in American Fork, was, needless to say, disappointed! But as the train approached American Fork, a multitude of Truman supporters overran the tracks and the Magellan was forced to brake to a halt. Her wish had come true!

Making the most of a providential situation, Reva stepped right up, but with a rule breaker. Instead of "Ladies and gentlemen, the president of the United States," she could not resist shouting, "President Truman, meet the people of the best hometown in the United States—American Fork!"

But Mr. Truman laughed and had no compunction in challenging the Judge's punch line. "No, Judge Bosone, you are wrong. The best hometown in the United States is Independence, Missouri!"

That evening in the Mormon Tabernacle, President Truman related how his grandfather, driving his wagons cross-country, came into Salt Lake City and how Brigham Young had befriended him.

The late president wrote the Judge in 1956, "I'll never forget our Utah campaign. It was a classic in its line."

The current clamor to install Harry Truman as a folk hero poses no surprise for Reva, who a generation ago was impressed with the integrity and trustworthiness of the man from Independence. As Reva stated in a recent address, "When he called you something you didn't want to be called, that's exactly what you were!"

The coffers of the state party were empty and most certainly the Judge had no funds to splurge on her campaign, so she shared a suite of rooms in the Newhouse Hotel with Grant Macfarlane, the state chairman. Her retinue was augmented by Sam Thurman, Jr., the eminent lawyer son of former Justice Thurman; Mrs. Scott Page Stewart, a former state chairwoman; young Lynn Cohne (now Arent), who had worked with the National Democratic Committee in Washington, D.C.; and Mrs. Carolyn Wolfe, who had held important positions in the Democratic party, locally, regionally, and nationally. Constituting the daily working committee, they met with the candidate and Ruth Penrose early every morning.

As the Judge, usually in a tailored brown or navy wool suit, walked briskly in each day, all eyes would stop at her handbag, the center compartment of which held money contributed for her campaign. With singular concentration they would ask how much and the candidate would dump out the contents. Sometimes just a few tinkles would herald the amount on the table. Be that as it may, Reva was a cash-and-carry customer then as now and insisted on no debts and no obligations. All newspaper ads and radio spots were paid for before they were run. And in every public office in which she served, Reva insured that every red entry was turned black before she vacated the office.

Lynn had prepared a large ad to cost $75 but a nervous crew sat on it for weeks until at last Reva jubilantly presented the committee with the accumulated greenbacks, releasing the dormant ad for publication the next day.

"Reva would go out and pass the hat—she wouldn't take big amounts from anyone. She used to say, 'I don't want to be indebted to anyone; even subconsciously I might vote wrong if someone gave me a huge amount of money.' I remember in the 1952 campaign, she turned down some pretty big sums," Lynn said.

Reva, in this day and age, never misses a chance to quote the amount that she, personally, spent on the campaign—*$1250!*

Every biography contains a few shockers. In the case of the Judge, who exerted the force of a fragile shoot pushing itself up through the pitiless sun-baked clay, to say that she prayed for defeat must arouse disbelief.

Only after most of life's accreditation has taken place and incredible accomplishments precede her name do we hear that Reva Beck Bosone did not really want to leave Salt Lake City or the bench or her cozy overage home on McClelland Street, that each night she sincerely wished upon that well-worn star that she would not win in the balloting, but that the vote would be close, of course (who wants to be skunked?). Perhaps it was the same feeling when all packed to go on a big trip she longed to stay put. Like the ancient limber pines of the West, sentimental roots kept her securely positioned in Utah. Even in the 1970s, living with her daughter in another part of the country, she is affected with pangs of homesickness that remind her of those she suffered as a young girl. Could she ever forget that summer so long ago?

THE SUDDEN gusty breezes that pushed through the sentinel firs made sounds like horses' hoofs and the young girl positioned on the big white rock would raise her head from its resting place on her knees to search the winding road for her parents' rig. Moments later, as the air carried to her ears the snapping noises of the nearby river which simulated the grinding of wooden wheels on a rock-strewn road, Reva would jump up with the joyous expectation of seeing her mama and papa riding toward her in the distance.

With every disappointment favorite memories flared up—the all-day ride to Pleasant Grove with her mother to buy bushels of fragrant fruit for canning, the new, sweet-faced doll with lace-trimmed clothes at Christmas, the accolades of her parents after her singing performance at the Opera House.

And then the forest sounds would jar her to the present. It has to be time for them to be here, she would repeat to herself in anguish.

"Reva, lunch is ready. Better come in now." Her new friends, Mr. Christy and his two young daughters who had been guests at the Grant Hotel and who had invited Reva to spend a month-long vacation with them at Deer Creek, were sympathetic yet concerned. Little did they foresee that toward the end of her stay she would spend most of three days on that rock in front of their new mountain cabin, desolate with homesickness.

After reluctantly leaving the rock one evening for dinner, Reva knew finally that her ears were not tricking her and she dashed out the door to greet her mother and father just arriving in one of her father's shiniest rigs and drawn by two of his sprightliest horses.

"Mama! Papa!" she cried as she flung herself into their arms. Surprised and upset that their sensitive red-haired youngster had been pining for home, they could see, nevertheless, that they were the answer to her prayers.

The next morning Reva hugged her two young hostesses, Ida and Margaret, in emotional good-byes.

"I really did have lots of fun and a wonderful time," Reva told them with a flourish, hoping they would understand that the only cure for homesickness in someone who had been away from home only one night in her whole life was the sight of her parents. Evidently they did understand, because Margaret, who matched Reva's age, became an over-sixty-year friend from the advent of that vacation.

The ride down American Fork Canyon was exhilarating—a rain the night before had dampened the dust on the road and left the trees slick with watered leaves, the brightness of the sun searchlighting the occupants of the rig through the tree branches. Reva slipped her arm through her mother's as she snuggled back on the seat and watched the rolling gait of the well-brushed horses—the world seemed washed and loving and . . . right.

NOVEMBER'S SHORT DAYS can be bleak, but more often than not the call of winter in the Rocky Mountains, heard through the leafless tree branches, is made in bright sunshine. The foothills below Mt. Olympus and Twin and Lone peaks are still tinged with rust, and above the 5,000-foot level, snow has settled through the brush to create a mottled effect, like putty in rock crevices. The clouds are often mere puffs high in the sky and the breeze has a certain chill, just enough to provoke a deep breath now and then. After the incessant productivity of summer, fall provides a welcome relief. And so did November 2, 1948, provide a respite from the hurricanelike commotion of politicking.

"When I ran for the judiciary I nearly always cleaned house and did the laundry on election day and then retired early," Reva said. "That was my intention on this election day. I cleaned house all right, but I received a call from headquarters that if I went to bed early, a crowd would come out and break down my front door if I didn't get up. So I decided to go down to headquarters at about 11:00 P.M.

"When I walked in, Grant Macfarlane grabbed me, shouting, 'Truman is making it, and so are you!'" The atmosphere was heady with victory! Somewhat overwhelmed, the candidate was kissed, hugged, and congratulated. The final results listed her ahead by 24,157 votes, and a celebration was in the making.

The titillating news of election night was the comeuppance of Thomas Dewey and the victory of Harry Truman, who had previously called public opinion polls "sleeping polls." He had said the public was not being fooled by them. Evidently not!

One can't know whether or not the president had a similar reaction, but when Reva was met with, "I'll bet you are simply thrilled," she put on her best act so far, the one with the happy mask. Why this apparent about-face?

"I suppose some people would ask," Reva volunteers, 'Why didn't you get out of the campaign when you knew you didn't want to be elected?' And I suppose my answer would be, 'It was too late. I had the nomination by then. And if anything, I had to live up to a promise.' "

Zilpha, understandably empathetic, experienced a touch of anguish herself. She was keeping company with the captain of the basketball team at Westminster College where she was enrolled and was most reluctant to leave. But she never suggested that she remain in Utah. To see her mother sworn in as Utah's Second Congressional District representative would be an unforgettable experience to be cherished a lifetime and a privilege that few daughters would ever have to remember.

Both mother and daughter chose to live up to the promise but they were scarcely prepared for what followed. The promise fulfilled spelled publicity beyond Reva's imagination, with requests for interviews and photographs from papers all over the United States. The fact that the Judge was a mother also heightened the interest—the domestic setting was a popular one for pictures of the attractive duo.

Necessary duties of cleaning up the cases assigned to her until the last week of December, boxing personal papers, answering enlarged stacks of mail, sorting, discarding, packing, and preparing her house for renters demanded her attention from the first of November to the last of the year.

Delineating between the important and the unimportant was dearly learned by the novice congresswoman in those first weeks following her election. "One day I received a copy of the Corrupt Practices Act from the clerk of the House of Representatives. I was terribly busy and when I saw this publication I knew *I* didn't need to read it so I dumped it into the wastebasket—a terrible mistake because it ties in with a cruel episode four years later!"

A book uncovered by an old friend, Caroline Perry, would have given Reva solace during those flurried weeks of preparation for Washington, D.C. By Edward W. Tullidge, *The Women of Mormondom,* published in 1877, says on page 527:

> They [the women] have taken action upon the very foundation of society-building. Already, therefore, the women of Utah lead the age in this supreme woman's issue; and, if they carry their State into the Union first on the woman suffrage plan, they will practically make women suffrage a dispensation in our National Economy for all States of the Federal Union. And it will be consistent to look for a female member of Congress from Utah. Let woman be once recognized as a

power in the State, as well as in society and the church, and her
political rights can be extended according to the public mind.

When the Judge was made acquainted with the book in 1952, she
realized that she had become the woman whom author Tullidge had in
mind.

Lining up a committee assignment and a top administrative assistant
were of chief importance before taking up residence in Washington. The
first was a natural for the new congresswoman—after all, she had studied
resources for years. It would definitely be the House Interior Committee,
where public lands, dams, irrigation projects, mines, and Indian welfare
were priority considerations.

Finding an administrative assistant Reva classed as a stroke of genius
by two friends, Carolyn Wolfe and Elise Musser, who suggested attractive Virginia Rishel, daughter of Bill Rishel, head of the Automobile
Association of Utah. With two degrees in journalism, she had served as
the editor of the *Democratic Digest* in Washington, D.C. However, having
never worked on Capitol Hill, let alone undertaken any secretarial tasks,
she disparaged her abilities in that respect in her reply to Reva's query.
But Virginia's superior intelligence, enthusiasm, and obvious integrity
impressed the congresswoman to look beyond mere typing and shorthand
deficiencies; Reva *knew* that Virginia would be her perfect aide. The congresswoman's knack for sensing potential was uncanny; a friend, Jack
Dixon, formerly of the Interior Department, claims that Reva qualifies as
the type of person who can pick up a chestnut and tell if the nut inside the
husk is any good.

A harmonious association between the two women resulted on a personal basis as well as in the workaday world. Sharing many habits and
characteristics, each seemed to understand how the other ticked. As
Virginia says, they even shared some of the same faults. "Invariably in
going through a door, we would both push where the sign said pull!"

"Knowing what assignment I wanted, I asked Virginia to contact the
Walter Granger office [he had been a member of Congress from Utah for
eight years] to set in motion an assignment to the Interior Committee. She
was dubious about my chance since no woman had been on the committee," said Reva. "Then she wrote that she had talked to Jerry Cooper,
chairman of the Ways and Means Committee, and members of the House
Interior Committee and was told it would be embarrassing for me to be on
a committee that discussed animal breeding!"

But the Judge had been exposed to the gamut, learning more than
she ever wanted to know, and had emerged from the background of court
experience still a gentle woman. Animal breeding? They had to be kid-
ding!

She wired Virginia to inform them that after hearing cases of sex perversion by human beings, it would be refreshing to learn about animal breeding, an explanation that evidently convinced the all-male committee, because she was appointed the first woman to sit on the Committee on Public Lands, second in a group of seven new Democrats!

Lo and behold, during the two terms the Judge served, she did not recognize any discussion on animal breeding. Actually there was one— which at the time went by her. After a committee meeting one day she asked her colleague, Wayne Aspinall, what a mounting station was, to which he gave her an amused sidelong glance.

As for irrigation projects and problems of land resources, as a teenager Reva had been involved in table discussions on these and related subjects. From her earliest years she had trekked repeatedly with her parents, who owned stock in the Pacific mines, to the lead, silver, and zinc mines of American Fork Canyon. Hauling ore had been a function of her father's occupation, of course. And one summer even young Horace, at the age of seventeen, had run a passenger and mail stage up that winding canyon road one day and down the next. Mountains, water, and mines were intertwined in the lives of the Becks, and Reva had sat for hours listening to the miners' tales of exhilaration and tribulation. Water subjects held particular interest, the Colorado River project presenting a special fascination, and she followed closely every proposal for its development.

Détente was a Bosone law long before the word enjoyed household usage. In Reva's estimation, too many welfare and resources problems clamored for her attention to waste time worrying over poor personal relationships. So if in her earnest manner she did not charm everyone with her forthright approach and if an acquaintance showed a lack of confidence in her or pettiness because of prejudgment, she would bide her time and look for an opportunity to alter the opinion. Chances were first rate that she would find it and proceed to a lifelong friendship with the adversary. With the exception of a former political opponent, a Bosone enemy is nonexistent.

A case in point concerned Judge James A. Howell, a Republican of Ogden and one of the most active leaders on the water problems of Utah and the West. When Reva first sat in on the irrigation committee meetings of the State of Utah, she simply failed to impress him. His indifferent attitude toward her could have remained exasperating if she had allowed it; he relegated her, she presumed, to the status of upstart in a man's world with a primer knowledge of natural resources.

So the formula for being accepted as a new member of a men's group was put to use immediately—keeping a meaningful silence—just until, that is, she knew she had acquired enough savvy, and then, by hell's bells, she'd let fly and command attention! After a few months, Judge Howell joined her league of supporters, spending much time in her office on trips to Washington.

"To see our friendship grow was one of the most rewarding periods in my life. He was big enough that politics made no difference to him. When he passed away I felt I had lost a dear personal friend."

National Legislator

LEAVING HER HOME STATE turned out to be almost traumatic for the Judge. During December, still issuing edicts from the bench to the tune of approximately a hundred per day, suffering from a severe head cold, interrupted by scores of often inconsiderate individuals demanding solutions to problems before she departed, answering endless phone calls, packing, and attending to the innumerable details that encumber an out-of-state move, the Judge was close to walking the fine wire of exhaustion.

Finally mother and daughter collapsed in their bedroom on the train taking them to Potomac country, looking forward to nothing more strenuous than watching scenery. Soon, however, they found they were being given preferential treatment. Although Reva's fight for a train limit bill was fifteen years in the past, the crew had been given the word that they were carrying a special lady, and nothing was too grand for the Queen of the Rails!

PHOTO: *Reva Beck Bosone, Member of Congress, 1948–52.*

Arrival in Washington, D.C., was made in drippy weather, doing little to raise their spirits. The two women registered at the Congressional Hotel (since demolished) on Capitol Hill and sat dejectedly in their room.

"It was New Year's Eve and there we were," Reva remembers, a shroud of homesickness clinging to them. "We decided to take a walk on Pennsylvania Avenue, but even the weather wept with us. The room was better than the street so back we came." They toasted each other with one small glass of wine and decided to hear the New Year in across the nation on radio, which would include Salt Lake City. Unfortunately, the network hit Denver and bypassed Salt Lake City, so the two let-down newcomers gave up and went to bed.

Virginia Rishel, meanwhile, plunging into the sphere of government proceedings with singular industry, had set up the Bosone offices with the aid of Elva Bell, administrative assistant to Walter Granger, in Room 1416 of the New House Office Building. Reva soon selected her staff and the characteristic busyness began. When the new congresswoman moved in, so did a few lush philodendron, ivy, and tiger plants. In Salt Lake City she was reputed to own one of the best collections of rare plants and shrubbery there.

A priority cosmetic project was covering the walls—which were in what her secretary called a "heavenly shade of government beige"—with autographed pictures of women colleagues in Congress. On the desk, photos of her daughter, brothers, and personal friends transposed a little of "home" to the big new position. Granger, avowed friend, and Elva, who had been with him as long as his Washington career, were of invaluable assistance in showing her the ropes. Reva's regard for Walt was of long duration, of course, since their 1933 legislature session together in Utah. And the regard was reciprocal—he introduced the Judge at the Democratic caucus in the House as "a lady in the parlor but a fighter in a legislation hall!"

Reva's participation in the Women's National Press Club Dinner honoring congresswomen resulted in a wedge of influence for the Judge during all her years in Washington. As Reva reviewed the scene that night of the elite of the nation's capital—the brass of Congress, high-ranking officials, and distinguished members of the press—she again gave a silent thanks to a mother who had lovingly tended and nurtured a wispy seedling of a girl in preparation for such honors.

After dinner the honored guests were expected to speak, and the Judge was startled to be introduced first by the mistress of ceremonies. "I never dreamed of being first! I hadn't prepared a speech because I felt I wouldn't be called on until later and by the time I was, I would have something in mind to say. You see, I hadn't been in Washington long enough to realize that protocol is sacred and seniority is the rule!"

Cornelia Lund, her Utah friend, had suggested that Reva just be herself in the sophisticated world of Washington. This prosaic advice could be somewhat disastrous to the milktoast or the boor, but the suggestion was apropos in the Judge's case—even in her more subdued moments Reva is apt to produce a precedent-scoring idea. So at this formal affair she decided to be first a drunk and then herself! Grabbing the rostrum to steady herself, she swung into action as the alcoholic who appeared in her courtroom.

"Jedge," slurred the Judge swaying to imitate the boozer, "Jedge"—"he" hiccuped several times attempting to say more. Finally, the inebriate steadied "himself" enough to look up and stammer, "Jedge, you here again?" Then she gave a quick resumé of her background.

When she sat down two (or more) minutes later, whispers queried, "Now, *how* can we follow that?"

This cameo appearance, she claims, opened the door to the inner offices wherever she went. The greeting was always, "I remember you. I heard you at the Press Women's Dinner." It also affirmed to the world of the press that Reva Bosone was super copy!

Grace Grether considered Reva a brilliant subject way back when the Judge was attacking such problems as alcoholism and traffic fatalities. A consistent admirer of Reva, the bouncy newspaperwoman doted on running breezily worded complimentary articles on the Judge's accomplishments. Close friends for thirty-five years, the congresswoman and the columnist complemented each other—Reva supplying the color and Grace transcribing it into clever word tones and hues. Asserting that Reva was one of the greatest judges in Utah, Mrs. Grether attributes her judicial success to a combination of a tender heart and a strength of character that wouldn't permit her to stoop. Referring to so-called "compliments" on the Judge's ability to think like a man, Grace stated that it's just too bad more men don't think like a woman!

In those first weeks in Washington, when each new (and old) member of Congress was sized up by a seasoned press, Reva was checked off as definitely not run-of-the-mill.

Tris Coffin of "Washington Daybook" wrote that new House members showed promise of the liveliest Congress. One included in the "up-and-at-'em" freshmen was Reva Beck Bosone, and he quoted Victor Hunt ("Cap") Harding, the cautious National Democratic Campaign director, as shouting enthusiastically, "Reva Bosone has a hell of a lot on the ball." And Drew Pearson in "Merry-Go-Round" called Reva "Capable, charming, keen mind; was a good judge in Utah and should make a good congresswoman."

The rapport between Reva and reporters has always been mutually beneficial. Never a purposeful seeker of publicity, she nonetheless left a trail of goodies for the journalist wherever she appeared. And never one to undercredit, Reva heaps glory on the press for hoisting her career on its shoulders.

The faithful media were favoring Reva and Zilpha with some publicity preceding an event in 1949 but the opportunity for them to perform together before an audience was thwarted. The stage of Constitution Hall was to be the showcase for the mother/daughter duo singing Zilpha's original composition, "Sophisticate," at an affair sponsored by the members of Congress. But Zilpha fell ill with the flu, causing much disappointment, especially since their photo had appeared in the *Washington Star.*

"The Interior Department of the United States holds the key to the prosperity and happiness of future generations," was Reva's long held opinion that influenced her choice of committee activity. The dream was at last a reality—she had acquired an assignment on the House Interior and Insular Affairs Committee, whose chairman made a special effort to greet her in her new office. Keeping a clamp on her tongue until she could contribute was still her strategy in this bastion of men's opinion. In other words, she was long on listening and short on "horseback opinions."

"I'll never forget when Congressman Comp [Compton] White of Idaho passed my chair one day in committee and leaned over and said, 'What can a woman know about this stuff?' " Refusing to get unnerved she shot back that he'd be surprised. She guessed that he couldn't possibly believe she was truly interested in the damage of the spruce bark beetle on the Colorado River watershed.

So she had a quick PR job to do! A few weeks later a mellowed Comp White never hesitated to confide in her in discussing his committee measures. And an added courtesy—he never hesitated to invite her to accompany him on his White House visits.

Included on important subcommittees, one of which was Indian Affairs, Reva asked again—why not? It was said she was just upholding her reputation for doing battle for those who could not do it for themselves. The battlefield was often the committee room. After intense preliminary work, the lady member of the Interior Committee introduced joint resolution, H. J.R. 490, which would gradually, after years, take the Indians off the one hundred–year policy of government wardship. In a conference Congressman Norris Poulson denounced her with, "All you want is publicity in this bill," spurring a few caustic words from the congresswoman after which the belittling Poulson was reported to have said, "This proves her hair is not dyed. It really is red," a color at that point which Reva distinctly saw! She was reported to have snorted that if she had been within three feet of that Poulson she would have smacked him down! (She had tangled on the bench with fiercer adversaries.)

There appears to be no documentation that the altercation ever took place (Poulson, who later became mayor of Los Angeles, was said to have gone into training), and true to the Judge's nature, she transcended the discord, applying her winning ways. The two wound up the best of friends.

She certainly was not neglecting the Indians during the rambunctious repartee. It was not difficult to deduce that there was not a single Indian vote in her district! Certainly no opportunist, she took genuine interest in their plight, conferring with committees of Indian tribes in her travels over the United States to learn their problems.

"Their lack of hatred and their intelligence impressed me greatly. What extravagance to have wasted and left untouched for so long the talents and brains of the American Indian!" she emphasized.

Knowing that many influential people in this country advocated the preservation of the Indian culture, the Judge asked the Indian leaders on her visits to the reservations what their culture consisted of; they didn't know! They did know one thing—they wanted to live like the white man. Every leader expressed this desire in 1949. In the comparatively recent insurgencies, however, it is evident there has been a change of heart in some areas. During the desperate Wounded Knee confrontations, Reva would gladly have paid her own expenses there if the eye affliction she suffers had permitted her to take such a mission. "I would have told them that it's too late for sovereignty. I sympathize with them—they're entitled to it, but it's not practical. I want them to have the same as the Danes, Swedes, Russians, Blacks. I have profound respect for the American Indian!"

She recalled an incident that scratches the memory like a snaggy fingernail. "In Phoenix, on a trip with the Interior Committee, there were a couple of Indian leaders with us. When we were in a restaurant they couldn't order a drink at the bar, so Wayne (Aspinall) and another member ordered two cocktails each and gave one of theirs to the leaders at our table."

Describing the congressional bill, the congresswoman said, "It provided that the Bureau of Indian Affairs should make a report listing the tribes then ready and willing to be 'put on their own,' and there are many. The report would be accompanied by suggested legislation and recommendations. Congress would then have something definite to consider, some plan to evaluate.

"The resolution provided also that later on the Bureau of Indian Affairs would present another report listing the tribes not ready for citizenship, telling why they were not and making recommendations to correct the deficiency. My bill did not contain any magic that would make the Indian ready for citizenship overnight. It was one of positive policy. It would have forced the responsible agency to view the complex problem from a new angle. It is one thing to set up a custodial agency; it is another to set up a preparatory agency."

Both Republicans and Democrats on the Interior Committee supported her resolution in the 81st Congress. And in the House, both parties were behind it. The bill hit a snag in the Senate; it was killed there in December 1950 by one dissenting vote on the "Consent" calendar (a bill on the Consent calendar can be passed by voice vote or it can be held up by the objection of one senator). That holdup was made by Senator Arthur V. Watkins of Utah! And so another round of intrigue that absolutely baffled the congresswoman lost the nation its chance at that time to help square it with the Indian, to let him compete with the white man and not remain subservient to him.

Rumor had it that in 1952 Reva might oppose Senator Watkins, a one-term judge in Provo before his election, if Congressman Granger decided not to contest him. This was worrisome to the incumbent senator because Reva's followers were legion by this time. Republican Poulson, sarcastic about the Judge's bill in the 82d Congress, had actually stood beside her in the 81st and helped her push it through the committee and the House. But a complete switch saw Poulson and John Taylor turn against the resolution. A new member, Frank L. Bow from Ohio, apparently a good friend of the two top men in the Watkins office, was an ally of Poulson and Taylor. The three banded together to snipe at Congresswoman Bosone, accusing her of selfish motives. Strongly resenting the accusation that publicity was her motive, she later recognized the reasons for their lashing.

"I did not run for the Senate, after all. Then after I was defeated for the House seat in 1952, Senator Watkins, to my surprise, introduced an Indian bill having the same idea in it as mine. Yet he was against the resolution when he thought I might be his opponent that year."

In the July 29, 1950, issue of the *Saturday Evening Post,* Reva's bill was editorialized as follows:

> Rep. Reva Bosone (D., Utah) has introduced in the House a joint resolution calling for an investigation of the American Indians "in order to determine the respective qualifications of such Indians to manage their own affairs without supervision and control by the Federal Government."
>
> Although we have come to accept as irrevocable the idea that Indians are "wards of the nation" and therefore especially fitted to be

herded into reservations and managed by employes of the Bureau of Indian Affairs, it is quite possible that Mrs. Bosone has something. It could be that the reason Indians appear to require Federal supervision is that they have always had Federal supervision. Mrs. Bosone believes that Indians have "the same inherent intelligence and capacity for performance as other Americans." She thinks they ought to have a chance to exercise these qualities.

Dean Russell, in a pamphlet published by the Foundation for Economic Education, makes an interesting comparison between the performance record of Indians and that of American Negroes, who were at one time treated as "wards of the nation" under Freedman's Bureau, of Reconstruction days. Soon, however, the former slaves were thrown upon their own resources, and the record of the Negro race in American citizenship is one of the finest bits of evidence in history of the ability of men to advance under conditions of freedom.

"Now," says Mr. Russell, "compare the remarkable progress of these former slaves to the lack of progress of the American Indians who were made wards of the Government; who were given state-guaranteeed 'security' instead of freedom with responsibility. In 1862 most American Negroes were slaves. Today they are about as self-supporting and responsible as other American citizens. Meanwhile the Indians as a group have become less self-supporting and more dependent on Government aid. . . . As has been proved by the success of many individual Indians, they have just as much capacity for understanding and advancement as the Negroes and the so-called Nordics. But today there are 12,000 Federal employes directly 'taking care' of the 233,000 reservation Indians who are still classified as wards of the Government. The number of Indian caretakers has been steadily increasing over the years."

The ambition of too many politicians is to return all America to the status of the "secure" Indians, but Mrs. Bosone may have struck an important blow for progress in the opposite direction. Instead of giving the country back to the Indians, it seems to us that America should at least consider the possibility of giving the Indians all the advantages, and risks, of life in this great country.

Among the few who took exception to Mrs. Bosone's idea on Indians' rights was Harold Ickes, former secretary of the interior, who feuded with her on the printed page. The badinage ended with a standoff, however, and a compliment from Ickes, "I think if I knew you, I'd like you."

The bill, generally accepted, was even okayed by Indian Commissioner Dillon Myer and Assistant Commissioner H. Rex Lee. Lee was asked how it felt to cooperate with a bill that would eventually eliminate his own bureau (which cost the taxpayers $80 million per year). "Well," he was reported to have said, "that's what we are in business for—to get ourselves out of it."

The *Salt Lake Tribune* joined the majority in a favorable editorial,

"Getting the Indian Off Uncle Sam's Back." While not always agreeing with Reva's policies, the paper conferred kudos on this one. "It may take a long time to get the Indians off the federal dole," the article stated, "but surely this should be the consistent aim of the Indian bureau, the Interior department and congress. House Resolution 490 is a proper step."

Water and Other Elements

"FROM MY EARLY CHILDHOOD in American Fork," Reva recounts, "I realized that water is the key to Utah's development. That is the reason, when I went to Congress, I took a place on the West's own big committee—the Committee on Interior and Insular Affairs. It is through that committee that all reclamation bills must pass."

Brigham Young, a pioneer in many endeavors, in 1847 was the first Anglo-Saxon adventurer to take water out of its natural bed for its beneficial use elsewhere—of necessity diverting a stream from City Creek in the Great Salt Lake valley to enrich planted crops. (Spanish pioneers and western Indians had instituted the practice earlier.) This act nullified the riparian rights principle which stipulates that each water user return the water to the stream undiminished and unimpaired for users downstream.

Reclamation as such was born in comparatively recent times—1902. It suffered a relapse in the 1920s when the easterners, in opposition, centered an attack on it. It was revived by the big development that began in New Deal days as part of the program of utilization and conservation of the nation's resources. During the twenty years of Democratic administration (from the early 1930s to the early 1950s), the government appropriated five times as much for reclamation as was appropriated throughout the entire thirty years previously.

In years 1951 and 1952, the coalition of Republicans and Dixiecrats that had taken control in the House habitually denigrated reclamation when funds were being considered. "Eight times the Republicans and Dixiecrats slashed away at the West's program," said the Judge, "and eight times the administration Democrats fought to save the full amount of funds needed for reclamation, land management, and other programs vital to the West. In most instances, the Republican-Dixiecrat coalition was successful!

"Every important development in our water setup in the last fifty years," Congresswoman Bosone declared, "has come through Democratic administrations and as a result of Democratic effort." So in this light she felt especially disposed to try her best for the natural resources of her state while a Democratic president still occupied the White House, know-

149

ing the House of Representatives was riddled with reclamation denouncers.

No one could dispute the fact that water was a commodity coming into short supply if a farseeing plan were not implemented. The congresswoman knew the importance of anticipating future demands in a burgeoning Zion (the land of Deseret, as were other states, was adding to the census fast and furiously), while stressing the importance of population control for a decent quality of life for the living and future generations.

The Colorado River Project, mammoth in scope and considered one of the important measures in Congress, was viewed with Echo Park Dam—Utah's big interest—as a wreaker of havoc by the Isaac Walton League, other conservation organizations, and the Army Engineers.

"The congressional delegation from the western states decided that the bill should not be introduced until the trouble with the Echo Park Dam part could be ironed out, until the opponents changed their minds, until the Army Engineers wrote a favorable report," Reva said. In the meantime, she poured on her most convincing words in behalf of this project which she reckoned was being emotionally propagandized. The Army Engineers were contacted and also the national General Federation of Women's Clubs, led by the capable Dorothy Houghton, whose mind was changed by the persuasive congresswoman.

Reva placed several items in the *Congressional Record:* a letter from Frank Ward, secretary of the Colorado River Development Association, taking exception to the statements opposing the dam by the National Park Service; a letter from Dr. Ernest Untermann, director of the Utah Field House of Natural History ("In this letter," the congresswoman states, "Dr. Untermann seeks to correct certain erroneous reports which have been published about the pending destruction of geological values by the proposed dams."); and a "clipping from the *Salt Lake Tribune* which tells how the Utah Federated Artists with spokesmen Lynn Faucett and Mabel Fraser at first opposed the Echo Dam Project because they feared it would endanger scenic values in the area, [but] found after a first-hand study of a special committee that this was not true, and voted to approve the project."

In December 1951 Congresswoman Bosone, heading a special six-member committee, called a hearing at the state capitol in Utah to determine what type of local opposition existed to the construction of Echo Park Dam in the Dinosaur National Monument. Only one of the witnesses who appeared at the meeting of more than one hundred persons disapproved of the project.

Her opponent in the political campaign of 1952, William Dawson, accused her of not introducing the bill in Congress. She defended her stand with the argument that the controversy of *national* objectors had to be minimized before the bill was introduced.

"It is interesting to note," Reva says, "that the project bill did pass after 1952, in the Eisenhower administration, but it passed without the Echo Park Dam. If Walter Granger and I had agreed to delete the dam part of the bill, it probably would have passed earlier. William Dawson and Arthur V. Watkins permitted Utah's important issue to be deleted!" According to news reports, Congressman Dawson's reason for voting for the bill without the Echo Park Dam inclusion was that it had a better chance of passing.

Paul Badger, administrative assistant of Utah's Senator Elbert Thomas, believed Reva was right in not compromising Utah's claim.

During the campaign of 1954, the Judge asked former President Truman at a small dinner party in Salt Lake City his views on the Colorado River bill and he answered, "It should have been fair to all the states. Since it wasn't—wasn't fair to Utah with the Echo Park Dam out—I would have vetoed it."

The present Flaming Gorge Dam, not too far distant from the site of the previous proposal, was a later thought for Utah's benefit in the Colorado River Storage Project—authorized in 1956 and completed in the 1960s.

Reva's ever present concern about the water dilemmas of the West and the world led her right into the $70 million Weber Basin Reclamation Project. Although both Congressmen Granger and Bosone introduced it in the House, and Senator Watkins introduced it in the Senate, it could well have been called Operation Bosone—it was literally saved by her hand.

Just after a committee hearing one afternoon on the Weber legislation, members of the subcommittee surprised the congresswoman by proposing to report out her bill with her name on it. Although this pleased her, she knew she couldn't allow it since Granger, a veteran member of Congress, had completed much work on his measure and was entitled to the credit. So be it. Shortly thereafter, the main committee on Interior reported out Weber Basin bill H.R. 799, which contemplated additional reservoirs on the Weber River and two conduits into Davis County. Also in the plans would be the dyking of Great Salt Lake around the mouth of the Weber and the pumping of fresh water onto the lower lands.

One day, after a conference on the Senate side at which Senator Watkins was present, Reva reported that he groused to her, "You shouldn't have reported the Weber Basin bill out of the subcommittee and main committee so fast!"

The congresswoman faced him squarely and challenged his sincerity.

"What do you mean fast?" she asked. "Aren't you for that bill? If you are, then you should be happy it was not tied up in the committee!" Senator Watkins' own bill was still in the Senate committee.

"Later on his measure was reported out of the Senate Interior Committee and passed," Reva remarked. "Walt and I could have held up his bill and passed Walt's, but we were more for the legislation than for the credit!

"Walt saw Joe Martin and then we both saw Speaker Sam Rayburn and arranged for the Weber Basin bill with Watkins' name on it to pass the House under suspension of the rules. We both knew at the time that Watkins never would have done this for the Granger bill had it passed the House first."

Since the Korean War was imminent, President Truman announced there were to be no new reclamation starts except for defense or emergency. After the Weber Basin Project had passed both houses, pessimistic rumors hung in the air. One evening Granger, who with his wife lived in the same apartment building as Reva, called her for a conference on a frustrating predicament. When she walked into his living room he was pacing the floor.

"The president isn't going to sign the Basin bill, Reva. *What* can we do?" His agonized proclamation foretold a death blow to legislation of the most vitally necessary reclamation project in Utah's history. Reva sat down, thinking desperately.

Senator Elbert D. Thomas popped into her mind first. He was up for reelection that fall, having rolled up an impressive record as chairman of the committee on Labor and Public Welfare; subcommittee chairman of Unemployment in Mining and Mine Safety; member of the Foreign Relations Committee; member of the subcommittee on Voice of America; Far Eastern, United Nations, and World Government; North Atlantic Treaty; International Wheat Agreement; Genocide; and Democratic Steering Committee. He was geared for a tough duel in the coming campaign but the doom of the reclamation project could disintegrate his future political career. If there was ever a time when a brilliant extemporaneous idea should be forthcoming, it was at this moment. And it came like the proverbial light bulb over Reva's head!

"Senator Thomas should see President Truman immediately," she declared, "put his feet under the desk, and remind the president that he, Thomas, has for years introduced and carried the responsibility of getting the most important administrative bills through the Senate and that if this bill is not signed by the president, it would help defeat Thomas in Utah. The president's signature is vital! The senator should plead his cause."

Granger stopped pacing. "Call Paul Badger and tell him that," which is precisely what the junior congresswoman did the next morning and Badger relayed the message to the Senator.

"At noon that day I was in a conference in my office," Reva recalls, "when Virginia came in to announce that Senator Thomas was on the line. When I answered I heard him say, 'Thanks, Reva, thanks a lot.' I asked whether it had worked and he said yes."

The president then made good his word and the bill was signed. A discouraging postscript in political development—despite Reva's last-gasp attempt, Senator Thomas did not survive the smear campaign waged by his opponent and he returned to private life.

Still more roadblocks! Even though the bill was signed, the Appropriations Committee announced there would be no funds! Believing that if the amount could be knocked just low enough to crank the Weber Basin Project into being it would have a chance, Reva contacted her friend, Jack Dixon, head engineer at the Interior Department, to set a reduced workable sum that hopefully the Appropriations Committee would allow to stand. He dug in efficiently to figure and calculate, reporting shortly that $1 million would put into motion the initial plan.

Mrs. Bosone then went before the committee with the Dixon report, again flashing her debating expertise, and stressed the low amount she was asking. Success! (Later, she understood the committee obliged her and left in $1 million from the original request of $70 million because they believed the president would strike it, anyway.)

Finally, there was only one more hurdle—she made an appointment with President Truman. He always had her sit beside him near his desk. "How's your health, Judge?" he would ask. "Bess read you had the flu when you were in Salt Lake." And a warm chatty conversation would ensue.

The Judge remembers that he had a copy of the bill on his desk. "I have always marveled at the brains of this man. He *knew* legislation. I told him that I had had the appropriation reduced to an amount that wouldn't do much but it would get the plans moving. After I finished my explanation, the president cautioned, 'Now keep this a secret—tell no one! I'll leave the appropriation in.' And he did, bless him. Believe me, I kept quiet. But that is why I consider the Weber Basin Project *my* bill!"

"At the dedication of the project in 1969," she related, "Senator Watkins took full credit for the passing of the bill, indicating he had written a strong letter to President Truman that convinced Truman to sign it. Surely he didn't know the president very well, for *no one* could scare him! I could not attend the dedication, although I received an invitation, but if I had, I'm afraid there would have been disagreement between Senator Watkins and me in rather forceful language."

And she adds, "I was always a bit disappointed that Senator Thomas and Congressman Granger never did reveal why the bill was signed and how the project got started. Perhaps it was embarrassing to give credit to a woman in a supposedly man's field. The admitting would have been a noble act. Judge Howell did know and was grateful."

Paul Badger, who moved to Salt Lake City from Washington, D.C., in the early 1970s, said, "Reva really sparked it and urged them [Thomas and Granger] to have a private conference; both of them made two or three trips to see the president. The Judge played a vital role in getting that approved."

In her ongoing role as "Mother of Reclamation," a term applied to her by the head of the Reclamation Association, Reva had enjoyed the achievement of steering the Weber Basin Project, with Walt Granger's assistance, through the House. Then in 1951 she introduced the first Small Water Projects bill, H.R. 2646.

In those war years federal economy was foremost on the public's mind. At the same time it was conceded that a national water policy was mandatory. Besides the West's weighty problems, the water picture in the East was changing drastically—increased population, increased irrigation, droughts, and floods had made former management practices obsolete. When confronted with having to cope with these vexations, the House Appropriations Committee called for a "coordinated program for the development of our water resources." The congresswoman punctuated that action by saying, "a nation, like a human being, is not healthy unless all parts are healthy."

Her federal bill was similar to the Little Fellows Reclamation Service, which had already been working well in Utah. The states that benefited were those whose problems were too small for consideration by the Bureau of Reclamation. Under the Little Fellows plan, numerous projects varying in cost from $5,000 to $100,000 had meant raised living standards for hundreds of people.

"I had been working with the Utah Water Users and the National Reclamation Association for the past two years in trying to establish this program on a national basis," said the congresswoman. The Bosone House bill sought a $5 million revolving fund to finance small-scale reclamation projects running under $1 million each. The revolving fund would provide federal funds for several types of projects; the amount to be repaid by the state involved would vary according to requirements in each case.

Because of jurisdictional disputes and general opposition, making reclamation legislation of any kind difficult to pass, the progress of the measure was slow. "Against the background of conflicting legislation, development of a water policy, the trend against duplication, and the recognition of states' rights and responsibilities, we had to consider the Small Water Projects bill," Reva told an interested group of water users.

The evolution of water rights is innately complex. The law of appropriation, which had superseded the doctrine of riparian rights, applied to the entire stream or river, not just part of it in one state, and this now constituted the basin-wide development principle.

What kind of basin-wide development should there be in relation to small projects and a national water policy? That was truly the billion dollar question. Certainly state responsibility would be a main concept, she concluded, not only for the good of the program but to help fix the concept of state responsibility in the national water policy.

Reva had the encouragement of President Truman, who approved the idea when she consulted him. In an address before the National Reclamation Association in October 1951 at Amarillo, Texas, she summed up:

> I close now with the reminder to you that the President of the United States favors the objectives of the Small Water Projects program; and with my own comment that the National Reclamation Association give serious thought to the fundamental problems involved; that you remember that America is evolving a national water policy; that you should make no compromises for expediency's sake but arrive at conclusions by objective analysis; that you should consider the line of demarcation between "farmstead water" and "irrigation water" as one of the chief control points in determining the part the respective federal agencies should play in water development; that the duplication of effort in this matter be resisted; that the concept of state responsibility be religiously adhered to, and, finally, that NRA seriously consider the proposition that the time has come, as far as small projects are concerned at least, to extend the reclamation idea to the entire Nation.

Obviously, complications abounded. Most certainly no help on this bill was forthcoming from Senator Watkins. "I knew if he were to take the same attitude he had on my Indian bill and the Weber Basin legislation," she said, "he would want it stymied until he could get the credit for it."

In any multifaceted legislation with wide-reaching ramifications, technicalities took time to be examined, placed under a strong light, scrutinized, and fit together in working order. But the bill's sponsor wasn't given the time—in 1952 Reva Bosone was defeated. In 1954 *seventeen* bills similar to hers were introduced in Congess! One of these was Senator Watkins's measure which eventually became law.

One of the smoothest functioning collaborations between a member of the House and a member of the Interior Department was that of Reva Bosone and Jack Dixon. The two worked together to lay the groundwork, if not always to reach their ultimate goals, for some heavy reclamation undertakings.

Dixon, as a member of the Advisory Committee of the National Resources Planning Board, had produced years before a manuscript with two other engineers on the planning of small water projects. During World War II their efforts to obtain the printing funds for this document went begging because of the abolishment of the board.

After Dixon acquainted Congresswoman Bosone with it, he was pleased to see she considered it a valuable manual, indispensable to those interested in the "what and why" of small-scale water planning. Earlier Dixon had showed her his Low Dams manual prepared in 1938 and sponsored by the National Resources Planning Board which became a Government Printing Office best-seller. Reva was so impressed with that first information guide, which could assist Utah among other states with its unique water problems, that she arranged for its printing as a committee report.

Now here was another treatise covering the project as a whole, appearing to be a boon to farmers with a special interest in looking ahead for water supply, sewage disposal and sanitation, flood protection, irrigation development, and land drainage. Reva introduced H.R. 322, so as to have it printed as a House document, and this report also became a high-demand item at the GPO.

A combination of talents and a desire to cooperate with each other proved mutually helpful. "Had she not arranged for that first printing, the manual would have been dead at that point," said the retired engineer at his Arlington, Virginia, home. He recalled their strenuous sessions in committee hearings and elsewhere in persevering for Reva's causes.

"She could fight like a wildcat!" he smiled. "She would fight just as hard for another project in somebody else's state if she thought it was a good one." And he added, "She would fight against it if she didn't think so."

Dixon tells of the time he was scheduled to be called on in a committee hearing, but prior to his appearance a congressman confided in him that he meant no offense but he was going to roast him on the spit! Jack, surmising the intended exhortation was for the benefit of the homestate voters and knowing he couldn't stop him, told him to go ahead if he had his facts straight. And so the legislator proceeded to lambaste Dixon in an uncalled-for verbal display.

In Jack's turn, he decided to inform the members of the committee about the secret warning of the hot-tongued solon, which completely deflated the effect of the man's vitriolic speech. After which, in the quiet of the dignified room, came a slow, pronounced clap of hands.

Bosone was making known her approval!

A priority when Reva first moved to Washington was to straighten out a district condition, also connected with water, the results of which were of especial benefit to those in the southeast section of Salt Lake City. As in the days of the Judge's traffic court regime, when the car accelerator would warn the cautious driver—Bosone, Bosone, Bosone—now when the kitchen tap pours forth water from Deer Creek Reservoir (fifty-five miles away), a soft voice is thought to be heard: Drink up—hope you like it! Through one woman's perseverance and charm, a soggy ending was averted. It began as a believe-it-or-not story, as the Judge words it, but true in all details.

Authorization and appropriation had been granted for the big conduit from Deer Creek to the edge of Salt Lake City. Reva says, "In spite of World War II and a lot of engineering difficulties the conduit was nearing completion, but it apparently was going to look a lot like an arm without a hand, because some place along the line—I didn't know where—the Terminal Reservoir had become lost! I had to find it."

Her first stop in Washington was to consult Michael W. Straus, commissioner of Reclamation, and he agreed that there was indeed a problem, but a terminal reservoir was not provided for in the contract and if Salt Lake City wanted one—and the conduit would be of little value without it—the congresswoman would have to go the whole route, which meant Bureau of Reclamation approval, Bureau of the Budget approval, presidential approval, congressional authorization, and finally congressional appropriation. Expletive deleted!

A call to action! Convincing "big, jovial, stubborn" Mike Straus that somewhere along the line a perfectly good terminal reservoir was wandering alone looking for a conduit was not easy. With persistence, laced with gentle persuasion, she camped on his doorstep until the white flag went up and the weary Straus either found the reservoir in the contract or put it there. "Frankly, I did not care how it got there just as long as it finally showed up!" she admitted.

So far so good, but getting the funds was another battle. To take the roundabout route through interminable channels seemed folly if she could start at the top (which has been an axiom in her life's goals). President Truman granted her an interview and listened to her story, watching a bit of histrionics as she pushed out her arm and figuratively removed her hand. The president caught the point and immediately cleared the way for budget approval of the project and the funds needed to get it under way. The reservoir now resides just north of Thirty-third South and west of Belt Route I-215.

Thirsty southeast residents of the Salt Lake Valley had reason to drink a toast to the crusader who assured them this indispensable liquid from Deer Creek long before it was possible had the reservoir been initiated as a special project!

Hill Life

"I WISH THERE WERE MORE LIKE HER"

UTAH'S BOSONE OFFICE was reported to be among the busiest on Capitol Hill! Perhaps this truism was due to Reva's occupation on a major committee, Interior and Insular Affairs, seven various subcommittee assignments; and service on a special committee studying deleterious publications. Then in March 1949 President Truman, recognizing her meritorious highway safety efforts, appointed her chairman of the Committee on Laws and Ordinances of the President's Highway Safety Conference.

Duties piled up. When floor leader of the House, John W. McCormack of Massachusetts, named Reva to be the Democratic member to address the House in its Memorial Day exercises she knew she had been

PHOTO: *With Admiral W. F. Halsey on deck of carrier* Midway.

uniquely honored. Mrs. Frances P. Bolton was asked from the Republican side. No other women had ever been dealt this consideration.

Twelve years earlier on Memorial Day, the record toll of more than one hundred traffic offenses in a town the size of Salt Lake City had provoked the Judge into changing traffic fines to save lives. Now in 1949, to the day, the congresswoman was to speak to the House of Representatives, eulogizing servicemen who had lost their lives.

At that time Reva created her own speeches; it was her forte, in fact, if she could claim a few minutes to call her own. However, strict privacy was necessary, with no interruptions, and this took some doing. Virginia Rishel was continually reminding the congresswoman about her composition. "I'm thinking about it," was her answer. And that was true. In moments of waiting or traveling she would contemplate the meaning of life and death.

But it was always rush, rush! She never had those valued moments to coordinate deep thoughts. Then came a trip with the Interior Committee to Ashville, North Carolina. On her return—still no speech. "There wasn't a minute to write anything!" But she was still mulling. On Monday morning she entered the office sans speech and Virginia, concerned over the rare opportunity for the Judge to make a powerful presentation, looked forlorn.

So that night, while strict silence was observed in the Bosone apartment, Reva wrote her speech straight through. In the morning she rehearsed it on her administrative assistant, herself a writer of merit, who could hear but did not see for the tears in her eyes; Reva knew she had done her job! After she had addressed the joint session, revered Congresswoman Mary Norton and John McCormack were the first to shake her hand. The floor leader paid his respects, "That's the best memorial address I've ever heard given in the House."

Her opening words on that solemn occasion touched the softer hearts in a hard-boiled atmosphere:

> Bright is the morning with glaring light when the sun rises in the east. Brighter still becomes its rays as the morning grows into noon— the most brilliant part of the day. As afternoon wears on, the heavens shade the brilliance with colors in full bloom—the sunset. Then the twilight gathers in luxuriant hues; evening descends and darkness puts the world to sleep.
>
> So it is with the life span of man. With great exultation a child is born! A smile is on every face. With each hope of life's expectancy— dreams are translated into reality. At the noon time of man's life— great in luster is his development, varied is his activity, and bright is his future. As life wears on, his colorful contributions envelope him. Twilight slows the pace but sweetens the path—night descends. He who was a child becomes a man, and in the evening of his life slips away into the night to rest forever.

After that she was encouraged by several members of the House to sign up with a New York City agency that would arrange speaking engagements, providing a supplemental income for the luxuries of life. But for a few activities she never charged; she was not about to make speechmaking a pecuniary affair. "In the first place, I usually talked of things about which I wanted something done. In the second place, if one is conscientious as a member of Congress, he/she does not have the time to make many speeches or write books. If one's time is thus involved, knowledge of legislation suffers—the staff is left with the work, and I've never been for that."

Unfortunately voters don't always distinguish between a politician and a statesman and the conscientious member sometimes has to bite the dust. John Carroll of Colorado made legislation his entire job. "For his kind of wonderful public service," says Reva, "he was defeated after one term. He was one of the best legislators I've ever known but the rottenest politician!"

Characteristics of the great are purported to be honest humility, helpfulness, and approachability, and hopefully every new member arrives in Washington well equipped with those attributes. But that does not always happen, and Reva comments on the type of member who begins a career in Congress with little background but with a position of power that he/she isn't about to let anyone forget. The sensible member appreciates that power, she insists, but has the good sense to keep it in reserve to be used on rare occasions. The rare occasions are momentous enough to make up for their rarity if they involve temperament, as they did once. This time it was Reva's temperament.

"In hearing after hearing I listened to a few members of the Interior Committee harass witnesses—American citizens who had come to the committee on their own, to be helpful, or at the request of the committee to give information," the Judge makes clear. "I have heard some of those witnesses bawled out and embarrassed severely by impatient members. I always felt sorry for the individual and I boiled within, but I held my red hair flat on my head.

"Finally, one day when a young lawyer from the Interior Department was trying his level best to answer questions, the usual members rode him so hard my temper flared and down came my fist on the counter. I shouted, 'That's enough! For months I have sat here and heard witnesses ridiculed and bawled out. It's wrong and it is not becoming to the Congress. If I were a witness I wouldn't take it and I don't think he has to take it either!'

"There was complete silence. Then the chairman resumed the meeting. Never after that was a witness frustrated—in my presence, anyway."

A temper, like a garden shovel unearthing a rampant weed, can eradicate a bad situation before it has a chance to cause complete devastation. In her 1950 campaign, Reva heard that a few leaders at the Labor Temple in Salt Lake City were withholding support of her. So requesting Joe Wilson, president of SLC Labor, to call a Sunday morning meeting of all the leaders, she spelled out in no uncertain terms her trials in fighting for labor in the two legislative sessions in Utah, that the best labor laws were original with her, that she stood on the floor of the House in the state legislature for hours pushing through their interests, and that she did not appreciate lack of support from them! She warranted loyalty and she demanded its expression!

"Afterward," said Reva, "young Dave Turner, secretary of the city organization who was too young to remember my labor hassles in the legislature, confessed that he had thought a woman couldn't fight. But he told me I could and that he was for me now. I didn't have any more trouble with labor. Some of them had forgotten; I reminded them!"

While she doesn't advocate blowing one's cool over trivia, Reva is very sure that a wisely timed steam valve release is the answer at times. Certainly a person who always holds back is about as interesting as clabber.

The figure of the great colonizer of the West, Brigham Young, was again involved in controversy, midway of the twentieth century. The State of Utah was planning to present a marble statue of the first governor of the State of Deseret to the hall of fame in the National Capitol. The proposed placement of this sculpture was by a window in a dark hall just off the hall of fame rotunda, as suggested by the eminent sculptor, Mahonri Young, a descendant of his subject. But the window looks out onto a wall!

Reva, who had just assumed her legislative role in Washington, scanned the site with a dubious eye—what honor is there for Utah's first member of this statuary group of the country's distinguished achievers cooped up in an inconspicuous uninspiring place? The spot was supposedly chosen by Mr. Young for his own reasons, which he no doubt considered logical. But for the practical reasons, Congresswoman Bosone considered a new placement in Statuary Hall not only more suitable but mandatory to command the respect the memory of this famous man deserves.

She hastened to call the Capitol architect, aware all the while that she was a non-Mormon hustling for Utah's foremost Mormon leader in the face of Mormon congressmen and the Church hierarchy at home. The architect told her confidentially that he also preferred the rotunda, that by the time other statues were placed in the little vista, no one would be able to see Brigham Young. Seeking another opinion in order to be objective, she asked the head of the Capitol guides his view without revealing that of the architect; his, also, agreed with hers.

With these concurring opinions added to her own conviction, she contacted the members of the congressional committee—the bill authorizing the action had already been passed by the joint committee—for a hearing to reconsider the measure. After this meeting, Utah's Senators Thomas and Watkins and Congressman Granger also expressed a desire for the change, and the committee voted to reconsider.

The impressive statue of a sitting President Young is now admirably situated between Georgia's Alexander H. Stephens on his right and Vermont's Ethan Allen on his left, benefited by the spacious and well-lighted atmosphere of Statuary Hall. A quarter of a century from that occasion marks the wisdom of the congresswoman's efforts.

"But I feel sure the sculptor, Mahonri Young (now deceased), never forgave me," Reva says. And others were opposed to her miniscule participation in the long-planned dedication exercises—introduction of Vice-President Alben Barkley, to be exact. She heard that the Mormons would work for her defeat because of that deed. Was the reason because she was not a Mormon, she wondered? And yet who else instigated the statue's move with positive results?

Aside from that, a certain intrigue had been built up among other congressional delegates regarding who was proper to present the monument. LDS President George Albert Smith noted in his journal, "I had apprehension because of some petty differences that had developed because of political jealousy, but it turned out to be a very fitting occasion."

During President Smith's visit in Washington, Reva dined with him in his hotel room and then rode with him and daughter Emily to the meeting in honor of Brigham Young.

Reva wrote the religious leader later, "It was wonderful to have you and Emily in Washington for a few days. So many of the Easterners who attended the unveiling were impressed with your prayer. They thought it was most unusual that you said something about presenting the monument clear of any indebtedness. This certainly made a hit with the Easterners."

Dubbed by a woman member of the press as a mover and a shaker, Reva was not content to "move" only Brigham Young to a brighter place; she had her eye on yet another forsaken representation in marble whose rights had been usurped. George Dixon, described as a shameless quipster, reported in one of his columns:

> Representative Reva Beck Bosone, new gentlewoman from Utah, has dedicated herself to a crusade. She is determined to move the big suffragette statue from the Capitol Basement.

Mrs. Bosone has nothing against suffragettes. In fact, she reveres their memory. She thinks the statue known to Capitol employees as the "Three Broads in the Bathtub" (because it gives just such an impression) is being discriminated against.

It's dark and dingy down there and the three suffragettes suffer in silence alone, without a single companion statue in sight. Mrs. Bosone wants them up in the main hall of statuary.

Please, Mrs. Bosone, let well enough alone! That statue is a thing of sheer horror.

It is obvious that Mr. Dixon's motivation in making the plea was esthetic rather than chauvinistic, but because of the possible suspicion of suppression, Reva's plea must have carried weight at one time or another—the "Three Broads" have been most conspicuous in the area of Statuary Hall.

Two future presidents figured prominently in Congress when Reva served. Richard M. Nixon, a member of the House, was an active member of the Un-American Activities Committee. He usually sat alone, as Reva remembered, and she surmised that many Republican colleagues were unhappy with his activities, which were widely publicized.

On the Democratic side was a young man called to her attention by one of her young women staff members who quizzed her boss about a rich, handsome congressman from Boston. Several weeks and a few of his speeches later, Reva made the acquaintance of Jack Kennedy. At first his conservatism was most obvious to her but she thought well of his demeanor. Then, when he often sat beside her, she came to know him better and admired him more. She was flattered, too, that he would prefer the company of a woman so much older than himself.

"Often when there was a windjammer in the well of the House making a speech for home consumption, Jack would pull out a paperback— always a serious book—from a pocket. My admiration grew, but always I wished he were less conservative!

"A few years later, after I was defeated and had returned to Washington, I observed Jack Kennedy—his record in the Senate was increasingly impressive. I told him so when I saw him on the Capitol train and in the Capitol." Reva sensed in him symptoms of deep sympathy and understanding of his countryman's misery and suffering when his campaign took him to improverished sections of the land. This compassion was later evidenced in presidential actions.

Along with the tragic memories, shared by the nation, of an assassination is a pleasant one that recurs to the former congresswoman. After President Kennedy's State of the Union address, Reva left the floor of the House and walked down a back stairway but was stopped by a guard before she reached bottom. He announced that the president would be coming so she and other observers ahead of her must wait on the steps.

"I was looking away when all at once I heard, 'Hello, Judge Bosone!' I turned and there was the president with his arm stretched to me over the people in front of me, and we shook hands. Jackie smiled. By Jack's cordiality she probably thought she knew me, but I had never met her. What a generous gesture he made—all I had expected was a hand wave!"

President Kennedy referred to Reva as his friend and former colleague and he asked Postmaster General J. Edward Day, who had appointed her to a top spot as judicial officer in the Post Office Department, whether he could announce the appointment. When he did, it created the widespread impression that she was a presidential appointment.

As for all sensitive citizens, the president's untimely death was a soul-searing episode for his fellow partisan. "I wept bitterly for the loss of such a human being," she disclosed. "I must say that Jack Kennedy will go down in history as a man whose heart was in tune with what this country needed and he was one who had the potential of accomplishing those needs."

Stuart Symington, then secretary of the air force, is one who remembered Reva's speech at the Press Women's dinner. This was a plus for the lady legislator who was in his office one Saturday morning to plead a cause—this time for the future of Hill Field Air Force Base near Ogden, Utah.

She had learned that this installation, one of the largest of its kind in the United States, was now in apparent danger of extinction, with a major move planned to the State of Washington. Hundreds of acres of Utah's most fertile soil (and Utah does not have a plethora of it on the flat) had been covered with tons of cement for this base. Obviously, it could not be recouped for agriculture or much else.

"Since the government has taken this valuable land, I can see nothing but a loss if the government closes the field or cuts its activities," she argued. Then she expounded on Hill Field's great contribution to the economy of the state and Utah's achievement in the war effort.

All the while Secretary Symington listened courteously, then replied, "I'll send a general out to Ogden to explain what we are going to do."

But Reva, fully aware of that statement's implication, exclaimed, "Oh, no you don't! I would have fallen for that a year ago, but not now! I suggest you send a general out to talk to the leaders of Ogden and Salt Lake City, find out from them why Hill Field should be left as is, then have the general report this to you." In her excitement over a possible home state calamity, the otherwise tactful lady had a fleeting thought on the propriety of her fiery reply.

The secretary leaned back in his chair, thoughtful. It was obvious he was conversing with a woman who knew her mind and her state. After a moment he answered, soothing ruffled feathers, "We'll do that, Judge Bosone, and we shall send you the general's report." In two weeks the secretary called the Judge to report that Hill Field would be kept open. Reva considered that decision fortunate for the rest of the country as well as for Utah because in two months the Korean War broke and Hill Field was vital to the war effort. Certainly this wise action of Secretary Symington's was viewed by the Judge with much gratitude.

Another air force official, General William F. McKee, who had been present in the secretary's office, was obviously intrigued by the motivation of the pragmatic debator and suggested while they walked out together that Reva get in touch with him personally if the air force could ever be at her service. Reva took him at his word and several significant functions were performed because of his thoughtful offer, one of which was assisting Reva and the Utah delegation establish the Air Force R.O.T.C. at Brigham Young University at Provo.

The advice of ailing Congressman John Dingell of Michigan struck a knowing chord for Reva. "Get away from Capitol Hill before you break your health as I did working in the office every night!" For five months the Congressional Hotel was the home of Reva and her daughter, but the high rent and its proximity to the office where the congresswoman felt compelled to put in many fatiguing night hours were minus factors for permanent residency. Apartments were at a premium in 1949, though, but when she was finally able to locate a large efficiency at the Majestic on 16th Street, she knew it was a move for the better.

Soon after moving in, Zilpha flew to Utah to spend the summer vacation and her mother began coping with Washington summers, radically different from those at the 4500-foot elevation next to the mountains. Lesson one was learning self-control in staying calm though continually damp in a sustained heat of 100 degrees with high humidity! Only two large fans comprised the cooling system.

Her compact apartment at the Majestic was adequate for a year, but Reva longed for a spot of grass to sit or walk on. So in June 1950, mother and daughter moved into a large, attractive garden apartment in Virginia with a side entrance. Reveling in a sense of freedom, the two westerners were like uncaged birds; prior to their Washington experience, they had enjoyed the vast spaces of mountain country at their disposal. Now grass, flowers, and beautiful birds around the quarters were a constant joy. And then, as though into every joy a little frustration must fall, it happened.

Not only was the exhausting summer heat an annual surprise to Reva and Zilpha but some visitors, or rather residents in the area, threw them into absolute shock.

"Cockroaches!" shudders the Judge. "It seemed they had been drafting all their forces to invade the apartment. Those creatures can throw me into a tizzy in a second—I can't take them! I always believed they meant dampness and dirt, and I keep a clean house. The attitude in Washington, D.C., is that they are everywhere and you put up with them. Frankly, if that city would crusade against them, I'm sure their numbers could be reduced.

"Well, I was too busy to think of moving again so I bought a spray gun. Oh, how I sprayed! I could keep them down for a while and then all at once a huge one would show its ugly self running up the wall!" One amused spectator, seeing her panic, tried to con her into believing they were water bugs, which just made her spray the harder.

In her long address to Westminster College graduates, Reva stated that she was afraid of nothing except a mouse, which isn't all that correct, of course, because cockroaches run neck and neck for scariness! An example of her reaction to the orthopterous insects was amusing news to the nation when it was included in a syndicated column. At a meeting of the House Interior Committee in her congressional days, John Saylor of Pennsylvania was expounding his beliefs on certain legislation when a big cockroach tippytoed across Reva's desk.

"A cockroach!" shrieked the horrified congresswoman in true-to-form fashion. Committee-type pandemonium broke loose. Congressman Saylor jumped up, pounded his desk, and shouted angrily, "That's the first time I have ever been called a cockroach!"

Reva was engrossed in getting away from the usually nocturnal pest and Saylor was preoccupied with the audacity of his red-haired colleague, but the humor of the occasion became almost overwhelming for the other members, who were so convulsed with laughter that they were helpless to come to the aid of the two confused victims. Finally, Wayne Aspinall managed to explain to Saylor what had happened and he was as embarrassed as he had been previously angry and hastened to apologize. Reva accepted and took a back seat. And presently all was calm.

The following summer (1951) Reva decided to give in to an air-conditioned apartment. The cheery and convenient efficiencies in the Boston House on Massachusetts Avenue proved most inviting, so the third and last move was made. Sans cockroaches, stifling heat, and cramped style, at long last this apartment seemed ideal.

"What a relief! Unfortunately, though," she lamented, "we didn't have long to live there—just a year—because I left in July 1952 for the National Convention and didn't return until after election day. Then it was a matter of practically giving away my nice furniture and packing my personal effects and office files, for then I was a defeated candidate."

Reva was first asked to participate on "America's Town Meeting of the Air" radio program in July 1948 in Eugene, Oregon. Senator Morse, chairman, who became a long-time friend of Reva, and the present

Senator Alan Cranston were among the participants discussing "How Should the United Nations Progressively Establish International Law?" A second invitation took her to a Town Meeting program in New York City to discuss, "What Is the Best Answer to Alcoholism?" for which a more authoritative participant could not have been obtained. Reva's prospect of meeting another panelist on the same rostrum, Norman Cousins, editor of *Saturday Review,* made this event especially outstanding.

The New York appearance was also the first time she had been paid for a speech—$100! She could not have been more surprised or delighted because just to be featured on this nationally prominent show bestowed prestige. A third invitation was extended but Reva bypassed this one because of a previous commitment. Evidence of her popularity was seen in a reply to a letter from Reva's brother Horace when Marian S. Carter, Town Meeting's acting program manager, said of the congresswoman, "It is just for the reason of her adaptability, competence, and being a ready debator that we have invited your sister to participate twice within the past year. As a woman, I feel along with the rest of our program staff that she is a great credit to us. I wish there were more like her."

Gratification comes to those who wait. Joseph F. Merrill of the Council of the Twelve in the LDS Church wrote the congresswoman immediately following the Town Meeting program on alcoholism.

> I listened last evening to the broadcast relative to the alcohol problem in which you participated. I send this to congratulate you most sincerely on what you said about the part that Alcoholics Anonymous played in the recovery of alcoholics. I was disappointed in not hearing any of the other speakers speak approvingly of what the A.A.'s are doing. I think these people are doing as fine a type of humanitarian work as any that I know. They certainly are satisfying the requirements of the beautiful parable in the twenty-fifth chapter of St. Matthew wherein it is stated: "Inasmuch as ye have done it unto one of the least of these my brethren, ye have done it unto me." I think the A.A.'s are entirely worthy of highest place for the unselfish work they are doing.
>
> A few months ago Mr. Tom Kearns told me how his group functions and how he himself is willing to go at a moment's call any time of day or night, dropping any and everything else he may be doing if called by a patron of his group.
>
> Further, I was highly pleased with your outline of the educational program of the Alcohol Board in Utah."

And again, a long-held conviction had been honored in a warm and appreciated manner.

Other activities that kept Bosone treading the mill to accommodate her constituents and her conscience included writing weekly columns such as "Life with Congress" for the *American Fork Citizen.* She had been appointed a member of the General Committee in charge of the 1949

Inauguration. She participated in "People's Platform," a CBS public affairs program. She belonged to the Congressional Breakfast Club which met every Thursday morning in the Vandenberg Room on the Senate side of the Capitol. That club meeting resembled the prayer meetings of years before where the membership represented various faiths. And she made important speeches, one of which at the Women's Bar Association of Baltimore banquet resulted in a note to the Judge the following day:

> Dear Judge Bosone:
>
> What joy you brought to all of us Friday evening.
>
> I haven't seen the men enjoy themselves so thoroughly for years and I know my husband came home relaxed and refreshed! Your delightful humor will keep us chuckling for months to come and we are most grateful—It was delightful!
>
> Thank you for taking time out of a busy constructive life to be warm and human and friendly! How much the world needs that warmth!
>
> We enjoyed everything you had to say and the delightful way in which you said it. Bless you!
>
> Cordially,
> MYRTLE FERGUSON
> (MRS. HOMER)

The congresswoman worked to bring about the appointment of a Fact Finding Board to investigate the controversy involving Kennecott Copper Corporation of Utah in 1949, which ended one of the nation's longest and most critical disputes. At the outset, the Locomotive Firemen and Enginemen called for a fact-finding procedure but the management declined, the issue at stake being "equal pay for equal work"—the same rates for men on the mine railroad as are paid to those who operate a connecting line owned by the same company.

The new congresswoman drafted a resolution for introduction in the United States House of Representatives asking President Truman to establish a fact-finding board. She announced her intention to the public.

It was reported that "This prospect of action by Congress and the White House helped persuade Kennecott to retreat from its adamant position." She was hopeful that an agreement would soon be reached in the strike that reportedly had caused an output loss of $40 million and a $10 million decline in business to Salt Lake valley merchants!

Summing up the first session of the 81st Congress (1949), the lengthiest since 1922, Democratic freshman Bosone commented in the press: "When you consider that there must be a meeting of minds of some 535 legislators, all of whom had convictions and ideas of their own, before any law can be passed I feel we have done very well. The accomplishments of this session of Congress have been of mighty significance both to the people of this country and to the world. We have lived up to our international commitments. Domestically, I feel the measures that will most deeply affect us are the slum clearance and low-cost housing bill, which is now law, and the Social Security bill which the House has passed and which the Senate is expected to act upon next session." And she listed two specific cases in which she was of service to her district: the Terminal Reservoir for Salt Lake City and the Weber Basin Project. An energetic record for a first-termer. (One woman compatriot, another first-termer, had not introduced a single piece of legislation in that period.)

Reva's optimistic statement contrasted crisply with that of Congresswoman Katherine St. George, Republican of New York, who was serving her second term. "I feel that the 81st Congress has labored and brought forth a mouse. The only big accomplishment has been a record in government spending. . . ."

Other women of Congress supplied during the year individual enthusiasm and dedication for various issues, materializing in their particular legislation. It was as diverse as the women who sponsored it: Senator Margaret Chase Smith and Congresswomen Edith Nourse Rogers, Frances P. Bolton, and Cecil M. Harden, Republicans; and Congresswomen Helen Gahagan Douglas, Chase Going Woodhouse, and Mary T. Norton, Democrats.

Mary Norton, from New Jersey, member of the House since 1924 who was fond of wearing silk ribbon suits, regarded by Congresswoman Bosone as one of the greatest of legislators, paid high tribute to the other women members. And then she said, "The first session of the 81st Congress ended on a high note of achievement." A supporter of progressive legislation, Congresswoman Norton had authored in her many productive years important bills for welfare reform. As chairperson of the Committee on House Administration, she was responsible for pushing through the House more than seventy resolutions and bills. A most qualified person to serve as president of the United States, was Reva's unreserved opinion!

Although a Republican, Maine's Margaret Chase Smith was another who would have Reva's vote if running for the highest office of the land. Norton, Smith, and Frances P. Bolton, a Republican from Ohio, were the strong women of the 81st, in Bosone's mind.

Noting Reva's close and loyal ties to her parents and her brothers, an observer would not find it difficult to understand her strong love and affection for her daughter. The two were like youthful companions. Nineteen-year-old Zilpha, pretty, tall, and willowy like her mother at the same age, possessed a striking figure. Her fair complexion contrasted effectively with her heavy, long, reddish brown hair. Talents in musical composition and lyrics and interpretive dancing won her hard-earned recognition in fields widely spaced from the political arena. Vivacious and accommodating, Zilpha was considered one of the most valuable assets in her mother's public career, and she was much too serious-minded to play the social scene for what it was worth. The ostentatious functions were shunned in favor of intimate dinners or dates at Annapolis.

In 1950 her mother treated her to a Puerto Rico trip; majoring in foreign languages at Trinity College and concentrating to perfect her pronunciation of Spanish, Zilpha was interested in gaining background experience for speaking the language fluently. When she returned she made a decision; because she had missed a semester in changing colleges when she moved to Washington, Zilpha was determined to take enough credits to graduate in 1951, completing college in three and a half years. Her mother believed the extra effort would place undue strain on her daughter's already involved life. She recalled her own trials of losing her faculty for quick memorization from such strain. But Zilpha accomplished her goal.

"The only problem I have ever had with my daughter," says Reva, "has been in trying to hold her back in studying. She was a fine student who took great pride in her work, but I think one can overdo." This serious application of a studious nature was responsible for Zilpha being awarded a doctorate in speech pathology from the University of Kansas, an accomplishment that thrilled her mother.

Ill-fated timing doomed two uplifting proposals by the congress-woman—one for world peace and the other for the youth of America. The Korean outbreak cut them both to the quick.

"I have long believed that the women of the world should declare a strike on war!" said Reva in the House of Representatives in January 1950, her proposal calling for the women of America to present a statue of Peace and Brotherhood to the women of Russia. "Women everywhere feel the same about war—regardless of the type of government under which they live or the language they speak. I believe this gesture of good-will and desire for peace would be very tangible evidence," she states, "not only to the women of Russia but to women all over the world of the sincerity and earnest desire of the American people to seek peace among nations." The idea of a peace statue was not original with her but the mat-ter of presentation—to whom and for what—indicated inspired thinking.

Reva made the same appeal in her address before the Women's na-tional Democratic Club. In answer to "What about the Iron Curtain?" she answered that it doesn't matter about the Iron Curtain. "We could crack or rip the Iron Curtain!" Then in the spring of the same year a more com-prehensive proposition for building peace, completely original with her, was explained by Mrs. Bosone, again in the well of the House.

"With security being threatened as never before in history, it is time we try another exchange—that of *mothers*. I don't mean a world conclave of women executives, but a delegation of mothers, two from each state, of all stratas of society to actually break bread in the homes of Communist mothers for a period long enough to become acquainted, a period long enough to convince Soviet mothers that the women of the United States are serious in striving for world peace."

The idea was apparently approved by many in Congress and had favorable comment from the American public. Drew Pearson devoted a column to its attributes. Ironically, a few weeks later the world was reading about the outbreak of a war and the "Mother Exchange" idea was mothballed.

But Reva could never let a good idea expire and so she fed it, nursed it along, and whisked it out in the right company at every opportunity when she returned to Washington. Her contacts were either overwhelmingly for it or feared the expense. She counters, "With millions of dollars being spent for only one weapon of war, why not a few thousands for live instruments of peace? Everybody else has had a hand at trying to win the peace. Why not give mothers a chance?"

In May 1959, Congressman David King of Utah introduced a resolution requesting the State Department to carry out an exchange of a hundred American mothers to Soviet homes. The idea, he said, was not original with him. "As some of you may remember, it was proposed to this body nine years ago by a distinguished citizen of my state and a former member of this body, the Honorable Reva Beck Bosone."

In 1960 the former congresswoman seized an opportunity to outline her idea with Finaida Fyodorova, executive secretary of the Soviet Women's Committee, in Moscow on her private visit to Russia and Scandinavia which included Denmark, her ancestral land.

"When we were about to leave," Reva recalled, "Madame Fyodorova said through her interpreter, 'Your idea is accepted.' I asked then with whom I should keep in touch on our plans and she answered 'with me and my office.' Then she presented Virginia (Virginia Rishel had accompanied Mrs. Bosone on the tour) and me with a beautiful pin and souvenir each. The pin represents an international conference of women held in May 1960 in Copehagen. We departed feeling that we had made friends and that Madame Fyodorova and her interpreter were sincere in their friendship for us."

Several later attempts to shine up the peace plan resulted in interested discussions but it was never given the strong shove into the serious mills of the Congress. It remains to be promoted by another member with compassion, courage, and a maternal instinct.

The success of the CCC (Civilian Conservation Corps) program was heavy in Reva's memory. Fresh from the experience of issuing court judgments on human misbehavior, she was attuned to the precept of prevention of crime. Filthy streets and rat-infested cramped yards were simply not playgrounds for children who aimed to stay on the side of the law, she knew.

"Anyone who has gone watercressing in the meadows, tromped the pastures gathering milkweeds, followed the winding canyon river, or breathlessly reached the top of a mountain knows the joy of being in association with the best in the world—Mother Nature." Lyrically put, the legislator's fond wish was for all young people to taste these delightful experiences. As a deterrent to juvenile delinquency, she introduced a modified form of the original CCC bill. Her reasoning was based on obvious urgency—4 million acres of national forestland were in need of reforestation, 100,000 miles of roads needed to be constructed in various mountain and wooded areas, and a million young men between the ages of sixteen and twenty-four were seeking work.

The congresswoman then presided at Interior Committee hearings where a group of Michigan educators explained their successful program based in part on the early CCC bill. But again, the interruption of war destroyed ideas, plans, hopes, and dreams besides devastating human life.

"In my first term in Congress I tried to get the Interior Department to sponsor a bill that would set up a research program to estimate the kinds and amounts of minerals in this country, a survey of our natural resources," said Reva of one attempt to improve a situation that is still critical thirty years later.

"The department was interested in the idea but, because of the cost, said it could not be done. As I remember, they estimated it would cost millions of dollars. But in order to control the natural resources of today it is still vastly important to have some idea of what we have," she stresses.

Gene O'Brien of the *Sun Newspapers* in Minnesota, an early admirer of the Judge, lamenting the energy crisis, wrote in a column in response to a letter from Mrs. Bosone that "The distinguished lady's cause put forth nearly a quarter-century ago, if acted upon possibly could have partially forestalled the crisis we now have on our collective backs. At least she wasn't asleep."

If a person is unfortunate enough to be unjustly accused of a criminal act, he could have no more forceful vindicator than Reva Bosone. One day in March 1951 she proved with good cause the word often used to describe her—outspoken!

Believing that character assassination is far worse than murder, Congresswoman Bosone explosively defended in the House a woman of renowned reputation. Charging Congressman Harold Velde (R., Ill.) with "misuse of congressional immunity, she called for him to withdraw from the *Congressional Record* his insertion: "The influence of Eleanor Roosevelt in the promotion of communism and immorality and indecency among so-called minority groups in Washington should be explored!" In Reva's opinion, Mrs. Roosevelt was "one of America's greatest women"; this attack was like dangling the red flag in front of the representative from Utah and Majority Leader McCormack, another of Mrs. Roosevelt's supporters.

Congressman Velde did not make his charge on the floor of the House but inserted it in the *Record* under permission to revise and extend remarks he had made in a short speech. Mrs. Bosone said that time-honored right "was never intended to be a means for an attack on character—an attack without a chance to defend." Saying he had intended nothing reflecting on Mrs. Roosevelt in his speech, he reconsidered and asked consent to withdraw from the official record those remarks, after which Reva agreed to withdraw from the official record her words denouncing Velde. And democratic leader McCormack, finding a scrap had been circumvented, sighed in relief. An editiorial in the *Miami Daily News* implied that a touchy situation had been altered by a "woman's shaming."

The stellar personalities or the old standbys back home—there's no difference as far as friendship is concerned; according to the Judge, once a friend, always a friend. And scores of folks looked to her to supply the "something" lacking in their lives—sympathy, color, encouragement, examples of courage. So uplifting letters flew from her office or house in seemingly unending numbers!

But out there in the great audience of political kibitzers were those who took issue with Reva's choice of friends. In 1951 a postcard from New York added contrast to the congresswoman's usually hospitable mail:

> Some time ago you had the brazen insolence to proclaim Eleanor Roosevelt the greatest woman in American history. She and her unholy set are responsible for the world's deplorable conditions.
>
> Anyhow, a thorough mental examination for you would seem to be of prime importance. Better still would be to put you behind bars to prevent you from doing more damage.
>
> C. WILSON

And as though to close in on the kill, another card from C. Wilson arrived two days later:

> The other day I heard you on the radio and found out to my consternation, that you had been and might be probably again, a schoolteacher.

What a misfortune for the poor children to have as an instructor a
mentally diseased nitwit, who considers the Hyde Park woman an
asset to our country. May the Good Lord have mercy on your soul.

Below the signature Reva has recorded her response for posterity—
"Amen!!*!"

Jumping into a cutthroat dispute among congressmen in the well of
the House and jumping into the middle of a bloody, knock-down-drag-out
melee in a street intersection have similarities! So one can understand the
motive, if not the display of courage, that possessed Congresswoman
Bosone one Saturday afternoon when she was driving with her nephew,
then living in Washington and working as a Capitol page. The joust involved about fifty black men slugging each other in a Washington intersection. Without a single fearful thought she stopped her car, jumped
out, and strode briskly into the confusion.

"Stop this! Cut this out! Get off the street and back there *now!*" she
commanded. To render decisions, to straighten out, to subdue—these
were her life's orders, whether they concerned a billion dollar legislation
or fifty belligerents in a slug fest.

As amazing as her action was that of the bruised men who promptly
broke up, backed onto the sidewalk, and wandered away. The congresswoman then strode back to her car, rejoined a shaken nephew, and
drove on, coming near to a collapse in a few blocks after a double take at
the risk she had taken. A characteristic sometimes referred to by
relatives as coming on strong was responsible for disintegrating a volatile
situation.

Congressmen Chase Going Woodhouse, Cecil M. Harden, and Reva
Beck Bosone, along with a number of other members of Congress, were
issued invitations to observe military activity for a weekend aboard the
carrier *USS Midway,* docked at Norfolk, Virginia. Reva instructed her administrative assistant to call the navy to accept. But when the navy
learned that Bosone, Woodhouse, and Hardin were "broads," they suddenly knew that somewhere in their ranks was a blooper-maker!

Well, ma'm, they stammered, when the acceptance was proffered by
Reva's assistant, naval regulations bar women from overnight accommodations aboard warships. There just were not "facilities" for
women, the obscene language would make it prohibitive, there would be
too much luggage, the women wouldn't be able to negotiate the ladders
and dividers . . . and the spokesman would call back later!

Not to be rejected and savoring the prospect of a once-in-a-lifetime
opportunity, Reva told Virginia to give him the word the next time he
called that the "facilities" are used by both men and women in the home
and the same could be used by both on a carrier! And that her vote in Con-

gress looked just the same as a man's vote—and it was just as important! And she would be ready to go!

The message was relayed. As one analyst stated, one simply does not go around insulting congressmen—*or* congresswomen—so, after some rather frantic high-level confabs in Washington in which diplomacy finally won out over tradition, Bosone and Woodhouse, who had also accepted the invitation, were allowed to go, along with newspaper woman May Craig. The other guests included twenty-seven male members of Congress, fourteen of their sons, and several newsmen. The admiral's quarters were assigned to Congresswoman Bosone and Mrs. Craig (Reva occupied the admiral's bed—"without the Admiral") and the cabin of the chief of staff was used by Mrs. Woodhouse. And from all reports, the three ladies had themselves an adventure.

"How silly the navy didn't want women on the carrier," Reva declared. "In the first place, the men took twice as much luggage as Chase and I. We gals climbed the ladders just as fast if not a little faster than the men," she bragged. "I wandered all over the ship; the men were so occupied with their tasks they didn't pay any attention to me and I didn't hear any offensive language. I couldn't see where we three women caused any trouble!

"The admiral's quarters were on the top deck right beside the foghorn. Because of a heavy mist all night the horn was sounded every few minutes. A hammock on the lower deck would have been preferred," she laughed. "But the admiral's quarters are far from being soft or luxurious; they are barely comfortable. Since then I have had a greater appreciation for the officers living in those austere conditions. Incidentally, the "facilities" were no different from those in a home."

The only incommodious incident took place when Reva, feeling seasick, took a Dramamine pill, which caused her to be drowsy at the precise moment she was conferring with Admiral William F. Halsey on deck. Other than that minor embarrassment, she thoroughly enjoyed this unexpected sojourn and had nothing but praise for the precision flight operations that Sunday.

Bundled in a fleece-lined parka, a kerchief harnessing her hair in the gusty winds, she posed for a photo with Admiral Halsey and W. H. P. Blandy, commander in chief of the Atlantic Command and the U.S. Atlantic Fleet, and although it was a happy trio, one presumes the smiling veneer of the distinguished gentlemen hid surprise at the turn of events.

"The navy got one vote it might not have received if the top brass had carefully checked out that original invitation list against women," the congresswoman commented. After the cruise, besieged by reporters, the women learned that while they were reveling on board as old salts, they were newsworthy to landlubbers as barrier-breakers.

"Why shouldn't we have gone," Reva asks. "I didn't know legislative votes had sex!"

May Craig suggested forming "one of the world's most exclusive clubs, consisting of women who have spent the night on a warship."

Several years later, former Congresswoman Woodhouse, the decorous member from Connecticut, former teacher and an organizer in women's organizations, wrote Reva that "the commotion of our presence in the domain specially set up for men always gives me a relished kick."

"And, dear grandchildren," Reva is heard to say these days, "did I ever tell you about my weekend on a naval carrier?

Woman vs Woman

IF POLITICAL OBSERVERS were gleefully anticipating a scrappy scene in the coming 1950 congressional campaign, the two women contestants befooled them. Reva Beck Bosone and Ivy Baker Priest, longtime friends, squared off by smoothing on lace gloves rather than boxing gloves—over a tea set rather than in a punch bowl.

Word had reached the congresswoman in Washington that the home state Republicans could not find a man to run against her, so attractive Mrs. Priest, national committeewoman of the Republican party of Utah, who later became treasurer of the United States, jetéd into the ring, with her strongest jabs accusing Reva of stretching toward socialism. This was all featherweight for Reva because at no time was she worried about Ivy's debating; however, Mrs. Priest had the edge in being able to start grass roots campaigning early in the spring.

Congress continued in session longer in 1950 because of the war development. Reva had not been in Utah since September 1949—shuttle diplomacy was definitely not her thing.

"I was never the member of Congress who kept chasing back to her district. In the first place I was too busy, in the second place I couldn't afford it, and in the third place I thought then as now that a good record in one's job should be sufficient recommendation for being reelected. The time and energy spent on buttering up constituents are better used in doing a good job. I would hope that voters could understand this. They would be a lot better off since the laws under which they live would be improved."

When Reva returned to the Salt Lake valley for her stumping stint, she found that the Republicans had grasped at the socialized medicine straw, denouncing the bill she had introduced in Congress. This issue could be and was dramatized as a monster in the independence-oriented state of Utah.

The first bout for both women on the same program was slated for the Jewish Women's Luncheon at the Unitarian Church. In ladylike action and forthright presentation the two women were on a par. Poised and assured, Mrs. Priest detailed her case against the legislator, leaning heavily on Reva's presumed proclivity toward socialized medicine.

Reva then rebutted with the true facts on her position regarding that

177

aspersion. It seems that mail from home had been beseeching her to devise a system that would insure the elderly against pauperism through the leeching of medical expenses.

"I had introduced a bill in the House that was like automobile insurance," she explained, "and at the time it was introduced I made the statement that the bill was dropped into the hopper in order for the committee to toy with an idea other than the Truman administration health bill. I stated that there needed to be relief from medical bills for the long protracted illnesses that so often consume the savings of a lifetime. Never did I say I was for socialized medicine! I love independence as much as anyone else and a whole lot more than some people!"

Essentially, Congresswoman Bosone's measure would have established a $50 deductible plan of national health insurance on a trial basis. It would provide that all medical bills up to $50 and all dental bills up to $25 be paid personally and then the government would assume responsibility for payment of all amounts over these sums.

Republicans in Congress evidently were solidly against any compulsory health program, including Senator Robert A. Taft, who was an outspoken opponent of the president's health program. The *Salt Lake Tribune* did not subscribe to Reva's idea either, saying, "First of all, there is no such thing as taking a dose of socialism on a trial basis and getting away with it. Once these things start there is no stopping them until a war from without or a revolution from within wipes them out." But many wondered where the escape would be from the savings wipeout from illness. The same widespread discontent with the high cost of medical care today existed a generation ago.

An editorial in the *Washington Daily News* discussing the differences between the two compulsory health plans was prefaced with a description of Reva Bosone's background in Utah and mentioned that such a career should assure more than just an ordinary knowledge of human nature. "Apparently Congresswoman Bosone has a hunch that a kicker in the Truman health program [which would cover all expenses] is the staggering cost of hypochondria. And she offers one of the most interesting suggestions yet trotted out on the subject. Not as the answer. Just as an idea. Something to be considered open-mindedly—to be 'batted around,' as she puts it, to see what kind of reception it gets."

Under the $50 deductible system, the column explained, there just would not be the incident where a physician, summoned by a health insurance subscriber, learned after a long drive to the patient's home that there was nothing wrong with the individual—he had just wanted to meet the new doctor in town.

The editorial concluded: "She [Reva] just humbly asks that we think it over—this idea of a $50 deductible brake on the self-pampering impulses of the human race."

The socialized medicine issue was driven home with such force and bitterness that in 1950 Senator Elbert Thomas, who favored a compulsory health insurance plan, was eclipsed partly by such charges against him; and Mrs. Bosone's narrowed margin of votes was attributable in part to that bitterness. Socialism and communism were equally matched, it seemed, for detestation.

The Democratic party program's claim that insurance is not socialism was backed up by facts that for thirty-five years reputed physicians in the nation had had their fees fixed in industrial accident cases by a state industrial commission meeting with a board of physicians. No socialism here, said the doctors.

Private companies, the railroads in particular, had stipulated that workers must pay for medical care and use the company physician. The railroads never branded that socialism.

In actuality, the government subsidized doctors in 1951 to the tune of $39,578,000 for research. "Creeping socialism" had already hit the medical profession but apparently the American Medical Association, which spent vast sums on denouncing national health insurance, did not regard this direct subsidy in the same light.

Certain representatives of organized medicine confessed to the failure of private enterprise to provide efficient medical and hospital care outside of skyrocketing costs, especially to the increasing indigent class. Dr. James Howard Means, professor of Clinical Medicine at Harvard University, said in the *Atlantic Monthly:*

> A learned profession has sunk or been dragged, in its political sphere, to a distressingly low level. . . .
> If organized medicine would drop its obstructionist tactics and instead devote its energy and money to the creation of adequate health plans like H.I.P. (N.Y.C. Health Insurance Plan) and Permanente (California Plan), it would more effectively forestall government medicine than it will with its present costly propaganda campaign and Washington lobby.

In the hometown luncheon debate that day between the two candidates, the hit to the solar plexus was Reva's reference to Republican-slanted *Fortune* magazine's call for a counterirritant for the medical care situation. Ivy was decked! The audience seemed foursquare with the incumbent Reva. In the large group were women who had recently house-guested doctors from England who were reportedly complimentary of the health care program in that country.

Reva's flair for rebuttal must have discouraged Mrs. Priest's inclination for discussing issues after that, which was not only disappointing but created a problem for the congresswoman in choosing a meeting topic. What's the use òf togetherness of opponents on the same program if one party won't tackle issues? And interestingly, the same issues that consumed the legislator then are timely today.

Near the end of the campaign trail, the Business and Professional Women's Club of Salt Lake City invited the two amiable adversaries to strike a blow for their particular issues at a dinner in the Hotel Utah. An overflow crowd charged the air with enthusiasm and anticipation.

Ivy, blonde and fashionable, who was introduced first as usual, announced that she could not stay long since another meeting later that evening was on her agenda. Then she proceeded to expound on the history of women's activities, which completely thwarted her antagonist. What would Reva talk about, having depended upon Ivy to set some sort of subject? The clubwomen were obviously crestfallen—they knew the history of women's contributions in general; they had come to hear the current views of two women in particular.

After Ivy's remarks, she asked to be excused. (But before she left the meeting, Reva found that they were both slated for that other meeting later in the Cottonwood Wardhouse, a meeting place of Mormon members.) In her turn at the BPW meeting, Reva, red-haired and fashionable, announced that she would not discuss issues in the absence of the opposition. The disappointed club members then implored her to change her mind, whereupon Reva insisted that the suggestion be put to a vote. The congresswoman heard no dissent, so she proceeded to elaborate on issues as planned.

"Incidentally, the next morning the BPW president called to say that Ivy was angry that I had taken advantage of her absence by discussing issues. The president placed the blame on Mrs. Priest, though," said Reva, "telling her that the women had insisted that I do that for which I had been invited!"

The Cottonwood meeting was in progress when Reva arrived and Ivy was giving her speech. Also on the program was Wallace Bennett, candidate for United States Senate on the Republican ticket opposing Senator Thomas, who preceded Reva. Ivy had not supplied a subject but Mr. Bennett obliged. The former president of the National Manufacturers Association revealed in his opening remarks that he had decided to enter politics because of his grandchildren.

Writer Barney Flanagan, who was present on that occasion, confided recently that the moment that epitomizes to him the essence of Reva Beck Bosone was her rebuttal to the senatorial candidate that night.

"Mr. Bennett is running for the Senate," Reva recapped, "because he is concerned with the future of his grandchildren. I, too, am concerned with the future of his grandchildren, but not only *his* grandchildren and *my* grandchildren, but I'm concerned about *your* grandchildren!"

Not only was this statement meaningful for Mr. Flanagan but for the entire crowd. In Reva's words, the house came down! "I shall never forget that night, for I've never given a speech that was sprinkled with more applause—from a Republican-slanted district!"

If there is a word that snugly fits Reva Bosone perhaps it would be FIRST. Ingenious, innovative, original, creative—all have been used in describing her. Stolen, lifted, borrowed, warmed-over—these are words that just don't fit her life-style.

Barney conceived a publicity idea for Reva in the 1930s and solicited the *Salt Lake Tribune* artists to compose a page in the center of which would be a photograph of Reva. Surrounding the inset would be drawings illustrating her accomplishments in education, teaching, authoring of important bills in the legislature, and national recognition of her work on the bench.

In the 1950 campaign Ivy Priest, if not coincidentally, evidently felt privileged to use the same format. Her flyer showed that she had taught in night school but no mention of where or how long; that she had "brought out" the Minimum Wage and Hour law for women and children, implying that she had introduced and sponsored the legislation (Reva and Ivy were not even acquainted when Reva pushed her bill through the two state bodies—later when the bill was made effective, Ivy sat on the Retail Store Board set up by the act); that she had been recognized nationally in safety (she had served on a committee for the National Safety Organization in Chicago, whereas Reva based her recognition on newspaper and magazine articles for her avant-garde programs in traffic control and alcoholism while a judge, and keynoting the National Safety Convention in Chicago in 1948 and the national convention of the General Federation of Women's Clubs).

With hindsight, Reva has every reason to believe that imitation is indeed the sincerest form of flattery.

THE WARM and close friendship between Reva and the president of the Church of Jesus Christ of Latter Day Saints, George Albert Smith, will remain a cherished memory of the former lady legislator.

"I would like to pay homage to one of God's children and one of the most Christian human beings I have ever known. President Smith was sincerely humble. He had no interest in the frills and froth of life; his habits were simple, as was the food he ate. He loved his fellowman regardless of the church to which he belonged. He served the poor and those who needed him. He couldn't keep an overcoat because he gave it to the first man who looked cold. He couldn't keep suits of clothes for the same reason. He insisted upon driving an old Ford when he first became president of the Church because he felt he could not visit the poor members of his faith in a Cadillac.

"President Smith was as fair as he was kind. He stood for right, regardless. A statement of his rings in my ears. 'Always stay on the Lord's side.' It is no wonder he was loved and respected by the leaders of all the various churches in Utah. Since President Smith was in tune with the universe he would have been a great spiritual man without being the president or head of any church. Bless him!"

And before Reva left for Congress in 1948 she was blessed by this great man; feeling his strong hands on her head and hearing his humble petition of the Lord, she felt tranquility with the world.

In 1950 President Smith had been in particularly ill health—he would leave his bed briefly and then suffer relapses, causing his daughter Emily and Reva grave concern. Whenever she could, however, Emily, a handsome woman of unshakable religious views, tried to assist Reva who was occupied that fall with the rush of convincing her constituents that she should be retained in office.

One night Emily called Reva asking about a letter she had heard was being circulated. The letter reportedly cast aspersions on Reva's character.

"I don't know of it, Emily," Reva answered. "Anyway, you know I'm not afraid of any letter."

"Reva, you had better get concerned. You are the most naive person I have ever known. As usual, someone like me has to protect you if you won't do it yourself. Now, please find a copy of the letter for me."

So Reva called her assistant for help and was told by Virginia that she had just come into possession of a copy of the letter and would mail it to Mrs. Stewart.

At Emily's urgent request, Reva came to the home of Emily and her father the next afternoon to review the letter and, also, a recent newspaper article that posed a problem for the congresswoman. The letter, issued by the chairman of the Law Observance Committee of the Salt Lake area stakes (several wards) of the LDS Church, implied a protest against gambling, horse racing, and prostitution. Listed were names of the Democratic and Republican candidates through which lines were drawn of all the Democrats (except the candidate for Salt Lake County attorney whose opponent was a Catholic). Since Senator Elbert D. Thomas and Reva headed the ticket and lines were drawn through their names, the overt assumption was that they were for gambling, horse racing, and prostitution.

Emily immediately phoned the Law Observance Committee chairman to ask how he knew Senator Thomas and Congresswoman Bosone were for all the practices mentioned. Evidently he had to do some fast improvising which wasn't too effective. Show proof, Mrs. Stewart demanded, which Reva imagined as she listened to the one-sided conversation caught the morals group leader off-guard!

After that conversation, Emily called the editor of the Mormon-influenced *Deseret News* requesting a retraction of the article that suggested which candidates should be elected but *omitting* the name of Reva Beck Bosone. The assumption by the Mormons would be that it was authorized by the head of the Church.

Not wanting to show any upsetting evidence to President Smith in his illness, Reva expressed her thankfulness for Emily's act of friendship, then left. She had been home only a few minutes when Emily phoned to say her father had called her into his room after the congresswoman had left. He had overheard part of the conversation and wanted to be filled in on the details. Emily said she then felt compelled to show him the newspaper article, whereupon he personally called the editor of the *Deseret News* instructing him to run a notice in the next day's edition squelching the implication that it had been authorized by the Church.

Nothing to that effect appeared as instructed so Emily reported to Reva that her father had again called the editor and threatened that if the statement were not included in the following day's paper he would give the story to the *Salt Lake Tribune* as he had been forced to do with another story years before.

The statement ran in the *Deseret News.*

"Wallace Bennett and Ivy Baker Priest should have denounced the letter as I did the smear on Senator Smoot in 1932," Reva protests. A story making the rounds in the early 1930s in Carbon County involved Republican Senator Reed Smoot, a candidate that year, to the effect that he had married a "madam" out of a brothel. Reva knew this to be false although she did not claim to be a personal friend of Senator Smoot or his new wife.

So in all her speechmaking in that campaign she opened with, "There is a story being whispered about Senator Smoot. I want to say here and now, it's a lie. If we Democrats can't win on issues and the truth, we shouldn't win!"

She adds, "I just thought it was the decent thing to do. Later I learned that Mrs. Smoot, a most charming and capable woman, had been managing the Children's Hospital in Salt Lake City. What real satisfaction in knowing I had condemned a lie concerning her and her prominent husband."

Even though others had not extended the same courtesy her way,

Reva's gratitude to President Smith for his special friendship was boundless. Just a few months after that occurrence, she was saddened to place in the *Congressional Record* the notice of President Smith's death on April 4, 1951.

> . . . I rejoice that President George Albert Smith was born and lived. Throughout his life he was a tremendous inspiration for good. It is impossible to measure the impact of his Christian spirit upon his Church and upon his state—and his influence spread far beyond the confines of both. He was, for example, one of the founders of the Boy Scouts of America, and an ardent worker throughout his life in that organization. . . . My life was vastly enriched by knowing him, and it is with deep gratitude to him that I pay tribute here today.

And more private is a sorrowful but precious memory of being called into his room by President Smith himself just four days before he died. In a calm voice, he assured her as she stood at his bedside, "I'm ready to go, Reva. I have made my peace with God."

Women and labor were still holding Reva, and her services to them, on a pedestal. Services, yes, but Reva—the woman—would never be comfortable on a pedestal. The antithesis of high hat, she's every inch the old shoe, insisting that one of her gustatory delights is bread and milk. And one can't get more old shoe than that! Old friend Sunday Anderson talked of the time she was recuperating from an operation and Reva, the busy judge, would drop by to cheer her up and chew the fat in the kitchen because "she always had time for her friends."

The momentum of the campaign increased with an appeal made to women by the Democratic Committee in its special bulletin: "Modern democracy—the program of the Democratic Party is human. It places human values above those of property. Its objective is people, their welfare and improvement. Wealth, property and prosperity must serve people. For the Democrats, these things are not an end as with Republicans. In their hearts, women find the Democratic Party and program much closer to their interests and needs than the Republican. Women will vote for human values on election day."

A letter from John W. McCormack of Massachusetts, majority floor leader of the House, didn't hurt the congresswoman's chances either:

> Dear Judge:
>   As a colleague of yours and as Majority Leader of the House of Representatives and of the Democratic Party, I want to convey to you the feelings of appreciation that Speaker Rayburn and I have for you and the outstanding work you have done for your people, your country and your state and for the Democratic Party during the past two

years. As a first term Member of the House of Representatives you have made an outstanding record for yourself. Your ability, your vision and your courage in serving the best interests of your people and of your Country have gained for you the respect not only of Speaker Rayburn and myself, but of President Truman.

I sincerely hope, as I am confident, that the people of your District will reelect you next Fall, enabling you to carry on in the great work that you are doing in their behalf and to make further contributions toward the progress of our beloved Country, both in the domestic and foreign fields.

Speaker Rayburn and I, I repeat, entertain for you, both as an individual and as a legislator, the strongest feelings of respect and confidence and we sincerely hope, as we respectfully urge, that the people of your District will reelect you.

With kindest personal regard, I am

Sincerely yours,
JOHN W. McCORMACK
Majority Leader

After Reva's victory in November the two women contenders remained congenial. The wish was fulfilled of one reporter who said early in the struggle, "Here is one race, however, in which the women have an opportunity to demonstrate how they can set a higher level in political contests than the men." Avoiding name dragging and reputation gouging, the two women congressional candidates in this *unprecedented* campaign were able to remain conscience free.

Hail to the women!

Back on the Hill

TEN YEARS before their admission, statehood for Alaska and Hawaii was strongly advocated by Congresswoman Bosone. She counted as close friends the congressional delegates from those two territories and the possession of Puerto Rico. When a bill was passed creating Puerto Rico a commonwealth, Reva was jubilant, and that country gave four House members, one of which was the Utah congresswoman, credit for its passage. She was referred to as the woman with the "golden heart!"

Congressman John R. Murdock of Arizona, chairman of the House Committee on Interior, dispatched Reva to Puerto Rico and the Virgin Islands for inspection and first-hand information gathering in connection with the proposed Organic Act since she would be unable to accompany the full committee in later hearings there. The Constitutional Convention

PHOTO: *Hill Field Air Force Base, Utah.*

was being held when she visited San Juan in November 1951. No outsider had been invited to address this memorable caucus, so it was an astonished and delighted congresswoman who contemplated her words before this distinguished convention, the members of which gave her a standing ovation as she took her place on the rostrum.

"To look into those anxious faces inspired me to make one of the best speeches I have ever given," she says. "That occasion lingers in my memory."

She was accompanied on the trip by Chairman Murdock's private secretary, Mrs. Virginia McMichael, and the two women, despite Reva's previous request of the islands' officials to forego any social events because of her fatigue, were prodded to busy fourteen-hour days their entire stay. Recalling her school teacher days and the persistent black dress, Reva regretted that she had packed, besides utility type clothes, only one moderately dressy black faille suit that she was sure would be adequate in the absence of gala functions in an energetic schedule.

So to the numerous receptions, elaborate dinners, and fancy parties that were planned in spite of her request, she showed up in black faille, compounding the torment of the exhausting humid heat of the islands. A worried woman acquaintance, noting her discomfort, presented the visitor with an exquisite fan which the congresswoman put to constant use!

The two women were housed at the ancient palace, La Fortaleza, home of Puerto Rico's Governor Luis Munoz Marin and the first lady, Inez, who made a most indelible impression of graciousness on Reva. Through tradition the governor, under heavy guard, did not leave the palace at night; minority groups for years had opposed the incumbent government. But the deference he showed the congresswoman in attending a dinner in her honor miles from the city of San Juan highlighted her trip. On a tour of the scenic island Reva was aware that the chauffeur shadowed her at every turn. When the party returned to La Fortaleza she learned that the chauffeur was just performing his duty as a police officer assigned for her protection.

In the Virgin Islands the congresswoman was intrigued to hear the blacks speak with a Danish accent, the island having been previously owned by Denmark, the land of her father's ancestors. From Governor de Castro she learned of the problems he was experiencing and the demands of the legislators of the islands, which seemed extreme. She did not favor a resident commissioner, so in addressing the legislature there she hoped to come across with diplomacy.

"To be explicit and firm in what I had to say and yet inoffensive posed somewhat of a problem. Apparently what I said was accepted because each member shook my hand afterward and Governor de Castro seemed pleased that I had taken a tremendous load off his shoulders that had caused him worry for months."

A law against segregation was in effect in the Virgin Islands—the respect for all races was most noticeable to the Judge. At the governmental level they worked together harmoniously. She found dire poverty but at the same time she saw progress toward overcoming it with housing gains and outer slum clearance. "I loved my stay in the islands," she said, "to learn the conditions and what makes the people act as they do. I found them a very friendly people."

But an unfriendly element which upheld independence had terrorized the United States Congress just the year before when a group of Puerto Ricans had entered the House gallery with guns blazing, resulting in wounded congressmen below.

"I was so lucky not to have been in the House where they would have had a good aim at me on the floor," says Reva, knowing she could have been a target because of her advocacy for a commonwealth.

Several years ago at a convention of the national Order of Women Legislators, one of the outstanding participants, who hailed from Puerto Rico, told the ex-congresswoman that a small group of radicals still operating in the islands was responsible for the 1975 bomb plantings in Washington, D.C.

"Since I was a member of Congress I have regretted that I didn't take time out to go on committee assignments to various parts of the world," says the Judge. "I worked so hard and so late at night that each day in the Congress took more and more physical energy out of me. The voter does not realize what a killer job it is." (Her reading of the daily newspapers usually began around midnight!) She introduced ten bills in the 82nd Congress.

Time and again she received the invitations! Once, before the Korean War, a special subcommittee of the House Interior Committee planned to visit all of the islands in the Pacific belonging to the United States. Seven men members urged her to join them, believing that the natives would have confidence in a woman, thereby giving the committee more credence. In spite of the navy's dictum that she was forbidden because of "no facilities," the committee members promised that if she decided to accompany them she could board the plane even if they had to stand on each side of her.

"You'll be able to get on board or there will be a hell of a lot of trouble," they announced, the navy being rendered puny in the face of all that power from fellow congressmen!

Convinced that she could accomplish much good, she was about to say yes when the reality of the hardships—two or three hearings each day and some traveling at night—hit her. Not feeling up to that strenuous regimen, she declined. The trip happened to be ill-fated for the group, however. Once the plane caught fire and all the members had to don parachutes, and at times the plane landed in water and natives of the islands swam out to carry the delegates to shore. The arduous trip was considered a cause of the sudden death of one of the committee members several months after they returned. Reva gave thanks that she had sat this one out!

Many invitations to visit Alaska were tempting because it appeared to be a particularly appealing assignment. The promise of a modicum of convenience and comfort almost had her on the way at one point. But she has yet to see that northern state.

An around-the-world invitation came from another committee where project hearings in which the United States was interested were scheduled. Reva decided that this opportunity was the most impressive of all, but perhaps too vigorous. Meet us in Athens then, coaxed the committee, who again maintained that the magnetic personality of the Judge would enhance their influence in the world. This just might be the ticket, she thought, and in her imagination she had her bags all packed. But for the first time her staff interfered. "Oh, no, you're in no condition to endure the rigors of a trip like that—they would bring you home in a box." So back went the suitcases under the bed.

The old dedication to the job surrounded her like a fortress. "I wish I hadn't taken my duties so seriously—then I might have had the strength to do the other things such as committee assignments. But Zilpha tells me I would do the same thing over again."

EVERYONE AGREES that the Snake River in Idaho tumbles through areas of grandeur unmatched in the country. (Evel Knievel will concede that it is very wide in spots!) Today the average citizen is ecology minded, but back in the early 1950s not everyone was so predisposed. The intended Hell's Canyon Dam on the Snake River was classified as one of those tremendous western projects. It was argued by true conservationists that one large project as opposed to several small dams would protect the incredible scenery from further desecration and offer more effective use of the water. But that stand was controversial—public power against private power!

Senator Morse of Oregon explained in a speech on March 7, 1952: "The great bulk of the entire cost will be returned; only 12 per cent is allocated to non-reimbursable purposes of flood control, recreation and navigation. Although this is a relatively small allocation, dollarwise, these purposes are highly important. . . . One third of the nation's hydroelectric potential," he informed, "exists in the Columbia Basin."

Reva was one of the few intrepid members of the Interior Committee who stood pat for the project. At the hearing, Mrs. Gracie Pfost of Idaho, who later became an influential legislator with a background similar to Congresswoman Bosone's in pulling herself up by her sandalstraps, also wholeheartedly supported the proposal of one large dam.

The lobby against it, however, was raising the dust with strong opposition in the media. To discredit the public power advocates, a leading Boise paper ran an editorial saying in effect that they bet Congresswoman Reva Beck Bosone's staff washed her bra and underwear (which had to set a record for remoteness to the subject of the debate). Idaho's Congressman Hamer Budge brought the clipping of this bit of ridicule to the hearing room and circulated it. The schoolboy tactics aroused Clair Engle, the ranking member of the committee, to pound his gavel and proclaim, "The next time something like that is passed around in this committee, I'll adjourn the committee!" Reva commented on the situation, "The Congress has a few small potatoes—not many, but a few. But gosh, why insult the potato?" Mr. Budge stood firm with private power.

At this point, it should be mentioned that the friendship between Engle and Bosone started with a charge. Bosone made tracks to Engle's office one day because she was told that the congressman said he liked Reva because she had a man's brain. Setting him straight that if she had brains they were hers, she proceeded to get along with him famously. Incidentally, another first in Reva's career might possibly include her shoe removal at official photograph-taking time when standing by California's handsome Congressman Engle, who appeared just a tad shorter than the Utah congresswoman.

The heavy lobby of the Snake River project won out despite its questionable ethics; today small dams clutter the scenic river in place of one large one. That constant howl for more projects which would have taken an even more drastic toll on the landscape should cease, however, now that the government has designated it a National Recreation Area.

ZILPHA'S DETERMINATION to join the air force after she graduated from college was a source of great happiness for her mother, not of course for the forthcoming hardships Zilpha would have to endure but because of her desire to fulfill the armed services role for the family. Sworn in on September 23, 1951, she entrained for Lackland Air Force Base in San Antonio, Texas, to enter officers candidate school, knowing in advance that since she was a congresswoman's daughter the book would be thrown at her. But she never realized she would be subject to a routine of cleaning more latrines and waxing more floors than any of the women in her class. She, as did the others, found the schedule an exhausting fifteen-hour day—every day—(and the accommodations were in musty, inadequate barracks). By Christmas she had won her officer's boards and was made a student captain, but graduation was three months away.

Brigadier General Wycliffe E. Steele, commandant, USAF Officers Candidate School, understandably wanted Congresswoman Bosone to present the graduation address of OCS in March, an honor she valued as the first woman in the history of the air force to perform this function. At the graduation ball at the base before the exercises, a surprise announcement introduced Zilpha singing two songs especially planned for her mother's pleasure.

Of the graduation program the next day Reva says, "To have the opportunity to look into the faces of hundreds of young men and women in the military uniform of their country was a thrill. To look into my own daughter's face was unforgettable!" Reva's memorable speech drew this written response from General Steele: "It was indeed meaningful and appropriate that someone as eminently qualified as yourself should connect the personal role of the new Air Force Officer with the tremendous challenge facing America today. I believe that these young people will long remember your challenge and the confidence that you placed in them to meet that challenge."

The following day Reva represented Congressman Olin W. Teague of Texas at the ROTC review held at Texas A. & M. College at College Station, Texas. "With top United States and foreign generals I reviewed the marching eight thousand handsome boys of that famous college, while Lieutenant Zilpha Bosone stood in the second line to review," she reminisced. Zilpha then flew to Denver for Intelligence School and her mother boarded the "Sacred Cow," the plane used by President Roosevelt when he was in office, to return.

"The generals who had flown from Washington, D.C., for the event at A. & M. gave me the center of the plane, President Roosevelt's quarters. I reflected as we cruised toward the nation's capital that this had been quite an eventful and memorable trip!"

After Intelligence School Zilpha exhibited some of the family temperament, necessary when women are sometimes nailed to the floor for no reason in a man's world. Assigned to Selfridge Air Force Base in Mt. Clemens, Michigan, on her arrival she caused shock waves among the base operation officers—the 61st Fighter Squadron with a female intelligence officer? Unheard of. No way. Out of the question. It was suggested that she accept reassignment to Eastern Air Defense Force headquarters in New York, which she surmised would be a desk job. After all, they said, there were "no facilities" for women at Selfridge—the standard cop-out.

With dander rising, suspecting sex discrimination, she informed those in charge that she was no pencil pusher, that she had entered the air force to perform a worthwhile service, that her grades had warranted an "Excellent" classification preparing her for fighter squadron duties, and that she had received official orders assigning her to that base.

"Try me for a month," Zilpha pled in compromise. "If I can't do the job, then you can reassign me."

A major, whose wife was a P-51 (single-seat fighter plane) instructor, listened sympathetically and then answered, "Well, why not? I don't see anything wrong with having a woman in a fighter squadron. Let's give her a chance!" This support swayed the vote her way and Zilpha became the first woman intelligence officer in an air force fighter squadron at the age of twenty-one.

And the old intimidation of "no facilities" was easily quashed. In the outbuilding housing, the facility that had been previously reserved for the squadron commander was henceforth designated, "Women."

Handling a job that involved unusual pressure, her likable nature and tireless attitude gained her respect from the base personnel, and her job—with required jet flights—was given worldwide publicity. Recalling those war days of the 1950s, Reva said of her precocious daughter, "She briefed the jet pilots each morning and at the end of the month had to stand by a bonfire until the last secret paper was in ashes."

While at Selfridge, Zilpha met and became engaged to First Lieutenant Arthur B. Crouch, a jet pilot with more than a hundred missions in three months over Korea.

Of the Heart

REVA'S RAPPORT WITH MEN would have to be classified as extraordinary! In numerous instances, no effort was too earthshaking, no favor too demanding if Reva Bosone requested it.

No doubt she had a "way," a way that began in the days of sibling coping. To live peaceably with three teasing brothers, she decided, she would have to adapt, extend herself, and, at times, compromise, which did not mean she abandoned her rights.

And because she managed to keep her self-respect with a sense of responsibility, she won her merit badge as a first-rate sister. What superb training for the many tribulations she was to endure in subsequent public life—with never a tear for career ups and downs. Competition with her brothers was considered unequaled preparation for later altercations in politics.

The Becks, who operated on the theory that what was good for the boys was good for Reva, and vice versa, always preached and practiced moral discipline, but they believed false modesty to be improper. Discussions on the facts of life were not suppressed—open conversations on touchy subjects incised many a boil of smirching and misinformation.

"There could be no finer background for one who was to associate with men," she avers. "I've been the only woman on many committees of men. I could speak their language. I have never been aware that I was a woman and they were men, so I have had absolutely no fear of associating with men in committees, on boards, or in legislative bodies. So far as I am conscious of it, I have never used a sex appeal approach. If I couldn't win an issue or a position on merit, I didn't want to win. To get anywhere on anything less than merit would have been an insult to my intelligence and ability."

Just because Reva had invaded men's dominion of the Utah state legislature, she could never quite understand why she was expected by a faction of the legislators—small, but nevertheless present—to be mannish and presumed to have been a tomboy who climbed trees instead of cuddling dolls. In recent years, of course, many women have been known to kick over the traces of housewifery in deference to more academic pursuits, but Reva was most certainly in the vanguard.

Fred Goerner, in his book *The Search for Amelia Earhart,* states that

Amelia had to work very hard at winning acceptance in her world just because she was a woman, but she suffered from no lack of femininity. As with the red-haired Amelia, red-haired Reva is feminine in every way, and she insists that one can be the feminine type and still climb trees, although she has never had any Tarzan inclinations.

Perhaps it was those tailored suits which were just gaining favor among women in the 1930s but incurring scant approval from men. Reva adopted this style because it just seemed correct for a woman lawyer and legislator. And she wore them to perfection (Reva and Rosalind Russell!).

But most of the masculine contingent saw her charm in spite of the tailored exterior. When the city judges of Utah were organized at a meeting in 1936 in Salt Lake City, Reva thought it generous of the men to elect her by unanimous vote the first president. Even more gallantry—a staunch Republican judge nominated her!

Her charm didn't escape the family, either, but they were used to her prominence. She was outspoken yet friendly, demanding yet appreciative.

There was always the trademark of red hair—genuine—variously described in news reports as flaming, Titian, brilliant, but really not as flaming as on the strawberry blonde side. Having clothes sense, she appeared publicly well attired at all times. Her groomed nails and hands were set off by one or more rings and the constant bracelet. "I feel nude without a bracelet on my wrist," Reva admits. Her feet are long and narrow, and at a home gathering years ago she removed her shoe to illustrate why she took such a long shoe size. Her big toe was the culprit, she used to say. Thin skin (part of the red hair syndrome) was lacking in Reva's personality and any wry comments a detractor might make about her feet were turned into a joke.

In her junior years, however, Reva confesses to a sensitive bent. She recalls the day a fellow student and good friend broke the quiet of the university Law Library with, "Reva, you have the prettiest legs I've ever seen but the damndest looking feet!" Flattered, flustered, and certainly furious, she doubled her concentration on the books and vowed that one day similar remarks would not bother her.

Exhibiting a genuine consideration for others, Reva was known for keeping silent until the propitious moment, which made good timing a constant attribute. Former Congressman Chet Holifield of California, who knew Reva in her congressional days, maintains her logic was well founded. Friendly, sociable, articulate were adjectives used in reminiscing about his former colleague.

Kenneth R. Harding, sergeant at arms of the United States House of Representatives and son of the late "Cap" Harding, Democratic congressional campaign director, recalls that more than twenty years ago when

Reva would return to visit Congress after her defeat, the occasion would resemble a homecoming.

"Any recognition the Judge received is because we all loved and admired her as a person and this is the way the whole house looked at her. Not because she was a Democrat, which she was and a darn good Democrat, but because everything she did was the right thing to do—that is why she was received as she was."

Harding continued, "Mike Kerwin, chairman of the Appropriations Committee, Public Works, of Interior, didn't naturally and automatically accept women in Congress and politics but he accepted Reva Beck Bosone.

"I used to be privy to some of the more or less private discussions of Speaker Rayburn, when he was with us, and John McCormack," he divulged. "I do know from personal knowledge the very, very high level on which they placed the services of Reva Beck Bosone. And this is one of the reasons, I'm sure, she was so highly respected. This is really a great personal tribute to her, and I'd like to make it a part of the record in passing it along. I'm sure she has heard it before, but I heard it with my own ears."

Senator Mike Mansfield, a colleague thirty years ago in Congress, has continued a correspondence with the Judge from Truman days to the present and says she inspires friendship. Judge William A. Duvall of the Post Office Department claims that in her tenure as judicial officer the men in the office had a real affection for her.

ALTHOUGH BERT was Reva's first love, Fred was her first infatuation. The two eighth graders walking home from afternoon school dances would hold hands, the limit of their romantic ventures. But the temperamental fluctuations of early teenage had them first as friends, then as opponents, and again as friends. The same type of ping-pong relationship continued with Bert at American Fork High School. Bert, who became the dean of the School of Business Administration at the University of Colorado and occupied high positions at Northwestern University and other institutions, was a tall, well-built young man with high native intelligence—like his teenage sweetheart. A leader in school, Bert was nevertheless romantically bashful with Reva and most unpredictable!

Manager of the basketball team, he with the team members were awarded beautiful white all-wool sweaters with a big red "A" on the side. All the girls at A.F. High regarded the gift of one of these sweaters a trophy and prayed the boys would give them up. Reva secretly longed for one.

Then one evening she heard someone bound up the steps of the family's apartment in the hotel. She opened the door to see Bert holding his newly acquired sweater. Pushing it at her, he blurted, "Take this and wear it!" The manner of presentation didn't matter—Reva was joyous.

"Huh," she says, "the next day did I strut that sweater! No other fellow had given his away, so I felt very special."

Bert's capricious qualities were sometimes vexing, though, due in part perhaps to Reva's penchant for arguing, which resulted in days of their not speaking to each other. Here, again, Reva's passion for syllogism was not always shared by members of the opposite sex.

The big spring dance was an event looked forward to with giggly excitement. Reva expected, as did her girl friends, that Bert would ask her for this important social occasion. But no invitation was forthcoming and she had to repeatedly shake her head to her mother's question, "Did Bert ask you today?"

Finally depression overcame her as the night of the dance arrived and no date. Most assuredly, she thought, no one else would think of asking her, assuming Bert had. As she sat at home taking down her hair—in turn, blue and angry—familiar bounding noises on the outside steps were heard. Then a loud knock. And sure enough, at 9:30 P.M., there stood Bert, dressed to the nines.

"Why aren't you at the dance?" he demanded when she appeared at the door.

"A darn good reason—you didn't ask me!" So here was an opportunity to turn her back, and Reva told her mother in another room that she refused to go with him.

Reva shrugs. "Well, my family was fond of Bert and they knew his ways, so Mother urged me to get ready and go." Relenting, Reva arranged her long red hair on the top of her head with a wide ribbon tied in a a bow in front, slipped on her pink chiffon dress, and the two were off to the dance.

"When we arrived, the kids had amused expressions on their faces. One of my girl friends told me later that Bert was there earlier and looked all around. They knew he was looking for me. Then they missed him and were not at all surprised to see the two of us come in together later."

After high school, the two students attended different universities and ended up in different cities, corresponding all the while, however.

A letter to her brother Horace in 1918 when the two were transposed—Reva back in American Fork between terms at UC and Horace trying his luck in San Francisco stock theatre—read, "Bert has been down this week. He was grand to me and wanted to be forgiven for how he had neglected me. When he got back to Salt Lake he sent me a box of Centennial chocolates and nearly half the drug store. He leaves today for American Lake as Sergeant (temporary)."

Each found a place in a different environment and married someone else. Then each was divorced and later remarried. Life catapulted them to separate heights but they always keep in touch. Looking back, Reva appreciates more than ever the respect and admiration they shared as two carefree but motivated young persons.

WHILE on the bench in Salt Lake City, Reva was in great demand at social events. A divorcee, with a background in law and with refinements cultured by her varied interests, she found that escorts were never in short supply. Due to job commitments, though, party going was selective.

But after a number of years of hedging the advances of fascinated squires, she called a moratorium on evening dates. She says, believe it or not, it was just too trying to maintain friendships after being forced to restrain a companion's amorous advances in the front seat of an automobile. What is there about a grass widow, anyway, she wondered?

In Washington, D.C., the affaire de coeur still posed problems. One fellow member of Congress used to pump his ego by broadcasting to one and all that his date was Judge Bosone, another member of Congress. She dropped him.

A colleague toward whom she was not romantically inclined expressed after many dates his devotion for her which ended that social alliance. As the song goes, he "said something stupid like I love you." They remained friends, of course.

One might imagine that the Judge's standards for a suitable mate were a trifle stratospheric. Many suitors tried to kindle the fires of passion. Just one succeeded. And as the stars would have it, he was married!

A distinguished millionaire member of Congress, he made a concerted effort to sit by Reva practically every day on the floor of the House. His much younger wife and he were prominent in the social register and their parties were the "in" occasions of the year. Reva admired the legislator because the luxury of his money and his social prestige did not interfere with his duties as a congressman.

Sitting side by side, the two were chatting one day between debate sessions. The Judge sighed that she had put up her last lunch for her daughter Zilpha because she would be graduating from college. The personable congressman exclaimed, "Look what you do—and my wife doesn't get up until noon after the maid has drawn the bath water!"

In the gripping, exciting, feverish, agitating, occasionally unsavory world of politics and lawmaking, the two would ramble on about how pleasant it would be to sit on the front porch in retirement. They recognized they were kindred spirits in many ways.

One day he explained that his wife would be visiting friends out of town and asked Reva to have dinner with him the next evening. Reva, characteristically honorable, told him that she didn't go out with married men, but if his wife would call her and give her consent, she would be happy to accept his invitation.

One will never know the wiles or rationale used by the congressman on his youthful wife, but she surprised Reva by phoning. With a tone of amusement she approved the proposed date.

So the gallant admirer escorted Reva to an elegant, intimate restaurant in Georgetown. The two realized joy in each other's company; their growing romantic attachment glowed as warmly as the candlelight on the table and the conversation lingered over comfortable interests that both shared. She remembers gentle laughter, a sense of well-being and contentment in just being alone together. The perfect evening!

Her car had been left on Capitol Hill, so her friend returned her to it. As they bade goodnight at the car door, he bent to kiss her. And Reva, longing with every feminine urge to submit but ruled by an iron ethic, responded in her characteristically above-board manner that she didn't kiss married men!

Well, anyway, the relationship continued happily. They seemed to be truly matched in compatibility, with the exception of political conviction. They usually cancelled each other's vote, saying, "Why would an intelligent person like you vote that way?"

Knowing she could have married the ardent congressman had he been free, she silently mourned his death years later.

Loyalty Impugned, Honor Questioned—Smear!

IN 1952 Senator Arthur V. Watkins was a fearful man. And all for naught! Fear led him to authorize others to smirch the long, clean, dedicated career of a woman colleague in Congress.

Reva was seriously considering the possibility of running for the Senate because Congressman Granger revealed to her that he planned to retire. Later he changed his mind and decided to run for the Senate. Reva then abandoned the senatorial race for herself, but the Watkins office was unaware of this.

One day in May 1952 a favorite reporter friend rushed into her office. "Judge, I've just come from the Watkins office and was told by Cardall and McKinney that they have something on you that will make you a lost cause!"

Reva chuckled at his concern. "Listen, if I'd done anything untoward, it would have come out long before now. This is my eleventh campaign, you know. Don't you believe it!"

"But Judge," he insisted, "if you'd seen their faces you'd know they mean business."

Reva recognized genuine agitation. "Well, we all know lies can be told and any fact can be distorted. But I'm not worried."

Worried, no, but this bit of news was disturbing. Reva knew she had never committed any act to cause her shame. So just what could the Watkins office boys be plotting? It would have to be wildly imaginative. How to find out? Perhaps by letting her name still be considered for the senatorial race.

Congresswoman Bosone did not have long to be curious. Sometime after the reporter's flurried visit, Reva's assistant walked into her office looking perplexed.

"Judge, Fulton Lewis in on the phone." Reva did not know Lewis personally, but she did know well the authoritative voice that perpetrated smears through the medium of radio. The issues he sponsored were Republican-oriented and those he fought were invariably of the Democratic party.

When she answered, he immediately asked, "Did your two secretaries give you contributions in 1950?" Taken aback, Reva tried to draw from memory. Yes, she remembered signing an affidavit during the campaign of 1950 on which contributions from her administrative assistant and her secretary were listed.

"What did you do with these contributions?"

Reva could not remember what was done with the contributions and being anything but devious answered him honestly, "I guess the money was spent." What else? Why this query?

"That's a kickback! Listen to my program at five o'clock!"

Kickback! Kickback! A loathsome practice she had always reviled! If a bomb had exploded in her hand, she could not have been more shattered.

"Don't you *dare* accuse me of taking a kickback," she snapped. But he was daring, and so she called him a skunk. (Son-of-a-bitch wasn't used too often by ladylike legislators.)

The brief conversation left her stunned. And then the thundering dawn—so this is the Watkins office black witchcraft!

Since there was no radio in her office, she and her staff barely had time to dash out to her car in the parking lot and turn on the radio. And there they listened as Fulton Lewis, Jr., on the Mutual Broadcasting System informed the nation that Congresswoman Reva Beck Bosone from Utah had violated the Corrupt Practices Act by accepting kickbacks from two of her staff members. He alluded to the affidavit listing contributions to the 1950 campaign of $400 by Virginia Rishel and $230 by Gayle Snow. And on and on he shot with his condemnation. He had his bead on Reva and she was his sitting duck, target of a particularly demoralizing personal attack.

With a string of well-chosen words he managed in a few minutes to rip the flesh of decency from her bones!

When it was all over, like the object of a well-planned ambush, she sat motionless. They were all in suspended animation. It can't be. It just can't be! Then they slowly realized why many Washingtonians had no use for Lewis. "You people out in the sticks," Reva said they told her, "are the ones who listen to him—not here."

That night Reva was deluged by phone calls from the press wanting a statement. Everyone prefaced his/her question with, "Judge Bosone, I know this is a political thing but . . ." She gave thanks for their confidence and tact. But what to say? What to do? She had above all committed no crime! Although numb with shock, there was no sleep that night.

"The next morning I picked up the newspaper with fear and trembling," she remembers. "I had pictured the headlines that these attacks often occasion. But thanks to the Washington press, there was merely a small story near the crease in the inside of the paper. They certainly didn't give much credence to the Lewis story. But outside of Washington it was a different story!"

The *New York Herald Tribune* carried the news with her picture. The Salt Lake City newspapers took the exposé route, as Reva expected. She was told, however, that when the story came over the wire to one of the two big papers in her hometown, receiving pressman King Durkee, a cub reporter at the Police Department when Reva was on the bench, said, "My God, of all the news I've had to print, I hate this the most!"

Fulton Lewis, Jr., continued blasting the congresswoman in four additional broadcasts with inflections, pauses, and innuendoes calculated to present the picture of a crafty opportunist, even distorting the facts of her two divorces.

Who, really, was the man behind the voice heard each weekday evening on Mutual Broadcasting System by 16 million people? In the book, *Praised and Damned* (1954), author Booton Herndon said that Fulton Lewis remained a storm center. According to Herndon, Lewis had been tongue-lashed by a president of the United States and on the floor of Congress, and many times he had been sued, but only two judgments were found against him for one dollar each. The *New York Times,* the *Washington Post, Time, Life,* and *Newsweek,* among others, had denounced him.

Mr. Herndon states that Lewis thought of himself as a "liberal in the traditional sense, neither right nor left, but straight down the middle." And he asserts, "Lewis has one bias—his patriotism."

On labor—originally he was for the intent of the National Labor Relations Act, but because of abuses he became favorable to the implementation of the Taft-Hartley Act. On the black race—Lewis claimed he wanted to see that group of people "stand in adulthood in America," but he believed Eleanor Roosevelt was doing them a disservice with her activities in their regard.

In Los Angeles a group called the Committee of One Hundred was looking for a man to run against the Democratic incumbent, Jerry Voorhis, who was voted the West's top congressman by the Washington press corps.

"It was necessary to find a man of impeccable background," Herndon says, "personal charm, and proven intelligence to conduct a successful campaign. And he must be a man of integrity and statesmanship in case he won." Lewis heard about the man they selected, Richard M. Nixon, and sought a meeting with him, from then, taking a personal interest in steering him toward the top. When Nixon's career was upgraded to the nomination of General Eisenhower's running mate, Lewis made his way to Nixon's side on that occasion. "Congratulations, Dick!" he said.

Herndon relates on page 98: "At the familiar voice, Nixon looked up for the first time. He could hold back the tears no longer, and his eyes brimmed full. 'Except for you, Fulton, it never would have happened!' he said, his voice breaking with happiness. 'And I'll tell that to the world!' ''

Close to Senator Joseph R. McCarthy, Lewis befriended the controversial finger-pointer at alleged Communists in this country many times, maintaining that McCarthy's desire to keep the American people safe was his—Lewis's—only interest. Fulton Lewis, himself, was bitterly opposed to Communists in government. Herndon writes that Lewis stated he knew that McCarthy had brought to light "literally hundreds of Communists, big and little."

But through a strange flick of fate, Lewis had to taste the same brew he had concocted for so many luckless citizens. Because of a Lewis investigation into apparent violations of his own County Board of Education in Maryland, which even usurped school lunch money in a gambling caper, the radio personality not only saw indictments of the political machine by a grand jury, but found *himself* charged on several counts. The charges were obviously superficial and trumped up, thought to be retaliation by the group he had persecuted, and all indictments on Lewis were dismissed or voted not guilty, but he was nonetheless stripped of membership in his beloved Little Brick Church by the Side of the Road, ending his long association with the Children's Choir which he had tenderly and painstakingly built up.

Apparently believing the accusations toward Lewis, the minister one Sunday morning, without mentioning his name, poured chastisement on the man who had brought so many in the limelight to their knees. Now deprived of privileges most dear, he was a crushed man!

Perhaps reflection on his undeserved downfall in this instance stirred thoughts of his own past brazen accusations without proper investigation!

Little wonder that Reva Beck Bosone would awaken in the middle of the night, agonizing over her undeserved persecution. And what was her alleged "crime"?

In all her campaigns she had filed with the proper governmental department the regular financial sheet listing all contributions. In the 1948 campaign in Utah, her first congressional contest, she had included the contributions on the financial sheet which was attached to a signed affidavit, then filed as a public document in the office of the secretary of state in the capitol building in Salt Lake City. The newspapers traditionally published the contributions made to each candidate.

Before the 1950 campaign, Reva's assistant, Virginia Rishel, placed the financial sheet on Reva's desk and said, "I've listed the contributions that Gayle and I want to give. Is that all right?"

"Oh, yes," the Judge answered, "I always list my contributions." Then she signed the affidavit.

If Reva and Virginia had read the copy of the Federal Corrupt Practices Act instead of the Judge tossing it, they would have been able to
avoid the embarrassing quagmire in which they found themselves. Those
setting out to violate the act would undoubtedly know it thoroughly.

The two women were not the only innocents in this case; several
members of Congress admitted to Reva that they had probably uninten-
tionally violated it themselves in some way. A Mr. Steele of the *New York
Herald Tribune* called her to find out the story on the alleged kickback
and during the conversation told her, "Certainly the law [Federal Corrupt
Practices Act] should be clarified because I believe several congressmen
have misunderstood it—in fact, there are thirty or forty other congressmen who I am advised have misunderstood the act." Reva has no doubt
that those members were honest, as she is, because corrupt and dishonest
acts are hidden, *not exposed in a public document.*

What constitutes a kickback? The basic principle is offensive,
abusive, and dangerous. A congressman, in order to finance his campaign, places an employe on his payroll to work either part-time or at
home. The employe receives a full salary, however. Then when the
monthly salary check is cashed, a portion of it—often as much as half—is
remitted to the employer, and the entire transaction is kept in murky
secrecy.

But sections of the law, prohibiting a staff member, for instance, from
paying the taxi fare of a member of Congress during a campaign, placed
irritating, unnecessary constraints on a legislator. Because of objections,
the act was then under scrutiny for change.

Much sympathy among Reva's colleagues over her predicament was
extended and compassionate calls and letters from Utah were being
received, the volume of mail getting heavier as Lewis's broadcasts continued. An Oregonian, former Brigham City, Utah, resident, sent the cor
gresswoman a copy of a letter he had rushed to the broadcaster:

> Mr. Lewis:
> 　Last night I happened to tune in on your program but did not turn
> it off, as usual, when I heard you mention the name of Congress-
> woman, Mrs. Bosone. I was so outraged by your personal attack upon
> her that I am writing you in protest at your cowardly, dirty, under-
> handed, character-smearing tactics.
> 　It is un-understandable that a man of your capabilities will stoop
> so low and characterize everything you do with destructive criti-
> cisms, not satisfied with giving your version of the "facts" but having
> to inject dirty insinuations and innuendoes as if these were necessary
> to strengthen your arguments. You must feel that your cases are
> weak or you would not resort to things that decent human beings feel
> are beneath them.

I wonder why, in the face of so many real injustices that should be righted, you would single out a woman who has done a genuine service in Congress, a service far above that of the average Congressman? I don't know the woman but I have followed her record, both in Utah and in Washington, and I think that anyone who would attack her as you have done, thru the injection of strictly personal issues—that are none of my business and none of your and most Americans are outraged at your misuse of them—anyone, but especially you because you overstep the bounds of decency so often, should be outlawed as a debaser of the ethics and values that make civilization what it is.

One builder-upper is worth ten thousand destroyers; you are a destroyer. Is the following and adoration of a stupid, half-civilized, emotional mob of the fringe of mankind worth it when just a small portion of that energy and intelligence, if properly directed could engender good-will, good feeling, encouragement and a will to make our Democracy function as it must if we are to survive?

You are to be pitied, Mr. Lewis, that you do not understand. Men of GOOD-WILL: that is what we need. Your Xmas service becomes a mockery in the face of these debasing tactics. I am sorry for you and for the people you so ruthlessly attempt to destroy. One thoughtless sentence and you can ruin the work of a lifetime. The tragedy you bring into peoples' lives! Is it worth it to you?

CLEMENTS HORSELY

The list of other friends volunteering help was long and strong. Walter Cosgriff, Republican, president of Continental Bank and Trust Company of Utah, head of Reconstruction Finance at the time, demanded, "God, what's wrong with this place? You can certainly count on me!"

Ray Murdock, one of Washington's most prominent lawyers, promised any service short of murder! Judge George Latimer of the Military Court of Appeals vowed to stand back of her 100 percent. Many busy senators had their clerks call in their support, with the opinion that Reva was the victim of a dirty trick.

Several lawyers of the Republican party who had practiced before her when she was a judge gave her their vote of confidence, one of whom protested that he would make no contribution to the party in 1952 if it would be used to spread lies about Congresswoman Bosone. Another Republican wrote her: "If this is a political gesture, made prior to an election, it seems cruel and unfair. If we as Republicans have to resort to these methods, it is about time that we were investigated, fumigated, and disinfected."

Joe Martin, Republican minority floor leader of the House, defended her against several Republicans who wanted to attack her from the well of the House. He refused them, saying, "We know she's an honest woman."

Reva, all this time, was desperate to explain her case from the well but was advised against it; let it die, the members said, or it will make more news. But Reva has since decided that she was ill-advised.

After the first Lewis broadcast, Attorney General James P. McGranery directed an FBI probe, requested by the congresswoman, of the charges against her and everyone who had ever worked in her congressional office. The investigator was informed by all that no one had ever given her money or had been asked to do so.

Then one day Congressman Byron Rogers, touched by the plight of his colleague, offered her assistance inasmuch as he had been attorney general of Colorado and claimed special insight into like situations.

As they walked together out of the Capitol and headed toward the House Office Building, he asked, "How about my going to your office and talking to each staff member in private to see what the score is?" Weary and disconsolate from all the accusations, Reva welcomed the positive suggestion and his kind offer.

"How did the girls give the contributions to you?" Rogers then asked.

Reva had no answer.

"Well, don't you remember whether they gave you the money in greenbacks or by check?"

She stopped as though lassoed. Until that moment she had not actually traced in her mind each small step leading up to the signing of the affidavit.

"No, now I remember—they didn't give me any money at all!!"

"Then why in the world did you say they had?" Rogers was incredulous.

"Well, I had signed that affidavit."

When they arrived at the House Office Building, Reva remained in her outer office while Rogers conferred with each staff member in her private office. After a lengthy period he opened the door and happily announced; "I find that no one has ever given you money for anything at any time, Judge. And the girls' contribution money was never used. It's right here in the safe!"

In the safe! What joyous relief and astonishment! From the beginning Virginia and Gayle, the hapless benefactors, had drawn blanks in recalling the disposition of the $630. Since Lewis first broke his story Virginia had been shaken and overwrought, blaming herself in the fiasco.

In retrospect, both the congresswoman and her assistant remembered that soon after the offices were set up, Virginia asked permission for the staff to secure a few important items in the small safe that came with the quarters. Reva always preferred using a locked file, so the safe was never touched by her. In the hectic routine of a congressional office,

Virginia and Gayle had assumed that the stipend was spent on the 1950 campaign.

When it was found intact in the safe, certainly the forgotten contribution could be considered a believable oversight, hardly the infamous deed precipitating a dark cloud of scandal. Virginia and Gayle, admired and trusted workers, both from honorable, impressive backgrounds, were the antithesis of the shifty poacher found in some political offices. So any faulting that ever existed was through innocence.

But Reva was quite sure that Fulton Lewis, Jr., would scarcely consider the episode a believable oversight, so she didn't burden him with the information.

Meanwhile, an informer pieced the story together for the Bosone office, revealing that Richard Cardall and Jim McKinney, the top men in Senator Watkins' office, had checked out the list of Bosone contributions in one of the Salt Lake City papers in the summer of 1950 and had made a note of the discrepancy. Taking advantage of Reva's innocuous act of including on it two modest sums from office workers, they meant to use the information as a sword whenever the propitious occasion arose. The big kill was planned for late in the 1952 senatorial campaign—too late for Reva to effectively counter.

She learned that when someone in the Republican National Committee had pushed the panic button and turned the news over to Fulton Lewis, Jr., as early as May, the Watkins office had bellowed and roared! Because there *was* time to answer.

But where could she start? It was such a gross distortion—an abominable accusation any time but worse in the light that she was not even a senatorial candidate! In campaigning for the House of Representatives that fall, Reva did defend herself; she told it like it was. But to get on network radio and dignify Lewis's "exposé" by answering each trumped up charge would have only fanned his fire-and-brimstone act. He would always have had the advantage of the last loaded word!

One morning at her desk, all the frustration, exasperation, and desperation peaked as she caught Congressman Ken Regan of Texas looking at her sympathetically through the outer office door. In a rare moment, she rushed to him and dampened his shoulder with her tears! (It is believed that others under similar circumstances might have been steady customers of the nearest bistro by that time.)

An addendum to this particular smear file concerns the attempt of certain Republicans to have a House committee investigate the congresswoman. Again the FBI reviewed the facts and again cleared her. Then the House committee cleared her; this was publicly irritating to the Republican-slanted *Washington Times-Herald,* which claimed a whitewash!

Kickback was a hot item in Washington in those days. Two Republican congressmen had been convicted of violating the Corrupt Practices Act. One was fined and given a suspended sentence and the other fined and jailed. The facts in those cases were contrary to those of the congresswoman's, but to counteract their bad publicity the Republican organization had closed in on a guileless Democrat. A *New York Herald Tribune* article reported: "Some Republican members of the House, aware of Mrs. Bosone's acceptance of political contributions from members of her staff, are reportedly preparing to ask the Justice Department whether it intends to enforce this section of the act on a bipartisan basis."

When the attorney general first instructed the FBI to check out the campaign contribution charge, Mrs. Bosone was quoted as saying, "I'm just grateful there's going to be an investigation." The *Washington Post* article with her remarks continued; "I couldn't have waited another day without asking them to do it. If they come up tomorrow to get the facts, it won't be too quick. They'll get all the facts and I have no fear of the outcome."

After a thorough investigation the Justice Department absolved the congresswoman. "This is a type of case which the department would not present to a grand jury," said a spokesman for the attorney general.

In October the *Deseret News* ran an article, dateline Washington, reporting a letter from two Salt Lake City attorneys demanding an inquiry into reasons for not prosecuting Reva Beck Bosone.

The response from Attorney General McGranery to Robert A. Collier, chief counsel, House Committee on the Judiciary, Subcommittee to Investigate the Department of Justice, is included in the article:

> Your information respecting this complaint is appreciated. In the light of the Parnall Thomas and Walter Ellsworth Brehm cases, it is understandable that to some it would appear that Representative Bosone also should be prosecuted. However, a number of differences exist. The Thomas case was a fraud case—payroll padding. The Brehm case involved the use of compulsion and coercion in securing the contributions from the employees. The Bosone case did not. In fact, the contributions to Mrs. Bosone were made without her knowledge, though she later learned of them when her secretary prepared and laid before her the printed form reports to be made to the Secretary of State of Utah and to the Clerk of the House of Representatives. It is clear that neither Mrs. Bosone nor the contributors were aware of the prohibition, else she would not have reported them. That, of course, is no defense but we found that the real difficulty lies in making the required proof. Technically, Mrs. Bosone is guilty under one section, the contributors under another, but there is no proof as to any of them except their own admissions. If they are indicted the Government can hardly expect the contributors to testify against Mrs. Bosone, or Mrs. Bosone to be a witness against them.

None of the persons could be compelled to be a witness for the prosecution. The letter . . . makes reference to the filing, on October 28, 1950, of Mrs. Bosone's sworn statements reporting campaign contributions. These statements constitute admissions on her part, but without corroboration, would not sustain a conviction. Later, verbal admission to newsmen and investigators were repetitions of the former admissions. An admission cannot be corroborated by another admission. The Government has no other proof of the contributions than the admissions. In these circumstances I have concluded that the violation which occurred here, if any, was not such a violation as should be presented. This conclusion is based, among other things, on the fact that there was not an intentional violation; the contributions were voluntarily disclosed by Mrs. Bosone; the persons involved were not solicited and made voluntary contributions; and that all persons involved are in a situation where they cannot be compelled to testify, without which there remains only the admission.

In connection with the report in the *Deseret News* of a letter demanding an explanation for dropping the charges against her, Reva recalled an incident involving one of the men who wrote the aforementioned letter. At a meeting she had attended in Salt Lake City, she heard a member of a prominent group declare, "Franklin Delano Roosevelt is insane!"

Reva said, "The remark was made with such vengeance that I thought it showed emotional instability. Of course, anyone has the right to disagree with any public servant. It was the way this remark was made that concerned me." The man was under consideration for a responsible position as a member of the Military Court of Appeals, but Reva believed that the administration, then headed by President Truman, should be aware of this man's expressed views before an appointment was made. The position was delegated elsewhere and evidently the reason filtered down to the attorney in question, who bore a grudge!

Next in line exonerating the congresswoman was the unexpected telegram on October 15, 1952, from Congressman Frank L. Chelf of Kentucky, chairman of the subcommittee investigating her case. Reva had made no contact with the committee, leaning on their discretion to weigh the facts honestly.

Ofttimes during the white heat of a political campaign when one's opponent is desperate for issues he seeks to drag into debate the honesty, integrity and character of a candidate. The Attorney General has ruled that for good and valid reasons no official action will be taken in your case. Officially I have supported the Attorney General's ruling. Personally I can say your legion of friends in the House of Representatives who served with you and who know you best believe in your honesty, integrity and ability as Member of Congress. You are entitled to be reelected and may God give you the courage to present your cause bravely and adequately and your good people the wisdom to accept the truth as it exists.

Sincerely,

FRANK L. CHELF, M.C.

After four grinding months, relief and gratitude crept into her feelings again, but nothing could ever compensate for the worry-wracked nights, the stomach knots, the taut nerves, and the terror of the treachery in the next office!

Postscript: Reva learned that Jim McKinney, one of Watkins's right-hand men, was none other than the son of Judge James L. McKinney of the Third Judicial District Court of Utah. Often, in righteous indignation or when she was desolate with heartache, she would wonder what the jurist's reaction would be to his son's enmity toward her. In the early 1930s, Legislator Bosone had been asked to help the threatened nomination of Judge McKinney, from the west side of Salt Lake City, and having many friends and supporters in that part of the valley, she agreed to give the nominating speech. "When I finished," she said, "he walked over to me and grabbed both arms in generous appreciation of what I had done. He won the nomination! How his son could be a party to a trick to ruin me is impossible to understand!"

In her statement of May 23, 1952, Reva said, "I am sure this kind of campaign will react against the person or persons who started it. I am a firm believer in the law of compensation." In this light, then, one views the fate of the other henchman in the "lost cause" ploy. Richard T. Cardall, with another man, was indicted by a federal grand jury in October 1960 on charges of conspiring to violate the registration and antifraud regulations of the Securities Act of 1933. In addition, Cardall was charged with committing perjury, suborning perjury, and conspiring to commit perjury before a federal grand jury. Cardall was disbarred by the Utah State Bar on July 12, 1961.

Paul Badger never felt Senator Watkins was the kind of man to pull off such a double cross, ascribing the plot to others. "The trouble with Cardall," Badger quoted Watkins as saying, "he thinks he's the senator." And later the senator did, in fact, fire Richard Cardall, he said.

Badger implicated Cardall with instigating the production of a one-time killer sheet, "United States Senate News" (Utah edition), the headline reading, "Thomas Philosophy Wins Red Approval." The aspersion in this spurious publication of the senator's alleged sympathy for Communists lost him the election and broke his spirit. Later Badger talked to the man from out of state who had ridden roughshod over Thomas's dedicated career. Walter Quigley, the adroit smearmonger, admitted to

Badger, "I can produce a newspaper or brochure on any member of Congress!"

Fulton Lewis, Jr., is deceased and former Senator Watkins died in Utah in 1973. In the fall of 1975 Richard Cardall and another man were found guilty on nine counts in the International Chemical and Development Corporation and Golden Rule Associates stock fraud case and given sentences in a federal penitentiary.

And a tortuous episode of 1952, written in memory, is laid to a restless grave.

The fountain of dirty tricks runneth over!

Congress adjourned early so members could attend the national party conventions in Chicago. Reva was assured by her colleagues that she would be asked to speak at the National Democratic Convention. But as the date neared and no invitation for her speaking services was received, she knew she had been bypassed because of the kickback story. Having been through the high water of the Republican purge, she was not about to let this snub get to her. But another in the same city succeeded!

India Edwards, director of the Women's Division of the Democratic National Committee, staged an important dinner for all the women at the convention. Prominent women appointees and others of the Democratic party were the honored guests at the head table. Other outstanding women who sat in the audience were introduced by the director. Reva, the only Democratic congresswoman present at the convention, sat unannounced! She was confident that Mrs. Edwards knew and believed the truth of the kickback story; just a word of explanation from her would have been oil on that troubled high water. But none was forthcoming.

And Reva again felt the heaviness of heart.

But back in Salt Lake City, true friends rallied round. The *Salt Lake Times,* a weekly newspaper, looked at the charge against the candidate for reelection for what it was and ran an editorial under the head, "A Dastardly Attack":

> Utahns would probably give but passing notice to the recent charge leveled against Reva Beck Bosone were it not that the implications arising from the accusations may injure the splendid reputation and prestige she has established during her four years in Congress and in turn hurt her chances for reelection.
>
> It is safe to say that no one in the Second Utah Congressional district and no one of her colleagues in Congress believe that Rep. Bosone did an intentional wrong. . . ."

Maryhale Woolsey, who composed the lyrics to the song, "Springtime in the Rockies," sent in her pledge of support: "Your record stands up mighty well, you know. We are proud to vote for you, and hope and pray you will be right there when the 'smoke' clears away. The only other place we'd rather see you would be in a still higher one and we have confidence that someday you will be.

"We too resent the attack that has been made on you, and it has not dented our regard for you. Honesty is NOT corruption, and if an error was made it should not have been kept back until the present time. I do not know of a single instance where anyone has been influenced to lower your standing in his or her estimation, because of that charge."

Although allegiance came with uncalled-for enthusiasm, Reva was continually fearing "nice" people. Her mother had a saying, "Nice people never set the North River on fire," a strange choice of words, but memorable. She interpreted "nice people," Reva said, to mean those who achieve a reputation of being nice because they overtly avoid controversy while they covertly engage in hypocritical acts.

Reva arrived in Utah in time for the Salt Lake County Convention. Opponent William A. Dawson, whom she had beaten in 1948, was counted by the congresswoman as a friend rather than an adversary principally because of a letter he had sent to Washington in the summer of 1951 in which he said, "I believe your record has been pretty well received by most people I have talked to except those who are prejudiced." It was later believed that Dawson had taken the friendly route because he was optimistic of winning another contest. Looking back, Reva commented sadly, "His back had not been up against the wall."

After Barney Flanagan, now on her staff, had exchanged a few words with Dawson on a downtown street one day, he attempted to convince Reva that Dawson was gearing for smearing—the former congressman had definitely sent out negative signals.

"Come on now, Barney, Bill's an honorable man," which now echoes hollowly in her mind.

Among key words bantered about during the nationwide campaign—Korea, corruption, communism—the last was the most treacherous. To be labeled a Communist sympathizer was political quicksand in the paranoid atmosphere of 1952. So Bill Dawson would spike his television talks with, "Now I think you should know this about Congresswoman Bosone . . ." and proceed to chew her up on conspiring with Communists while, she was told, he glanced everywhere but into the camera. Her votes in Congress came under his indignant blasts, intimating that she had always followed the Communist line.

Her friends knew the chance was about as likely as her wearing a size six shoe! She abhorred the Communist precepts, but she had been shocked at some of the Republicans who in frenzied and hysterical language shouted that Washington was a hotbed of Communists. She reminded her constituents that every government employe undergoes a rigorous FBI investigation—without klieg lights—and if anyone's loyalty is challenged, then the FBI undertakes an even more thorough investigation.

As experienced members of Congress know, lawmaking does not take a direct route. An example could be the Smith Act, which precluded Communists from working for the government, but it also meant that a housewife, for instance, innocently signing a peace petition, which was later found to be Communist-inspired, would be forever prohibited from holding a government position. The bill had ominous reverberations—native citizens would be bound and tied. Twenty voted no and Reva's penchant for voting her conscience went against her as less courageous House members shamefacedly voted to please a constituency not likely to comprehend the intricacies of the bill. It was common knowledge that many of them were opposed to it but rather than wrangle with their district voters, they found a yes vote easier.

The *Washington Post,* the *Baltimore Sun,* the *St. Louis Post-Dispatch,* and the *New York Times* called the dissenters twenty brave congressmen!

Bill Dawson called Reva dangerous!

A bill presenting a blank check to a new governmental bureau, the Central Intelligence Agency, was another which took courage and strong fiber to vote against. If this bill were passed, vast sums could be squandered with no check whatsoever on their disposition and accounted for solely by certification of the director. Other sections of the bill labeled it alarming. Congressman Emanuel Celler (D., N.Y.) protested, "This bill would throw out the window all immigration restrictions. Fascists, Communists, syphilitics, and lepers could be brought in. This bill illustrates how the cold war is unhinging the nerves of some of our high military authorities." But once again thoughts of the sacrificial lamb in the election booth struck terror in lawmakers' minds, and the bill passed! A member who had raged against it on the floor came up with a yes vote!

Only four, including Reva, voted against it. She was queried on a broadcast over WMAL–Washington and KUTA–Salt Lake City on the reason for her vote. "Because I thought at the time I voted no that it was dangerous legislation. We were giving blind authority which may lead to giving up some of our liberties, and in this blind authority I could see that we might be losing some of our fundamental rights that are vital to every American."

The chairman of an important committee who voted for it later apologized to the congresswoman, perhaps recognizing scrupulous ethics when he saw them. "I didn't want to spend the whole campaign defending my vote," he said. "I had to do that once before, and it's god-awful. I hope I haven't lost your respect!" But he had, and the bill has since been termed a monstrosity.

The book, *The CIA and the Cult of Intelligence,* written by Victor Marchetti, a former executive assistant to the CIA's deputy director, and John D. Marks, a former State Department official, claims the federal government spends $6 billion a year on intelligence and covert activities! Authorized manpower includes 16,500 but also tens of thousands more as mercenaries, agents, consultants, etc. The contested book presents the organization as seeking to impose foreign policies by covert and usually illegal means in secret and deceptive methods by what is established in the cult as the Clandestine Services.

Authors Marchetti and Marks say:

> It encourages professional amorality—the belief that righteous goals can be achieved through the use of unprincipled and normally unacceptable means. Thus, the cult's leaders must tenaciously guard their official actions from public view. To do otherwise would restrict their ability to act independently; it would permit the American people to pass judgment on not only the utility of their policies, but the ethics of those policies as well. With the cooperation of an acquiescent, ill-informed Congress, and the encouragement and assistance of a series of Presidents, the cult has built a wall of laws and executive orders around the CIA and itself, a wall that has blocked effective public scrutiny.

This exposé of the intelligence community states that while the CIA was created for intelligence gathering and the coordination of intelligence activities of other federal departments, two-thirds of its funds and manpower has been used in the last ten years on covert activities.

The authors report: "Under the Central Intelligence Agency Act of 1949, the Director of Central Intelligence (DCI) was granted the privilege of expending funds 'without regard to the provisions of law and regulations relating to the expenditure of Government funds; and for objects of confidential, extraordinary, or emergency nature, such expenditures to be accounted for solely on the certificate of the Director. . . .' "

Speaker Carl Albert wrote former Congresswoman Bosone in October 1974, "You were prescient in your vote against the formation of the CIA. The new congressional reorganization gives the Foreign Affairs Committee special oversight for military intelligence. I have supported CIA intelligence gathering activities, but I certainly do not condone any subversion of other governments."

So Reva, while reviling the abuses of CIA liberties, has the satisfaction of having feared not and being proved right! But her hostile opponents that year, one of whom was Bill Dawson, squeezed a lot of mileage out of her no vote on the CIA and used the exhaust to great 1952 preelection advantage.

Yet, if Reva Beck Bosone, teacher, attorney, judge, and legislator had possessed any Communist tendencies (attributed because of her vote), her daughter Zilpha would never have received "top secret" clearance while serving as an intelligence officer in the United States Air Force. Anyone familiar with investigations of this nature doesn't doubt the comprehensive and exhaustive measures taken to insure classified status. Red means hair in Reva's case.

But to Bill Dawson, red meant Reva!

"I have never regretted my votes because I think it is the stand I took in voting my conscience that has kept the respect and affection of my former colleagues," she asserts. "Their letters to me never cease to be warm and kind. My advice to a person beginning in politics would always be—vote your conscience; it pays off in the long run and leaves you with an unblemished ego to give you confidence and courage."

And, she added with emphasis, "There is no price that can be put on self-respect!"

As she concluded a campaign address one night in Springville, Utah, she was given a long handbill which was labeled from the headquarters of William A. Dawson. At a cursory glance the content struck her as being humorous, but on further reading she detected the crass nature of the put-down regarding an incident in Congress.

The 82d Congress had been tagged with many titles. President Truman dubbed it the "second worst" Republican Eightieth. Senator Wayne Morse called it "The Do Nothing Congress"; Congressman Abraham J. Multer termed it "The Do Nothing Right Congress"; Congressman Walter B. Huber's name for it was "The Tuesday to Thursday Congress"; Congressman Louis C. Rabaut's contribution was "The Horsemeat Congress." Reva Bosone thought that "The Dogfood Congress" was the most apropos. It was inspired when a Salt Laker sent her a can of dog food with a note: "If we don't get a good controls law, we'll all be eating this stuff." Washingtonians will remember hard times when huge signs about horsemeat—making a point of soaring meat prices—were displayed in butcher shops! Reva was singularly disposed toward combating the consumer's high price burden.

After receiving the can of dog food, she brought to the floor of the House a touch of horseplay on the high cost of living. She held up the can of canine rations and melodically sang a few bars of "The Old Gray Mare, She Ain't What She Used to Be." The effectiveness of this brief melodrama was manifest when a national journalist in his column complimented her method of making a point. After her vocal rendition she explained her reasons for singing, to the rapt attention of the gentlemen in the audience, according to Fred Othman in the *Washington Daily News.*

"With that Mrs. Bosone sat down. This seemed a shame; hers was the liveliest speech her conferees had heard in weeks."

But Mr. Dawson in his handbill implied that Reva was crocked on the floor of the House, crooning a song with her eyes rolling in their sockets. A trite, twisted version of a whimsical episode, developed to present a vulgar image! That intent alone was just an absurdity to the congress-woman. What was deplorable to her in another part of the sheet was the ridicule of her two divorces.

She could not help but reflect on the type of honor of a man who pro-fessed his special friendship (which she had inferred from his preelection letter), and he remains the one and only opposing candidate to whom she will not speak.

The Democratic State Committee, with Milton Weilenman, chair-man, bristling from charges that Mrs. Bosone's voting record made her a "leftist," filled in with facts what Mr. Dawson had left unsaid. Dawson had announced no specific program of his own, evidently content to ride the trail of denouncing his opponent on the CIO News summary, which reported that she had cast thirteen "right" (votes determined important by the CIO) votes out of sixteen.

Those votes, all of which seem pertinent to today's problems, were not explained by Mr. Dawson, so the committee obliged. The con-gresswoman had voted against turning the wealth of the Tidelands over to three states—California, Louisiana, and Texas—because she wanted the royalties from the $50 billion undersea oil pools to go to the school systems of all the states. The Supreme Court had twice upheld the owner-ship of this oil by the United States. Did this a leftist record make? the committee wondered.

She had voted for the extension of Social Security. Is liberalizing Social Security, which Dawson seemed to favor, leftist? the committee asked.

And Mrs. Bosone had voted against the use of the Taft-Hartley law in the steel strike because she didn't favor further government intervention. Her judgment was justified when the strike was settled by collective bargaining shortly afterward.

She had voted against amendments designed to take the heart out of price controls during the emergency. On two of these votes, a majority of the House had voted as she did. On the other, 169 were with her. Lots of leftists in Congress, evidently!

Congresswoman Bosone had voted for public housing in military and defense areas when abundant evidence was presented that families of servicemen were being forced to live in renovated chicken coops and pay high rents. Leftist with Bosone, the committee asked, or families of soldiers in squalor?

She had voted against cutting funds for public power lines important in rural electrification programs.

Mrs. Bosone had voted against the Subversive Activities Control and Communist Registration Act. The *New York Times,* the *Washington Post,* and the *Philadelphia Inquirer* had blasted the act as a threat to traditional American liberties. The sponsor of this bill, Pat McCarran himself, in the 1951 session had urged amendments to clear up certain portions. After that was accomplished, Mrs. Bosone had voted for those revisions.

She had not voted against requiring government employees to pledge their loyalty to the United States, as her adversary claimed. The loyalty law was on the books when Mrs. Bosone went to Congress. She and 129 others had voted against a rider to the National Housing Appropriation bill because they thought it completely unworkable. The Senate had insisted upon rewriting the amendment. Then Mrs. Bosone had voted for it.

The committee held that Dawson was aware of Mrs. Bosone's stand on these issues when he wrote that revealing letter on July 13, 1951, stating, "I believe your record has been pretty well received by most people I have talked to except those who are prejudiced." Further, the committee said that Mrs. Bosone had cast about 400 record votes in her four years in Congress—none can be successfully challenged on the basis of honesty, patriotism, and conscience and her God. She had not known at the time she voted whether that vote would be approved or disapproved by any group.

In a radio talk Reva expatiated on her vote rationale, referring to Bill Dawson's attack of disloyalty. With acerbity she remarked:

> If someone questions your loyalty—pay no attention to it—it's only politics.
>
> If someone questions your honesty—pay no attention to it—it's only politics.
>
> If someone, who knows that he is dealing in untruth, calls you a leftist—pay no attention to it—it's only politics.
>
> If someone says you are a radical and knows that he deals in more untruths when he says it—pay no attention to it—it's only politics.
>
> Just why is it, ladies and gentlemen of the radio audience, that some people are so constituted that they can do everything within their power to blacken the name and reputation of a fellowman and then salve their conscience by a shrug of the shoulders and the statement—"Oh, you know, it's only politics."
>
> I have said before, and I repeat it now, that in all of my past campaigns I have always considered my opponent an honorable person and I have always acted accordingly.

But as my opponent this year, Bill Dawson, proceeds with his campaign of frenzy, frustration and falsehoods, I must perforce change my beliefs that candidates can differ in philosophies and still be honest and of good conscience.

My opponent has spent most of his campaigning time in telling anyone who would listen to him that I am disloyal, dishonest, a leftist and a radical, and he bases all of this on a record which he says I made in Congress but which he does not have the courage or the honesty to disclose to you.

Perhaps the most shocking of Dawson's tricks were the large ads that appeared in the papers near election time. The most offensive one that ran the day before the election pictured a white uniformed doctor pointing his finger:

More Straight Talk to Walter K. Granger and Reva Beck Bosone about Socialized Medicine:

We who challenge your vicious plot to foist Communistic control on freedom loving Americans through Socialized medicine want to know why you haven't discussed your plan in the current campaign.

We want to know why you haven't told the voters of Utah that Socialized medicine was never intended to provide better medical services to the people.

We want to know why you haven't told the voters of Utah that Socialized medicine was originally established to make the people feel obligated to the government . . . a plan to strengthen centralized political control.

You know, Mrs. Bosone, and you Mr. Granger, that the source of the un-remitting and relentless drive for Socialized medicine is the Kremlin-controlled American Communist Party.

And yet both of you have made repeated efforts to secure national legislation that would clamp this Communistic scheme on every citizen in America. . . .

Libel, certainly! And serious thought was given to bringing suit when Horace drew up the papers, but perhaps the continuous deep stabs of the opposition had numbed their hearts and minds for such an action.

Dawson emerged victorious. Although others disagree, Reva has always felt that he would have won without resorting to the use of such defamation. The trend was set; Republican candidates were flying high with Eisenhower. She thinks few Democrats could have survived, especially in a pivotal state like Utah.

The effects of this contest crippled the psyche of many in Reva's campaign. And her three brothers suffered vicariously through the smears—they were outraged by attempts to tarnish the allegiance of their respected sister. Willing to accept the consequences under fair competition, they rebelled at their Republican party's unconscionable political devices. Loyal friends who had volunteered their efforts wilted through the cruelty displayed, promising never again to watch her submit to that kind of abuse. Reva herself was spent physically and emotionally by being forced to combat the incessant lies.

But her daughter, when informed of the election outcome, gasped, "Thank God! Now I'll have my mother longer."

A few days following the election a luncheon was given in Reva's honor at the Newhouse Hotel. She was overcome by the dedication of the ninety-nine women present. In times of great emotional inspiration, Reva habitually sheds tears, and they rolled on this occasion, but there were those Republican women who, on hearing this, said she wept in defeat.

Understandably, it takes a special kind of moral and visceral fortitude to be a good loser. A political participant should not, for his salvation, have a low pain threshold in campaigning. "The way one loses," Reva will say, "Is more important than the fact that one loses. Of course, it isn't sweet to be defeated, but it is a passing thing and to be expected.

"The shock of facing such smears, however, never quite wears away! The rumor noose does not break your neck; it breaks your heart. Montana's Mike Mansfield, for instance, could not even talk about his happiness at being elected to the Senate in 1952 because he and his wife were still bitter about the smear campaign that was waged against him. The distortions and vicious innuendoes used by supposedly reputable people are unbelievable."

Smear II

SOON AFTER the incendiary campaign, the commotion of the election, and the closing of her Washington office, Reva prepared for the wedding of Zilpha and Arty which was to take place on December 30 in Memorial Hall in Memory Grove, Salt Lake City. The color arrangement of the hall evidenced the sunny personality and originality of the dark-eyed bride who was radiant in a distinctive gown of delicate lavender. Her attendants were gowned in shades of the same color and all appointments were infused with a lavender tinge, creating a beautifully unified effect.

The surprise of the sentimental ceremony was the composure of the mother of the bride. "To show what can be done if sufficient determination is used," said Reva, "I didn't shed a tear!" The handsome couple left three days later in uniform for their military base in Michigan.

"For weeks I had never stopped, pressing more and more activities into each day," the Judge said. "A flu bug was looking for a fertile place to light and chose me!" Reva was recuperating from the severe bout when she received the news in January that Zilpha was seriously ill. She quickly enplaned for Detroit, near which the air base was located. "Sometimes we can't understand it at the time, but I sincerely believe my defeat saved my life and made it possible for me to care for Zilpha when she needed me."

After Zilpha's recuperation, Reva returned to Salt Lake City to find there were more hours in a day than she had remembered in her previous frenetic schedule. Cultivating a clientele in her law practice required patience, so such fill-ins as guest speaker appearances and getting after the earwigs and rose blight in her garden were fine, but killing time has never been one of her crimes, and "as life slips by, one realizes with a jolt just how valuable a day is!"

One bright day Sid Fox, former owner of a radio and TV station in town and one of her faithful friends who had offered her fifty free spots whenever she campaigned, suggested to her that she would be the perfect personality for a television show. Having enjoyed participating in her own radio program, Reva was inclined to think highly of the idea. So Fox conferred with Ben Larsen, manager of KDYL radio and TV, and the show, "It's a Woman's World," was previewed. Airing four times weekly, Reva considered the opportunity a special challenge inasmuch as she presided for the full thirty minutes, the format including a variety of guests discussing subjects of current interest. A friendly disagreement at the start between Larsen and Bosone was ironed out when Reva convinced him that a "powder puff" approach was not what the majority of women admired. The show proved her claim and brought an upbeat response.

But it also turned out to be a definite burr in the saddles of some of the most active and vocal Republican women—those who traveled the safe way through the lives of the candidates they sponsored, those who favored striking the opponent through the anonymity of organized partisan women. As individuals, many could be counted on to shrink from stepping out from the crowd. There were those of high integrity, of course, but the lowest of them caŝt a pall over the organization.

At one Republican Women's dinner in the Hotel Utah, Reva was duly informed, the question was asked of the speaker whether Reva Beck Bosone had any right to be called Judge. Being a lawyer himself, the speaker replied in the positive, assuring them that anyone who has been a judge could use the title. He added that some men who had been on the bench for only a short time used it while Mrs. Bosone, after all, had been a judge for twelve years. Her informant said this reply silenced the women on the subject. (A side effect of the 1949 Press Women's dinner episode in Washington was the rather permanent reference to Reva as " Judge." She couldn't care less, one way or the other.)

Soon after "It's a Woman's World" debuted, the Republican women held a meeting—topic: How to reach the sponsors so the program could be killed. All in the name of politicking—discrediting a possible candidate for Congress in 1954! One could say their deviousness and cunning were well practiced by what was leveled at Reva's unsuspecting sponsors.

One program featured ski clothes and interviews with various ski champions. Jules Dreyfuss, son of the now deceased owner of the Paris Company, supplied the clothes and accompanied the group of skiers to the studio. Dreyfuss watched the program in progress and expressed pleasure with it. Immediately following it, he received an excited call from his store manager saying that a woman had called to report that he should have heard Judge Bosone ridicule the prices of the ski togs she was exhibiting on her show. Quite obviously Dreyfuss reacted to the guttersniping with disgust—the ladies' plan had backfired. But it didn't in every instance!

Each sponsor would receive a call every day of the program. Reva's friend, Dave Romney, phoned to report his disappointment that she should make such an unkind remark about the Utah Symphony Orchestra, of which he was president.

Baffled, she pressed for an explanation. Well, his wife had received a call that Reva Beck Bosone had remarked on her TV show that what the State of Utah needs is the Opera Project, *not* the State Symphony.

"Dave," she protested, how could that be when I said while I was interviewing the director of the Opera Project and two of his students that perhaps Utah could have both! I cited the success of the symphony as an inspiring example and at no time played it down!" To this day she is not sure that Romney believed her, but she knows he certainly could have asked anyone who watched that particular show.

To ease a fraying situation for all, Reva suggested quitting the show—the sponsors should not be harassed by nuisance calls, she told Larsen. But he argued, "Nobody's going to tell me how to run this station! You'll stay. Besides," he added with a grin, "my mother would never forgive me. Your program's one of her favorites." She had been a local radio personality herself and was now in retirement.

So the show continued for several months. The harassment also continued, but there were just so many sponsors and in time they considered the dirty tricks a hazard of the occupation. In retrospect, Reva ponders on the infantile aspects of the partisan scourge, leaving the observer to suspect a telling lack of maturity and character among a group of politically motivated women.

Until her last campaign she could solidly count on the women. As ever present as death and taxes is jealousy, and psychologists admit that women may have a harder time with this fear than men. "Even in my own party," said the Judge, "there were those who jumped on any story that could cast a shadow on me. Women have a tough time reaching high goals in the world—each woman who makes it builds for the next woman who tries. Maybe the daughters of the vindictive women who are so anxious to ruin me may have to face what I did. It won't be easy for them unless it can be shown that women have been worthy of their praise in the past!"

A "spaciousness of spirit" prevails in her philosophy of life, however. "The reason my feet of clay don't extend to my knees, I think," Reva explains, "is that I have high self-respect. I can truly say that I have never been jealous. My mother recognized this early in my life."

To quote Dr. Nyla Cole, associate professor of psychiatry at the University of Utah, from a newspaper article: "The sine qua non of maturity and getting along in the world is being able to allow another person to enjoy something which you are not in a position to enjoy at that time without defensiveness, resentment and competition. Be able to take pleasure in someone else's good fortune and hope you will get the same respect later on in your successes."

The five-month show was terminated on Reva's wishes when she again traveled back to Michigan to be with Zilpha for six weeks after another serious illness.

The ultimate honor for the program was the Zenith Television Award from Chicago for "Excellence in local programming," with a tribute to the Judge for her distinguished service.

THE SUMMER OF 1954—could Reva Beck Bosone ever forget it?

No one would question that politics was Reva's way of life. Even after the mauling and battering of 1952, the possibility of legislating again was a consuming idea; she had accumulated so many plans that could not be forever submerged. So it was really not difficult to be talked into running again for Congress.

After two years Reva believed herself psyched for "come what may!" The heinous smears were behind her—there surely were better ways of combatting them if they should again appear. Issues had changed, situations were different. And she knew a sizable percentage of the Utah public was solidly behind her. But best of all, Zilpha, now a civilian, would be home to lend support while she waited for her husband's tour of duty in Newfoundland to end.

Campaigning on a shoestring (Reva never did have any side pockets of resources), she substituted stamina for dollars and was in a state of perpetual motion. Devoted supporter Walter Anderson worked gratis as her manager. Barney Flanagan left his job in Washington, D.C., to offer his invaluable services and Caroline Perry was the equivalent of her executive secretary—both laboring for no remuneration. Other friends offered their services to make contacts and distribute literature. Reva is fiercely loyal to this type of dedication. Interesting to note is that no volunteer ever made outsize demands of her when she was elected to public office.

The first sex discrimination she ever experienced in a major campaign fell in this period. "It is pretty hard to believe in this day and age that anyone would seriously consider that 'Congressional work is a man's job.' Yet I was told that Rick (Warwick Lamoreaux), my opponent, and his supporters tossed out this expression everywhere they went. They did not attack my record openly. They merely belittled it. But there was no smear, and Rick and I came out of it as friends."

Reva was just not able to appear in every spot in the Second Congressional District, and lavish parties and dinners for important Democrats were above the budget; with no salary coming in there was diligent penny watching. Despite limited funds she topped the nomination vote over Lamoreaux, former member of the Utah House of Representatives and the State Senate, by more than two to one in every district!

But how unfortunate that she won so handily in the primary! The effect was terrifying for the Republican Committee who once again sounded the alarm for their incumbent candidate, Bill Dawson.

"It would have been much better if I'd just squeaked through," Reva recalls. "As it was, the fight was on—the meanest one I can imagine. I don't think any candidate who has ever run for public office has been exposed to more distortions, half-truths, and downright lies!

"Being a non-Mormon had never made any difference up to 1954," said Reva. The Church had always been neutral as far as Reva's campaigns were concerned and she had never regarded it as unfair. "The Church of Latter Day Saints was always good to me. News of the Church's participation in the campaign that year came to me from its members because I was not aware of it. If the Church did participate it was definitely wrong, for one of the great American principles is to keep the church and state separate." But it has been noted that LDS Church conservatism was being strengthened in that period.

Major partisan activity within the Mormon Church over the approximately 150 years since its inception has changed. In 1974 a leader of the faith was asked by a *Salt Lake Tribune* reporter if a good Mormon could be a liberal Democrat and he answered, "I think it would be very hard if he was living the gospel and understood it."

And yet Dr. Stewart Grow, whose doctoral dissertation covered the Utah Commission that supervised early Utah elections, asserts in a report that if early Mormons had followed a political line there is an indication that most of them would probably have become Democrats. Three distinct periods of early political history mark the Mormon community. The pioneers were so isolated that no real political party existed; the Church and politics were connected. In the 1870s a local party trend divided the residents into the Peoples party, basically composed of Mormons, and the Liberal party, mainly non-Mormons. The Peoples party tended toward the Democratic side and the Liberal party toward the Republican, but neither was a real part of the national scene, according to Dr. Grow. Then in the 1890s, as Utah was striving for statehood, all leaders decided that there should be affiliation with the national party lines, which assisted notably in achieving statehood in 1896.

In this 1954 campaign Democrat Bosone soon found herself in a life/death struggle for her career. Incongruities popped up everywhere. One could hear that Bosone was antiminority! Reva greeted this news with open-mouthed amazement—she, who had a record of championing minorities in Congress. Preposterous stories, obviously figments of troubled minds, spread like pollen in a spring hayfield. "When a party has to twist and ridicule the truth, there must be a lack of issues and public record on which the person can be attacked. This consoled me somewhat," Reva offered.

Being a charter member and the first president of the Women's Italian-American Civic League in Salt Lake City and the originator of the All-State Italian Day, Reva was always invited by the league to speak at its annual function, as she was this campaign year. But the Italians who did not attend the affair were called or visited and informed that Reva had refused to be with them this time. A small number of disillusioned voters—but any lie pours its vitriol!

The Women's Legislative Council of Utah County is a large organization of capable women who devote a meeting each campaign to hearing the candidates. Reva attended the session, utilizing her ten minutes in a discussion of the pertinent issues of the Colorado River Project. After driving the forty-five miles back to Salt Lake City, she was called by her friend, the Jewish Rabbi, who claimed he had been told that she had spent her time at the meeting berating Jews. He admitted he found it hard to believe of Reva, but evidently a woman leader in community affairs who had been present at the council meeting dropped into a Provo Jewish business establishment to inform the proprietor that Judge Bosone had really taken after the Jews!

How far could they go? Apparently, much further!

"I'm going to vote the Democratic ticket except for Judge Bosone. She was so mean to her son he became retarded and had to be put in the training school!" was heard in the land of Zion. Reva threw up her hands—ridiculous! They couldn't be serious!

But it *was* serious. It was heard everywhere—an organized smear! Smear, schmear, shock! Overheard by one of her workers was, "Are they trying to send that old drunk back to Congress?" Her charitable work with alcoholics and her involvement with the State Board on Alcoholism—with but a slight variation—was used to confuse her constituents.

She was made to appreciate the old saying—that a half-truth is like a half-brick, more effective because you can throw it further.

Expressions covering the district front: "She never appeared on the floor of the House without being plastered to the gills!" "She gave wild parties in her Washington apartment and got drunkest of the lot!" "The reason she was a leader in education for alcoholism was on account of her son, an alcoholic under treatment in the Provo Sanitarium!" How surprised one district was to learn she had one daughter, no son! And confidante Sunday Anderson discloses, "I have never seen her take a drink!"

Reva fills in, "No member of Congress could accuse me of ever appearing any place in Washington at any time intoxicated," a fact that scarcely needs elaboration, but she presumes there probably was a section of her constituency that was unaware. "I gave one staff dinner in my apartment in the four years I was in Congress," she said. "I was just too busy to go social."

Virginia Rishel relates the story of Reva's visit to her apartment after a devastatingly exhausting day. Flopping into a chair, the congresswoman told her assistant in all seriousness that she felt so tired that perhaps a mild drink would revive her—something like a martini! And Virginia still chuckles over the Judge's inference of the martini's mildness, knowing she had suggested it from a lack of knowledge of the drink's ingredients.

Regarding the "rumor noose," she tells the story of the two friends who met on the street. One said, "I hear there was a fire in your place last week and it did $10,000 damage. Is that true?" "Oh yes," was the reply, "that story is approximately correct. Only it wasn't a fire, it was an explosion. It wasn't $10,000; it was $1,500. And it wasn't last week. It's next week."

Women who had been extremely cordial were baring teeth. The Salt Lake Council of Women had always been an ally of Reva's among organizations in town. But the day Reva was a speaker, a chill wind blew from the audience. Icy tendrils of air worked their way down her back as she was introduced on the podium. Sunday told her later that a woman sitting behind her mumbled to another, "Imagine sending a woman of her reputation back to Congress!"

Another friend of long standing, in fact, since her husband had instructed Reva in high school, admitted she suffered a severe headache every Thursday after a weekly meeting in which she felt obliged to defend Reva from vicious never-ending scuttlebutt. The friend was one not easily subject to headaches.

"The reason for the rash of rumors about me can be summarized, I believe," Reva said, "by analyzing a conversation of two 'anti-Bosones' overheard near an elevator in the Newhouse Hotel about a month before election day. The two agreed that the 'way to whip Bosone is to ruin her name with the women.' That strategy—the desire to win regardless of how—is behind practically all political rumors." To anyone with political ambitions she is quick to caution, "If a person takes a definite stand for or against anything while in public office, there is going to be an 'Anti-Your-Name' society in the hometown."

But an incident of real pathos had the most withering consequences. As the underworld knows that the vulnerability of a marked person is usually through his loved ones—get at the proposed victim through the wife, husband, or children—so did political zealots in this campaign.

The Judge arrived home one evening to find her daughter distraught. Relating what happened, Zilpha said she had answered the phone to hear a woman ask for Mrs. Bosone. After the caller learned she wasn't at home and that she was talking to Reva's daughter, the woman said, "You'll be interested in a program on Kall Radio at 7:30 P.M." And Zilpha thanked the caller whom she remembered as having a sweet voice.

Zilpha switched on the radio at the appointed time and heard a group of women's voices chanting in unison—"Why? Why? Why?" A mistress of ceremonies announced there were many women present who were going to ask questions of *Mrs.* Bosone. Zilpha sat listening, becoming more heartsick by the moment.

"Now, Mrs. Bosone, the women of Utah want to know why . . ." and each voice rehashed the votes in Congress that Reva had explained in the 1952 campaign.

A Dawson newspaper ad utilizing a similar idea set forth in bold type: "But Utah women have been having a look at the FACTS. These facts tell us you have consistently yielded to the pressure of influence groups who would sacrifice the welfare of Utah and of the nation to satisfy their own selfish ends!"

As a consequence of the depraved harassment of her mother, capped by the cold-blooded apprisal by the woman on the phone, Zilpha became permanently alienated from the Utah that had dealt her mother such blows. Witnessing the potent forms of cruelty, pettiness, jealousy, and hate, she grew to loathe this campaign, and it left her with indelible scars. In later years when her mother has suggested her retiring in Utah some day, she is adamant. "Never!" No amount of convincing evidence that thousands of voters remained loyal to her mother has changed her mind.

The notorious radio program had evidently been recorded to be presented Friday before election. Aired at regular intervals frequently throughout the day, Reva was able to hear it herself at home. "After that purge, I was the Red Judge or, at least, the Pink Mrs. Bosone!"

The name of the woman who asked the question, "What about your reputation in Washington, Mrs. Bosone?" was announced as Lavon Brown. Reva caught her breath—could that possibly be "our" Lavon? The youngish voice was incredibly familiar. Reva and Zilpha exchanged a long look. It was true! An added insult to the ever-throbbing hurt of this campaign, mother and daughter recognized the voice as that of the daughter of Ina, a favorite cousin of the Beck family!

Lavon, a former Miss Utah at the Miss America pageant in Atlantic City, who had been featured and highly promoted on Reva's TV show. Lavon, who had assisted in receiving gifts at Zilpha's wedding reception. Lavon, who with her mother had socialized on the most convivial terms with Zilpha and her mother. The same Lavon!

Of course they were aware that Ina and her husband Denzil were strong Republicans. But no one could accuse Reva of being discriminate in her affections because of a party difference. "In a free country with a two-party system," she says, "I have a lot of Republican friends I respect and love."

Denzil Brown had aspired earlier to the state chairmanship of the party but had lost. To prove his loyalty, he and Ina had feted Dawson at a gala affair in the early part of the campaign and now their daughter eagerly worked for Reva's defeat at Dawson's headquarters!

The reward for this backstab was assumed to be a job for Lavon in Bill Dawson's office in Washington. It materialized with Dawson's victory but presumably fell short of the glamour hoped for; Lavon was not long in the nation's capital. But long was her mother Ina's remorse. She continually sought, via a cousin, a visit with Reva, but Reva insisted on a public apology.

And so a few years later Ina died, still asking to see Reva yet still not complying with her request. But Reva, not customarily one to bear a grudge, regrets not having granted Ina's wish.

The ugliest word on the campaign trail—SMEAR—was a constant intruder for Reva in 1954. So many rumors were flying that it was difficult to keep track of them, let alone rebut them. One was so vile, Reva learned, that no one would repeat it to her!

Another of Bill Dawson's misrepresentations concerned Reva's absenteeism at several subcommittee meetings. All congressmen know there is an age-old problem of getting to all committee meetings. Reva was clued at first that the way to get good marks was to touch down at each one (she belonged to seven committees) in the morning to be listed present and then attend full time the one she preferred. She considered this practice—token appearances—a gimmick intended to dupe the voters and she would have none of it. Instead, she was faithful to one committee meeting each morning, the one having a controversial issue or where a vote was to be taken.

Dawson, as a congressman, had to be familiar with committee rounds, that a person can attend only one meeting at a time, but Mr. and Mrs. Joe Doakes back home, ignorant of the legislative process, are easily confused by the workings of Congress. And so, according to Dawson, compared to his attendance record, former Congresswoman Bosone had been shirking her duties!

Of interest is a Dawson quote from the Lehi newspaper: ". . . we must insure the people of Utah that they will have mature legislation in Washington and that Ike and Dick have the dignified, honest, and hardworking Congress that will allow them to clear our nation's Capitol of the the dishonest people who now run our government."

The election was approaching fast, and unbelievably, miraculously almost in spite of "operation smear," Reva's prospects looked promising. On October 16 a news headline showed that "Bosone Takes a 5–4 Lead Over Dawson." Overcoming the hits of her antagonists, she was swinging the trend her way—a great tribute to a dedicated citizen who had always beaten the drum for Utah in the nation. Because of her untainted campaign program, perhaps her public on both sides was realizing the value of integrity.

But about two weeks before election day she and her staff sensed a peculiar change in the atmosphere. "There definitely was a feeling against Bosone, but we couldn't put our finger on it." It was a sort of ambiance of vilification, more powerful than the jabbing smears. This was like nerve gas as compared to tear gas. When Dawson didn't deny, at a prestigious dinner both candidates attended, that there would be a last minute surprise, Reva was immediately leary but she could not sniff out anything as deadly as what transpired.

The day before election a cleverly contrived letter purporting to be from fellow Democrats was widely circulated:

> Fellow Organization Democrat!
> The DEMOCRATIC WORKERS have been pounding the pavements for the PARTY, while BOSONE has been giving the fruits of a Democratic victory to her Republican friends.
> A Democratic Congress set up the U.S. Military Court to handle Veterans' cases—it is composed of FIVE DEMOCRATS AND ONE REPUBLICAN—Bosone worked for and secured one of these appointments for a Republican. The salary of this job is $17,500 per year or $175,000 for the 10-year term. This job was charged to the Democratic patronage of the Second Congressional District of Utah.
> When [Governor] Lee was elected, hundreds of Democrats lost their jobs—. Many O.P.S. jobs were available but Congressman Bosone helped many Republicans get these jobs—while YOU and YOUR FRIENDS, who really elected her, were neither consulted nor considered for these appointments.
> The Democratic party to be successful cannot tolerate that type of candidate who puts her personal ambition above that of the party by giving our opponents the fruits of victory.
> VOTE FOR DEMOCRATS THAT ARE TRUE TO THE PARTY!

That was the clincher! And a gross distortion of a good-hearted deed! The true facts by Reva: "While I was in Congress, a law was passed setting up a Military Court of Appeals. President Truman appointed two of the three judges—a Democrat from New Orleans and one from Rhode Island. By the time I found out about it, he was considering the Republican member.

"George Latimer of the Supreme Court of the State of Utah was among the candidates. When I heard this, I enthusiastically did all I could to swing the appointment for George. If the Democratic spots had been filled, why shouldn't Utah have an appointment, even though Republican?

I'm happy to say that George Latimer was appointed. It was common knowledge in Washington how it all came about."

But the letter insinuating that Reva had become a *traitor to her party* was circulated to every member of the Democratic organization in Utah and to all schoolteachers, erroneously stating that there were *five* Democratic judges to be appointed. A shot in the heart! The damning epistle was signed by two Democratic women. Both are now deceased.

That an affluent party or organization was involved in financing this letter was taken for granted. Sent too late for Reva to obtain adequate TV and radio time for rebuttal, it accomplished its mission. Victim silenced!

Following election day the *Deseret News* ran an editiorial entitled, "Men Worthy of Utah," with the opening sentence, "Utah's voters chose their men well yesterday."

Calvin W. Rawlings, the national committeeman of the Democratic party in Utah, and a Mormon, wrote Reva that "under the circumstances" she had made a wonderful race. The next time she saw him she asked what he meant, to which he replied, "In spite of the activities of the Church," meaning that the strong conservatism of the majority of the LDS membership, as reflected from its high officials, could not help but clash with the more liberal principles of the former congresswoman.

The day after election, Church members who were Democrats kept her phone sizzling with reports of unfair tactics. And when the Democratic State Central Committee met, there ensued a heated discussion by members of the Church on its activity in the campaign.

Typically, defeat did not eat at Judge Bosone, but she took another look at the oppression she had just endured. "It's amusing to look back to my girlhood. I thought people meant what they said and said what they meant. I believed that if a thing were right, people would recognize it and support it. I believed that everyone had sympathy for his fellowman in his sufferings. I believed that every 'nice' person was a good person. And had I remained a schoolteacher, I still would believe in the foregoing, for by nature I am naive. Well, I still want to believe in people.

"My heart went out to my devoted friends—they took defeat so hard. Barney left for Washington the day after election, and when he was about to step onto the train, he turned to me and said, 'I'd rather work for you and have you defeated than for some other candidates and have them elected.' Bless him."

Reva never shed a tear for losing, as usual. But the smear left her with an altered opinion of a certain strata of her fellowmen. From her experiences on the bench and in politics, she says that under the cloak of business, politics, and church, crimes are being committed daily that are as horrendous as those of criminals in penitentiaries.

"And they will continue," she insists, "just as long as people shrug them off with—that's business, or that's politics. It seems to me that our homes and our schools have failed signally in instilling a sense of moral responsibility in these vast areas of endeavor. Otherwise, how do you explain the legends of 'nice' people cheerfully participating in the thousands of crooked deals and brutal character assassinations of each election year?

Job Hunt

EATING HUMBLE PIE would be, in the chronicles of some notables, an unseen chapter. Not so in Judge Bosone's book of experiences. With an open, expansive personality and a view of life to match, she considers the struggle with the stormy putdowns a valuable test of character. And if someone can learn from her humiliation, it was not in vain. The ship of a public life, steered by unselfish motives with ambition, leaves in its wake the inevitable sludge of jealousy, envy, and covetousness. Often one does not realize to what extent this is true until that public career has been terminated suddenly by the constituency and the person is forced to seek another type of employment.

PHOTO: *Being sworn in by Postmaster General J. Edward Day.*

The 1954 campaign and election were in the past for the Judge. Her daughter and son-in-law, houseguests during the Christmas holidays, swathed memories of unhappy times with loving-kindness and the special joys of the season. Never one to dwell on the morose, Reva also was caught up in the spirit of the festivities. But shortly after New Year's, the military couple left Salt Lake City for Arty's new assignment in Duluth, Minnesota.

"It surely isn't easy for a mother to walk into a home alone just after her children have left. It's so empty! But I could not indulge in pity—I have been fortunate in having such a beautiful daughter, now happily married." Looking to the future, Reva planned to resume her law practice and, come summer, vacation in Duluth. And her bevy of friends had already made known their demands on her time.

One day at a social gathering Emily Stewart and her daughter proffered the idea of substitute teaching until she could decide what her long-range plans would be. The teacher shortage had been played up as a real dilemma in newspapers, radio, and television. The Judge felt a lively spark—what a wonderful suggestion! Who cares what people might think about the step-down in status—she had always wanted to wind up her life teaching school and what time could be better than now? Too, the funds she had been able to save from past salaries were diminishing rapidly, and having no retirement to fall back on, immediate employment seemed mandatory.

She made an appointment with Dr. M. Lynn Bennion, superintendent of schools in Salt Lake City, presented him with her record of teaching experience, and expressed her desire to be a substitute (at $10 per day!).

After a silence he remarked, "Of course, it is difficult to fit one in where one's teaching is so limited."

That stab could have dispirited a weaker soul, but Reva proceeded to list the subjects she was qualified to teach and added that three of the largest high schools in the area had requested her speaking services. But reinforcing her first impression, the Judge saw there was simply no rapport—no attempt by the administrator to even pay courtesy to an interviewee with polite conversation—just embarrassing silence.

Why? she pondered. Because she was a controversial Democrat? If the smear was in question, the superintendent knew several of Reva's close friends who could have straightened him out.

This incident tended to be morale deflating, but no one could say the Judge owned a pampered psyche, so, realizing why certain people do certain things, she continued in her search for a job. On a trip to Los Angeles the prospects of involvement with teaching, law, and young people had her applying at the dean's office of the University of California in the hope of becoming a law instructor. The dean of the department was absent from his office on Reva's visit so she submitted a copy of her background to his secretary who was openly enthusiastic after reading it. A young law professor walked by at that moment and the secretary showed it to him with a flattering comment. Glancing at the resumé, he said flippantly "If you want a job, I understand the University of Wyoming is looking for someone," and sauntered away.

Back in Salt Lake City, Reva learned that her friend Myrtle Austin anticipated resigning from her position as dean of women at the University of Utah. Other friends thought the Judge might be interested in filling the upcoming vacancy, so she contacted Dean Austin who revealed that it was indeed an interesting job but hardly challenging enough for her political friend. Looking at the job from another perspective, Reva believed it just might be suited to her—toned down, certainly, and low key compared to political life, but nonetheless an opportunity in a field close to her heart.

In congressional days she had always been at the disposal, if humanly possible, of A. Ray Olpin, President of the University of Utah, whenever he was in Washington and solicited consultation with her. Once when he asked to see her, she informed him that her only available moment in the day's packed schedule would be at ten o'clock that evening in her apartment. He accepted this generosity and appeared at the set time. So, after an intensely pressured day, Reva listened as President Olpin detailed his particular problems in Utah.

Now perhaps he could be at her service in her earnest search for a job. On her first and second phone calls to his office he was not in. On the third, he told her he was so occupied that an appointment with him would be impossible. She could talk to someone else if she wanted.

Far from being proud, the Judge visited the department and was interviewed by an assistant to the president. After the required background and qualifications were presented, she again expressed her love for teaching and her desire to work with and advise young women.

"But Judge Bosone," the man uttered, "you would have to be able to interview" (which is comedic relief now but was definitely not at the moment).

She applied to several law schools; if she received an answer at all it was to notify her of no vacancy. One exception cheered her—the dean of the Denver University Law School wrote a kind letter explaining his regret that there was no opening, for "you certainly are qualified." She declared, "Finally someone admitted it!"

A friend's comment on job hunting came to mind; the woman had held a high state position and lost it with the change in administration. In her quest for a new position she concluded that one should have an ordinary background, not an outstanding one, in order to succeed. Analyzing her own brushes with men employers, the Judge makes a judgment: "An employer who has the security of his own intelligence and capabilities has no fear in hiring someone with an unusual background."

In all her experiences, one of the most chilling occurred during this unsettled period of her life. There has never been a time when the Judge has not had time for students; in fact, she has usually given them priority. As a member of Congress she stressed to Virginia Rishel that young people would always have an audience with her, if at all possible. So in keeping with this policy in later years in other capacities, she was still happy to assist them if they asked.

One evening in the autumn of 1956 a University of Utah student phoned the Judge asking for an appointment to discuss her political campaign of 1954 about which he was writing a paper for his class. Reva set a time, and the military veteran, about twenty-eight or thirty years of age, appeared at her home shortly after and showed her a printed copy of a report of her campaign she had not known existed. She was repelled to read lie after lie in this summation written by the student's professor. She figured the professor knew it was untrue or he would have mailed her a copy, which is accepted procedure in such cases.

Step one was to point out the glaring errors and correct the record for the student, who was taking notes. As she was scrutinizing the report, he sauntered over to her chair and knelt beside it as though trying to read what she was reading. Then he said, "Judge Bosone, you're a most attractive woman." Taken aback, she chose to toss off the remark lightly and change the subject quickly. Old enough to be his mother, she was puzzled over a silly compliment from a student who had a wife and baby.

Other than the foolish comment, the conversation went well. He asked for another appointment to check a rough draft of his paper with her. The Judge was anxious to keep the professor's distorted report but the student promised that he would bring another.

About a week later he showed up at her home for his second appointment with said rough draft. Reva inquired about his wife and baby, but he answered that they had left him. The air seemed to thicken. He then asked her after a brief conversation about the paper to go for a drive with him to get a cup of coffee, to which she replied that she didn't drink coffee at night. Well, then, would she like to just go for a drive, which of course she wouldn't. Her guard was rising as his expression became more intense. Doing some mental squirming at this point, she was trying to line up ways to usher him out!

He then asked for a glass of water; she saw no harm in obliging him this favor—she could gain time to think. But he followed her into the kitchen, and as she was filling the glass she noticed his eyes shifting to the various doors. At that moment, panic took hold. He was tall and husky;

she was tall but had no preponderance of muscle nor athletic prowess to fend him off. Alone with him in the house, she was in a totally vulnerable position.

One of the better stocks-in-trade of the political professional is the ability to think under stress and Judge Bosone has been blessed in her career with a phenomenal sense of timing. Opportunely, it didn't desert her.

"My two nephews who live here should be home at any moment," she blurted out. "They're a bit late. They study at the "U" library."

The young man could not hide his surprise—evidently contemplation of this eventuality was furthest from his mind. Drinking the water, he returned to the living room and she hurried his departure. Locking the door after him she fell limp into a chair, feeling the ravages of fright!

Certainly if he had attempted rape she would have had him arrested, and to clear himself he would have alleged that she was receptive to his advances. A fantastic story for the opposition in her public constituency! And what a sullied reputation she would be left to cope with! Family and friends would never swallow it but her adversaries would not only swallow it but would swish it around in the mouth like fine wine!

It did seem as though the would-be lothario could have been put up to arranging such a tryst. Unreal, grotesque—but the pieces seemed to fit.

Apparently indomitable, the student called again to say his report was completed and that he would like to drop it by that evening. The Judge, sustaining her cool, informed him that she would not be at home but he could prop it by the mailbox. It was never left and she inferred that he planned on meeting her again in person. But she never saw him again or his final draft.

A year later, when she was a member of Senator John Carroll's staff in Washington, Reva received a letter from the professor-author of the offensive printed campaign report, asking a favor. Surprises never ceased! Posthaste she conveyed to him her shock that a man of his reputation would sign his name to such flagrantly false propaganda about her! In equal posthaste, he answered that he had put the report away and never intended to use it again. It was the same as an apology, but the Judge views the incident with revulsion and contempt.

LAMENTING her anxiety in job hunting was not her way—friends were not encumbered with her woes. Of necessity she pursued her law practice, trying to strengthen it to a point of profitable return. Regarding those years following the smear, Lynn Cohne Arent commented, "I don't think people ever realized what it did to her financially."

One particular event added extra purpose and meaning to her life; she received a phone call from Zilpha and Arty in Michigan one early morning to tell her they had adopted a baby boy, named Timothy Peter. Always of the conviction that adoptive parents rate high esteem and praise, Reva was as ecstatic as the new mother and father. In fact, after the phone call, to keep from exploding with happiness she stepped out in the back yard, set her resonant voice at "loud," and literally announced to her devoted neighbors on either side, Hazel Wach and Gladys Wagstaff, that she was a grandmother!

A few years later Zilpha and Arty adopted another baby—a beautiful girl named Christy Amanda Zilpha. Both times the parents and the grandmother felt the same emotional stirrings. "Nothing can equal birth by adoption," Reva beams. "I couldn't love my own blood grandchildren more!"

In the political arena she was always on call to help. The national election year of 1956 drew the enormous Bosone energy for the Harriman-for-president campaign, and Reva led the action locally. Failing to gain the nomination, W. Averell Harriman, governor of New York, wrote in August: "Now the Convention is over I want to tell you how grateful I am for the very effective work you did for me during my campaign and at Chicago. I will always be proud and honored that I was your choice for the highest office in our land and that you were willing to put in so much time and effort on my behalf."

He avowed the pleasant association they had had. "Your support and friendship have meant much to me. Let's keep in touch, and continue to work together for the things we believe in."

Three long years of challenges of another kind were straining her ever present optimism. The accumulation of all the "don't-call-us, we'll-call-you"'s put her in what she describes as a low valley. There was no chance of her becoming a misanthrope, but the rejections, creating a standstill, were galling! Being a woman of faith, she prayed that God would take her by the hand and lead her.

Very suddenly one night in early January 1957 the Judge decided to fly to Washington. A longtime friend, Mrs. Dorothea Merrill Dryer, and her husband had given her access to their townhouse, when vacant, which now was an invitation that Reva was happy to accept. A Republican administration was in office and possibilities for employment, Reva assumed, were remote, but she felt that she was being directed to the nation's capital.

Within a few days she met Senator John Carroll of Colorado in the Capitol who benevolently offered her a job in his office until she could find a position of her choice. She accepted but was bewildered to find that her duties consisted of answering calls, greeting visitors, and keeping the scrapbook!

Utah evidently had no monopoly on insecure "superiors." The decision to keep the Judge in her place, she reasoned, was that of the administrative assistant. Whenever anyone stopped by the office to see the Judge, this man would make a demand such as, "Bosone, I need the scissors! Will you get them for me?" Her visitors sat openmouthed.

She was never consulted about a legal or legislative subject or asked her opinion about reclamation or Indian affairs on which she had much expertise and on which the Carroll legislative assistant worked. At one time a secretary even grabbed some mail out of her hands because the Judge had made a few marks on it as she customarily did in her own House office. The presswomen wondered why she endured the indignity. But not having a crystal ball she was unable to see her future's outline. And a paycheck was necessary!

Not understanding the shabby treatment she was receiving, the Judge finally suggested to Senator Carroll that she leave. "I never said why I should leave," she said. "I figured he could see why. But he was good enough to advise that I remain until I found a position, for which I was grateful." And one presumes she must have wondered why she was being guided to this form of nemesis.

She could take heart in the continual expression from her loyalists back home, however, in their warm homecoming receptions. On a trip in 1958 the Salt Lake City Airport boasted fifty cheering fans to greet her. And in those moments, who cares about the ungraciousness of the world.

Then in May a genial former colleague in the House, Roy W. Wier, congressman from Minneapolis, wanted her as legal counsel for a permanent subcommittee of the House Education and Labor Committee he was then organizing. This opportunity came none too soon and Reva became her own boss, glad to get away from the supercilious attitude of the Colorado senator's underlings. It was a job with stimulus, and she enjoyed the renewed motivation until her duties were terminated with Wier's defeat in 1960.

Again the Judge was in the marketplace for a job. A logical appointment for the assistant secretaryship in the Interior Department the year of the incoming Democratic administration of 1960 would have been Reva Beck Bosone. Here was a position for which she believed she was highly qualified. Stewart Udall had become the new secretary of interior, always considered a man's province, and Reva was keenly aware that a woman had never filled the position of assistant. But surely there had never been a woman more equipped to occupy the spot, a view shared by congressional colleagues Clair Engle, Eugene McCarthy, Robert Bartlett, and David King, among others. John Murdock, former chairman of the House Interior Committee, pushed laboriously for her in this behalf, as did good friend Senator Wayne Morse.

"But finally I knew there was no chance," she sighed. "This was made clear when I heard that Mrs. Udall stated that a woman's place is in the home!" David King, congressman from Utah, told her that Udall indicated he favored young men for the top jobs in the Department of the Interior. The other job Reva aspired to, commissioner of Indian Affairs, wasn't offered, either.

Another low valley for the Judge! Knowing that she had pursued every channel to find her niche in Washington, she resolutely decided to face west and return to Salt Lake City to take on the practice that her brother Horace had abandoned to become a city judge.

This proposed move incited a flurry of complaints among the Utahn's friends. Barney Flanagan, a constant champion of the former legislator, believed there was yet another area she should pursue. He sympathized with her disappointment in the unsuccessful quest of the Interior post but wrote her that she was a natural for the Health, Education and Welfare Department where Senators Herbert Lehman and Abraham Ribicoff and Mrs. Eleanor Roosevelt, among others, recognized her a leader in the field of social and educational matters. In those areas she would not have to "surmount the obstacle of being a woman, I know it makes you mad to be denied positions just because you wear dresses, but going back to Salt Lake City is not going to change that one little bit." And he lectured, "Now, don't throw away a lifetime of effort just because some folks who wear long pants say you do not belong in their ball park."

And he chided that when the opportunities started rolling (Kennedy's progressive thinking in social areas would soon be tangibly felt with great changes, some believed), where would she be? In Salt Lake in "that house that Virginia and I are again considering hitting with a tornado?" The McClelland Street abode had received some good-natured razzing—the Judge, with sentimental attachment, had hung on to the homestead too long, according to her cohorts!

During this period, others of Reva's supporters were unhappy about the possibility of losing her from Potomac country. To the inquiry, "How about the treasurer's job?" she repined, "Huh, no challenge in that!"

The Senator Frank E. Moss office then asked permission to send her background material to Postmaster General J. Edward Day. Reva objected strongly at first, aware of nothing in that department that would suit her talents or desires. They persisted and she finally acceded, but she expected nothing.

In a few days the Moss office reported that Lou Doyle, general counsel of the Post Office Department, sought an interview. According to the Judge, there was immediate rapport between them, and Doyle recommended her for the two-pronged position—judicial officer of the Post Office Department and chairman of the Contract Board of Appeals (she had not known the latter existed prior to their meeting). Subsequently, the Moss office informed her that Postmaster General Day requested a meeting with her.

"What a welcome and wonderful atmosphere I walked into when I entered the office of General Day. In the middle of the interesting interview I said it sounded as though he was offering me this exceptional position. He replied, 'Yes, I am, and I hope you'll take it.' "

She surmised he was curious about her age, an immemorial unmentionable, when he asked, " Judge Bosone, how's your health?"

"Well, General Day," she answered, "I have all my own teeth."

Settling back in his swivel chair, he laughed, "You'll need 'em!" Enjoying his easy, relaxed manner, Reva saw a man "with the security of his own intelligence." And to her great interest, she learned later that a member of his family, an aunt, had distinguished herself as a medical doctor.

As usual, Reva has never known the salary of a new job until it was accepted. Her first inquiries were about selecting her secretary and obtaining a parking place. But it fired up her ego to learn that the salary was skyscraping compared to that denied her at the University of Utah. And ego-warming was the fact that she would be the highest ranking woman in the United States Post Office. With 709,000 employes, 107,000 of them women, it comprised the largest civilian department of government. And a third ego-warmer—the high echelon of the Post Office Department had always been sized up strictly as a man's bailiwick!

Having never knocked down any walls for the sake of showing up or rescinding the power of men, Reva had been shunted and shamed in her efforts just to contribute. Those who sought to humiliate her had never succeeded in lancing her self-confidence, however. She kept faith in that invincible product—Reva Beck Bosone. And now the rejections were being reversed into a glorious victory. As one newspaper labeled her, she held forth as the "First Postal Lady."

The office of judicial officer had been created by Congress just a few years earlier. Judge Bosone's role was in the final appeals; her legal decisions were written on the entire record of a case, as would be those of a state supreme court justice. In other words a woman had the last word.

If the words Post Office Department dredge up an image no more colorful than gray to slate, the Judge's newly acquired duties tended to dispel the notion. Her decisions were pronounced on a wide range of appealed cases. Besides violations of the second-class mail regulation, fraud and obscenity cases were prominent on the agenda and lively subjects they were indeed. A fifteen-page departmental decision was prepared on a fraudulent scheme for the sale of a breast developer. Among other decisions issued were those on obscene magazines, a falsely represented sexual device, and a circular advertising bawdy phonograph records and nude male photographs; and once again Reva's judgments were called upon to deal with human frailty. Her position did not require her to sentence the violators but to inhibit the mail and have it marked fraudulent. The Justice Department adjudicates the most flagrant cases, where a federal judge can fine and/or jail the defendant.

The basis of a typical case would involve the complainant charging the respondent with conducting a fraudulent scheme by obtaining remittances of money through the mail by means of fake and fraudulent pretenses, representations, and promises. Reva also rendered decisions in matters of whether the appellant constituted a certain organization as claimed, for instance, thereby entitling such organization to a second-class permit for mailing privileges. Often many months were required to form a decision on a case.

The Judge brought to the job her usual poise and that certain reserve that proved her aptitude. Back in congressional days when she had spent time on the Select Committee on Current Pornographic Material, she felt compunction to hide certain lascivious photos so the eyes of her office staff would not be accosted. (But a former staff member admitted that Reva wasn't able to hide them all that well!)

She wrote her former congressional committee crony, Clair Engle, that she was surprised she liked to write legal opinions. "I find it most interesting and sometimes refreshing to keep my nose in the law books." And she was apparently handling the facts of her cases adroitly. "It was a great thrill last Friday," she added in her letter, "when I found that my second decision had been affirmed by the federal court."

Aside from in-office research and decision making, she served as Postmaster General Day's emissary to various conclaves throughout the country. In July of her first year she represented her boss at the Girl Scouts assemblage at Button Bay, Vermont, presenting the commemorative stamp address. In referring to that momentous occasion, the Judge finds difficulty in describing it; certainly, it was startling for pure numbers—10,000 senior girl scouts, 1700 leaders, approximately 250 girl scouts from foreign countries, and 20,000 visitors. Another commemorative stamp ceremony in which she substituted for General Day was sponsored by the General Federation of Women's Clubs and took place at the Plaza Hotel in New York City.

In the Far West, post office dedication ceremonies in Utah (Santaquin, Provo, Grantsville, Wellington, Nephi, Lehi, Honeyville, and Salt Lake City) and Colorado were enriched by her timely message, always delivered in a rich contralto voice. Since no training is ever wasted, one could guess the Judge siphoned from her earlier oratorical experience to visibly sway her audiences. Those in rural areas were given the same direct, sincere discourse as the urban dwellers. Having hailed from the most countrified atmosphere, she claims there is no more important sense than horse sense, and there is an abundance of that in grass roots communities.

A reputation for originality and bouyancy popularized her as a guest of honor about Washington. As in her congressional days, with her social life as well as with her professional career she put forth a greater measure of effort than was expected. Whether she was at the piano accompanying a singing group, regaling an audience with a precise imitation of a political figure, or just conversing, Reva interposed color. Clinton McKinnon, a friend from congressional times, wrote that she always had a way of putting zip into everything. Her insatiable affair with life could make a "happening" out of any occasion she attended.

The honors and the slights have been interspersed in the Judge's life, with the contrasts the deepest in the 1960s. A booklet compiled in 1966 by a governor's committee (of women) entitled "Women in Utah" omitted any mention of Reva Beck Bosone, and she was ignored by the University of Utah when Law Dean Samuel D. Thurman submitted her name in 1968 for a Distinguished Alumni award. Stinging, to say the least, but certainly overpowered by the crowning recognition by the University of California at Berkeley, celebrating its Centennial Year, of thirty-nine of its most distinguished alumni, among whom was Reva Beck Bosone. The ceremony was documented in a history of the university, *There Was Light,* edited by Irving Stone, with a chapter contributed by each honored alumnus. Reva, representing the field of government, was one of four women so honored.

"The book is a portrait of America from the time Lillian Gilbreth was graduated in 1900, the year Rube Goldberg entered, to Robert Douglas Haas III, a fourth-generation graduate in 1964," to quote Mr. Stone. The Berkeley commemoration was held in April 1970, the year this compilation of fascinating essays was published, a "labor of love" that occupied Mr. Stone for eighteen months.

Garff Wilson, a member of the Centennial Publishing Committee for that event, earlier (in 1965) had invited his former drama teacher to be his guest at his production of the Greek classic, *Antigone,* at the university in Berkeley.

In thanking Dr. Wilson for his hospitality, she wrote of another honor that had come to her.

> Within a week after Supreme Court Justice Goldberg resigned, I received a long distance call from Utah saying that there was a movement going on to have me considered for the vacancy left by Goldberg. Well, it was a tremendous movement—grassroots and unbeknown to me. This thrilled me no end. The President and the United States Attorney General were bombarded with wires and phone calls

from my friends in Utah. Later I understood that one couldn't turn on
the TV or the radio out there without hearing the announcement that
friends of Judge Reva Beck Bosone should wire or call the President
and the U.S. Attorney General in her behalf. Of course, I knew there
was no chance of my getting this position. The great thrill and
satisfaction came in knowing how all my friends in Utah were again
showing their faith in me and their loyalty.

I think this is the second time that a woman has been considered
for a vacancy on the Supreme Court of the U.S. Judge Florence Allen
of Ohio at one time was considered. She was a distinguished judge. It
was a wonderful thing to have my name in the pot. Abe Fortas was
appointed. I know him. He was a very fine appointment.

In the summer of the same year, the Judge, as honor guest of a grand
fete in Utah staged at the home of Governor Calvin L. Rampton, piped,
"I've had my funeral! Now all that has to be done is dump me in the
ground without any ceremony whatsoever. You know, it's pretty nice to
smell the flowers and hear the wonderful things said while you are still
alive."

More than 500 Utahns came by that Sunday afternoon in veneration
of the tall, spunky daughter from American Fork who "lends dignity to
our state." Reminded of a remark by a Westminster College girl friend:
"We have to look up to you whether we want to or not," Reva noted that
those happy folks not only had to but wanted to!

"I've been blessed. I've just been enormously blessed!" could be the
quote of her life.

In the post office position, with a set vacation time, Reva indulged in
some private overseas travel. A visit in England with Zilpha and Arty, stationed there, and their two children was the cynosure of the 1962 summer
for Reva. The grandmotherly type, she wrote Christy and Timothy at
Christmas:

> I have a feeling that Santa Claus is going to be very good to you
> both on Christmas per usual. I cannot wait to see what he leaves you
> and what reactions you have. Be sure to be very good so that he
> doesn't change his mind or get mixed up and leave your presents at
> some other home . . .
>
> Timothy, honey, right after Christmas I want you to write me a
> long letter and tell me all about what happened for I shall be anxious-
> ly waiting. I wish I were to be with you on Christmas Eve and
> Christmas morning but you live too far away and it is a bit expensive.
> It won't be too long, though, before you are in America and Grandma
> can be with you in spirit. Now where do you think my spirit should sit
> at the breakfast table Christmas morning? You just imagine that I am
> with you and that you two are arguing where I am to sit. Do you want
> to know something? I just loved that argument because it flattered
> Grandma to know that each of you wanted me to sit beside you.

Then a summer tour with Zilpha and Virginia Rishel to the southern countries of Europe rounded out the busy year of 1963. Reva has a thankful heart that she was able to do that much sight-seeing because in 1965 the creeping robber, glaucoma, began to appear.

In 1966 the first debilitating effects of insidious cataracts were exacting a toll. Besides that, incorrect medication causing grievous side effects with periods of intense suffering put her life in jeopardy. Consulting another medical opinion just in time, she pulled out of the physical slide, but she is in the 5 percent of cataract victims for whom surgery is not entirely successful.

Her last public speech as judicial officer was ad-libbed at an Equal Employment Opportunity in Postal Service Conference before several hundred top level post office employes who had convened from all over the United States at the Presidential Arms in Washington. The ovation, when she completed her speech, booms in her memory today—five bows were necessary to still the clapping hands. She felt the accolades that day could launch her imminent retirement on a smooth sea.

On January 20, 1968, she did manage her departure from the judicial post and entered private life with its varying demands. Postmaster General Lawrence F. O'Brien, succeeding John A. Gronouski, succeeding J. Edward Day, was adamant that a party would be the fitting tribute for the Judge, even though she hedged on encouraging any observation of her retirement. And although a friend claimed Reva generally has the last word, on this day O'Brien was the winner. The department reception room was full to capacity and resounded with tributes. Her secretary, Mrs. Ida Miller Hines, assured her she would never have another boss like her!

Wishing her happiness, each man kissed her as he walked through the reception line even though he may have just been introduced. Surprised by this extra show of approbation, Reva decided it was the only way to be retired!

The *Salt Lake Tribune* editorialized on January 19, 1968:

> Retirement is a difficult step to take when the person involved is being nagged by apprehensions of things being left uncompleted. Fortunately for Utah's Reva Beck Bosone, who leaves public office Saturday after 40 years of service, there need be no such anxiety.
>
> During a long and distinguished career, Mrs. Bosone has contributed lasting accomplishments to the fields of law, government and public affairs in general. She has helped expand the scope of human understanding and women's role in a democratic society.
>
> Throughout her adult life, Mrs. Bosone, a Utah native, has successfully demonstrated the leadership capacity a woman can bring to matters of public concern. She practiced law, served in Utah's state

legislature and became a Salt Lake City municipal judge at a time when such functions were still generally considered "for men only."

Further, she was the first woman member of Utah's congressional delegation, serving two terms from 1948 to 1952. Her precedent-setting achievements continued as she rose to be judicial officer in the U.S. Post Office Department, highest position ever held in the department by a woman.

As City judge, Mrs. Bosone worked for rehabilitation of alcoholics during a period when drunkenness was classified as more of a crime than an illness. Her vision in this regard helped change public attitudes and official policy here and nationally.

Retirement is not the end of Mrs. Bosone's public involvement. She intends to volunteer her energies to "benefit my fellow man." It does afford an opportunity to formally sum up her unique past record, allowing Utahns and other friends across the country to express their sincere respect for 40 years of top quality service.

Varying Demands

RETIREMENT! What does it all mean? Dimming vision has forced her to quit the consuming professional life; in spite of surgery her eyes have given her the pink slip. Ideas still fly about in her mind with the frequency of popping corn. Vitality of that force can never be suppressed; the intellect, the conscientiousness are intact. And so the wise among her friends and acquaintances have learned to take advantage of her more relaxed schedule to importune her to make speeches and plan proposals.

PHOTO: *At retirement ceremony with former Postmaster General Day and Postmaster General Lawrence O'Brien.*

Lazy days are nonexistent! Dwelling in the past is indulged in only on dark days—dark in the sense of when she is bedded by the flu or forced inside by extended inclement weather.

With sufficient eyesight to read well-defined letters with specially prescribed glasses, she has built up a correspondence with several hundred people to a labor of love of tremendous magnitude. Using a heavy black felt-tipped pen on typing paper, she writes boldly on straight lines, flipping the bottom of the page over to start at the top on the other side.

Her rhetoric leans on the chatty side, as though she is asking the recipient to pass the coffee and Danish, please. A word of thanks, a witticism, or a compliment wins the reader's affection at the outset, then a comment on the political scene or a topic of current interest adds the punch. Diversity of those interests is apparent:

> I'm for the Equal Rights Amendment as much for the men as I am for the women. Many men get a rotten deal in this life.

> I just don't know how people with large families are eating. A friend of mine in California said he all but blew up when he had to pay 39 cents a pound for potatoes.

> Last week I was so burned up with Congress wanting to pass a pay raise bill, I called several Members and talked to their chief of staff and did I say what I thought!

> Broadcaster Howard K. Smith is a great man!

> I'm for the universities recognizing informal education and have advocated this for a long time. Years ago the biggest dam in the world was built in India. The chief engineer from the United States had no degree in engineering; he was an eighth grade graduate. I thought he should be able to apply to a university for a degree in engineering and receive it after presenting his history of accomplishment. What difference does it make how one gets his education as long one gets it? Schools are often repulsive to minds of originality.

> I have tremendous respect for the acting profession. We need surcease from the strain of living.

> Some nursing homes are unbelievable! There have been some terrible cases of neglect and fires around here.

> I think Judge Florence Allen who was born in Utah was the greatest woman lawyer in the United States. Her life history is stimulating— she had a hard time getting admitted to a law school. In her life I believe she received 23 honorary degrees. It was I who asked Dean Myrtle Austin of the "U" to propose her name for an honorary degree. Judge Allen was a dear friend of mine and should have

landed on the U.S. Supreme Court. When she was 72 a group of us women in Washington, D.C., proposed her name but her age stopped her.

[After hearing of the vast sums collected by congressmen for speech-making around the country] I accepted very few speech invitations when I was in Congress and to this day I have never charged a fee for making a speech. Oh yes, my expenses were paid. In Kansas when I spoke at a Unitarian Church they offered me the usual honorarium and when I refused it they were surprised.

And all her letters are basted with down-home exclamations. Advice, rarely given, is always packed with cotton—"I believe I would do" thus and so. So after reading a Bosone letter, one feels satisfied as though the refreshment was well digested.

But if her ire is ever aroused, watch it! Senator Sam Ervin, before he gained Watergate Committee prominence, sponsored his version of H. J. Res. 208—Equal Rights Amendment. It played up the physiological or functional differences between men and women. To Judge Bosone this warped excuse never fails to light a fuse. She shot off a letter to the southern senator.

Just what do you mean "physiological or functional differences?" Are you referring to menstrual periods and menopause? You men certainly go through a menopause. My long life's experience would not attach significance to these in determining one's ability to function in a field of endeavor that a man or woman chooses. The decision should be up to the individual man or woman. Believe me, there is no difference.

And the senator replied with a letter sent to objectors of his resolution that was just another explanation of his views, which only succeeded in causing more consternation for Reva. Telling him he really knew better than to justify such discrimination with his physiological (or is it psychological) differences, she jostled his reasoning with a gram of his own medicine.

"Maybe what is wrong with this country is that too many men are going through the menopause." And she needled, "I just cannot imagine a man of your stature using such ridiculous reasoning." Then in conclusion, "Women only want to be people—that is all."

But other letters yielded softer responses. Marion G. Romney, Second Counselor in the First Presidency of the LDS Church, writing in 1974, brought a tender smile from the Judge. "Hearing from you reminded me of three things—law school days, Utah House of Representative days, and my practice when you were on the City bench. It has been a long time ago, but those experiences are very dear to me."

Dallin H. Oaks, president of Brigham Young University, was appreciative when he wrote in 1972: "You may be interested to know that I was one of the first to benefit from your efforts in the Air Force ROTC; I was a member of the first class enrolled in the Air Force ROTC program at BYU, where I was a student from 1950 thru 1954. I clearly recall your fine service in Congress during that time."

Harold B. Lee, former president of the LDS Church, now deceased, whose wife is a Soroptimist sister of the Judge, had been a long-time friend of Horace Beck and Reva Bosone when he wrote in 1972: "We have respected you because of your ability, because of the service you have rendered not only to the city and state but also in the Congress of the United States."

One bitter episode in Reva's political life was not enough over the years to whittle away her keen respect for the LDS Church's major accomplishments and many of its distinguished leaders.

Almost daily a memory of President George Albert Smith passes through Reva's mind. "One of my Mormon friends told me he is trying to convert me!" she smiles. "But he never did talk his religion to me. He loved me no matter what I believed—he loved people. Oh, if we had a world full of President Smiths and Pope Johns!"

A TIDY HOUSE now, as always, is tantamount to peace of mind. Reva quotes her mother, "If you will keep in mind what is important and what isn't, you will amount to something." Mrs. Beck insisted on the kitchen, the closests, and the bathrooms being kept sanitary. Dust wasn't as bothersome. In other words, graffiti in the dust on the coffee table was more excusable than a mildewy clothes closet or a spattered kitchen cabinet. But Reva, being fond of stirring up the nest, irons with gusto and dusts with a flourish. Her Washington, D.C., friends refuse to believe that she is now engrossed in a goodly number of daily domestic chores.

At other times in her so-called retirement, she may be attempting to shorten a convict's allegedly undeserved confinement at a state prison. Or she may be giving her ideas on handling alcoholics to a municipal judge who has requested them. Another day she may be formulating plans for a World Conference of Leading Women to discuss remedies for explosive population—which she has considered for more than thirty years to be the world's number one problem—or pollution, or war. She boosted the idea of a survey of natural resources in order to protect the well-being of future generations. This survey was adopted by the eminent organization, the Washington Forum, composed of thirty outstanding women in business and government, of which the Judge served as the second president.

Reva has busied her herself as a member of the National Board of Women's Medical College of Pennsylvania—the first appointed from Utah, she believes—serving for twenty-five years. She involved herself with the SIR Club (Statesmen Involuntarily Retired), the purpose of which is "To keep the camaraderie of former members as it once was, to reminisce, to express opinions on important issues before the Congress, and if thought advisable, to lend the influence of the group to support important programs." Reva was chosen its first chairman.

Or on the domestic scene Reva may be having a heart-to-heart with the family pet dog, Tor, a rare Hungarian Vizsla, who has an affinity for the Judge's pens—they offer just the right amount of resistance for his sharp teeth. So lanky that he is fond of resting his front paws on a sitting person's shoulders, he has been with the family for years. In fact, there has seldom been a period in Reva's life when a dog hasn't figured prominently, either professionally or privately. "If there are no dogs in heaven, then I don't want to go there," she insists.

In 1937, which was soon after Reva became a judge, a brindle bulldog, Tiger, was exonerated in a sentimentally publicized case in Salt Lake City. It seems that Tiger had attacked the dog next door and the victim's master had brought suit. The Judge keeps an image to this day of that underslung-jawed dog sitting inside the bar awaiting sentence.

Tiger, after investigation, however, was found to be ordinarily gentle and loving. (Perhaps provocation had a lot to do with his burst of temperament?) Well, his master received a few admonitions and Tiger was let go free, last seen by the Judge sniffing his way out of the Public Safety Building thirty-eight years ago!

In these more leisurely years, there's time for fudge! Though not taking easily to the role of chef, Reva slings very tasty fudge, her favorite food! In fact, it could be a specialty of the House of Bosone (and modesty is not featured here). "I make the best fudge you ever ate!" she declares.

There's time, too, as there always has been, for giving just dues—like the glowing letter she wrote about an accommodating postwoman; the postmaster tacked it on the office bulletin board and also sent it to the regional office, which, in turn, proffered the postwoman an award. Needless to say, the surprised recipient, who was making a living for her four children, had a great day because a letter of appreciation was written.

Commendations in recent years have taken the Judge to her hometown. The first Annual Susa Young Gates (an early women's liberationist) Birthday Party in March 1973 drew Reva to Salt Lake City as a guest of honor and for an honorary membership in the local group of the Utah Women's Political Caucus, the sponsoring organization.

One of several books in which Reva has found her life capsulated in print in a most positive manner is the engrossing *A Minority of Members: Women in the U.S. Congress,* by Hope Chamberlin. In an earlier recognition she, with eight other women in the United States, was given special attention on the cover of *Ladies of Courage,* written by Eleanor Roosevelt and Lorena Hickok.

In her element that day in May, Reva stood at the Westminster College dais in merciless sunlight, hatless and scriptless, pouring forth to the 1974 graduates her story and counsel, which expanded from a twenty-minute speech to an almost hour-long epic. She was tickled to speculate that the standing-room-only status in the area of the stadium set aside for the ceremonies was attributable in part to her presence. Memorable is the quip of student Mary Wilson, the intermediary between the college and the Judge in Kansas, who informed the audience in introducing her for an honorary Doctor of Humanities degree that the former congresswoman attributed the important decisions in her life to temper, "which may lead one to believe that her temper was triggered very often!"

In September 1974 Reva attended the dedication of the Living Fountains at the Truman Memorial Library in Independence, Missouri. She met again Major General Donald S. Dawson, who had served as the late president's administrative assistant. "I was thrilled to see his instant recognition of me," she said modestly. "I had many contacts with him, but just think, that was twenty-two years ago!" She is always naively pleased to discover she is "rememberable."

John McCormack remembers and told his friend from Utah in 1975, "In my years in Congress, with thirty years of leadership in the House, you were one of the great members I served with."

Judge Bosone entertained "her boys" at a lavish luncheon buffet, complete with sentiment and nostalgia, in the Sky Room atop the Hotel Utah in April 1975. Fourteen former members of the Salt Lake City Police Department who had served when the woman magistrate presided talked of old times, current doings, and the future's prospects. At one large table in the glass-enclosed room overlooking the valley, the members of the party—all past seventy—relived earlier exploits on the force with a judge who always had their respect. Former Police Chief L. C. Crowther commented, "We need more like her now."

In the fall of 1975 Reva was overwhelmed by her selection as one of the ten outstanding mothers in the history of Utah! Chosen as one to represent Utah in a bicentennial publication titled *Famous Mothers in*

American History 1776–1976, she deems this an unusual honor in the Mormon state.

A colorful documentary on Reva was broadcast by KUTV, Channel 2, NBC, to five western states in February 1977 and again in June of that year.

And she is still chalking up "firsts." In 1977 she became an honorary member of the Order of Coif, the first and only woman so honored by the University of Utah College of Law.

On her visits back home the invitations inundate her, many of them from the "slaves" of her campaigns! One of those, sidekick Sunday Anderson, a former state legislator herself, chirped, " Just think, Reva, I was eighty in March!"

"You can't mean it, Sunday!" marveled the Judge, eyeing her youthful appearance. "Stop lying about your age." And with mirth, "I have never lied about my age—I've never told it, but I've never lied about it!"

So, armed with a compliment in disguise, Reva, according to Sunday, will offer up at a gathering of the gals, "There's one thing about Sunday Anderson—she lies about her age!"

But a definite Bosone command: "Don't you dare die on me," friend Sunday is heeding to the fullest.

The actress in the proficient Reva slips out every now and then as most anyone will vouch who has been the receiver of a phone call. Inasmuch as her voice is richly low, it is often disguised as a man's. A joke going the family rounds concerns a relative who was hoodwinked by her impersonation to a state of exasperation, only proving that Reva can still be the actress. Each day a cause to pursue adds to the feeling that for the first time in her life she aches to be twenty-five years younger and a member of Congress. "I'd be raising hell!" she exclaims.

According to those in contact with the Judge, she continues to help cheer, uplift, and inspire, and so combats the tedium. Always solicitous, she places shut-ins at the top of her letter list. The Judge is a pushover for a television plea to bail out an unfortunate from a particular predicament; for years the Shoeshine Boys project for orphans in Vietnam, led by Dick Hughes, a former pressman, has been a special target for her gratuities. A never-ending string of contributions emanates from her residence which she now shares with her daughter and grandchildren.

The years have wrought the inevitable changes—the Beck family has been cut in half with the deaths of Filcher and Horace. The former well-oiled link to home with the weekly beautifully composed letters of Filcher, the long newsy jottings of Horace, and the less frequent but always innovative letters of Clarence found Reva rummaging in the mailbox in keen anticipation. Now, with the link broken in two places, news is less in variety and kind.

Zilpha, now divorced, resuming her maiden name, excels in a professional career. Her beautiful daughter Christy has chosen to work in the business field. Son Timothy, who graduated from Yale in 1977, distinguished himself at age 17 as the 1974 nationwide winner of first place in musical composition sponsored by the National Music Teachers Association. Grandmother Bosone will dangle any participle in an instant to extoll the virtuosity of her daughter or grandchildren, ". . . for of the abundance of the heart his mouth speaketh."

Since she is continually being asked for advice, the Judge, teacher first, jots down a few guidelines, wise words, mottoes, and conclusions:

> Do right and fear not!
> If you expect thanks, you'll be unhappy all your life.
> If you want to do missionary work you can find plenty of it to do right around here.
> In my mind, a home isn't a good one for the child unless there is discipline. If there is imagination and understanding in that discipline, there aren't going to be too many problems with the children.
> One can often judge a person by his hands.
> If world peace is not secured, it isn't going to matter much what happens, for the next war will not prove who is right but who is left.
> I have reached the age where I make plans, have strong desires to fill them but am not disappointed if they are given no opportunity.
> A conservative votes with his head, a liberal votes with his head and his heart.
> I ran for myself, never against an opponent.
> One doesn't need a thick skin to become a public official because callow individuals should never be elected.
> I stand before you tonight—unpromised and unpledged.
> The American people must take a new look at government and those who carry responsibility. The average voter, if he is to be an honest and intelligent voter, must pay more attention to government between elections and use his brains more during a campaign. Great blocks of our voters, intelligent and smart in their chosen fields, are often gullible in the field of public affairs and vote for or against someone for some petty and inconsequential reason, ignoring completely important items which should be weighed carefully.
> As long as we fight our political battles on an emotional basis we will have a fertile field for the rumor noose. It will always be hovering above emotional campaigns, just waiting for some unscrupulous hand to twirl it over the wanted head.
> People can always be pretty nice on someone else's money.
> We must abide by the laws and when we think some are wrong, seek to change them—by law.
> Give me the teacher who knows her subject and if she loves

young people and has horse sense, I'll show you a successful teacher.

If we can catch the mentally slow children before truancy age and keep them in school, we can prevent most crimes, I believe. I have concluded that the majority of criminals are of slow mentality and truancy nearly always is a forerunner of criminality.

I made decisions, maybe not according to "Hoyle," but according to what I thought was justice.

If I were to die tomorrow I'd have no regrets.

Reva's voice takes on a ringing quality. "Yesterday I addressed a Unitarian Church in Kansas. It was a fine audience that seemed to like what I said. One young man from New York City came up to me afterward and said, 'I disagree with you.' I thought we were in for a pleasant argument. He continued, 'What do you mean speaking of the twilight years of your life? You have a long way to go before reaching old age!' Wasn't he kind?"

Cal Rawlings, a district attorney in Utah in earlier times, with a long distinguished record of activities in the Democratic party, is convinced that the future of women in high public office depends on whether or not a reformation of the system of the election of senators and congressmen is enacted that will outlaw contributions of tremendous sums of money to campaigns, which often results in politicians selling themselves to private interests. In Mr. Rawlings' opinion, women would not be as tempted as men are to accept these vast sums if offered, but usually those offerings are not *available* to women, making their opportunities limited. However, it is fairly easy to imagine that if a woman of Reva's exceptional calibre and background were to run for Congress today, she would command the attention and money that are lavished on selected male candidates.

As the system goes now, Rawlings believes that the feminist movement would advance if it encouraged more women to become involved as Reva was and then pointed to their achievements as the hallmark of what a woman can do.

"One thing Reva did by being a judge was to raise the image of women in politics and public office. She let the public know that she could be an outstanding public officer.

"I can say this about Reva," he continued, "a person's success depends largely on his or her unselfish contributions to worthy causes, and by that standard, Reva Beck Bosone stands tall! Honest, knowledgeable, and loyal, she was one of the finest stalwart Democrats we ever had in this state and she made one of the greatest contributions to this state and the nation of any woman I ever knew!"

THE LIGHTS of early spring leap through the window, alighting on the Judge who sits looking out at the never-changing profile of the Wasatch

Mountains where she is on a visit to her hometown. From across the room one seems a slim woman—a professional, hair slightly fluffed, figure in a pink wool suit of couture style, a long line of legs, with feet together in pretty, simple pumps. The chunky bracelet has given way to a narrow bangle, but two or three large rings are quite noticeable on her hands. The green eyes, now enlarged by thick-lensed glasses, are the only feature distorted. A cane is propped nearby, evidence of a recent successful hip operation.

The stereo has just delivered a raucous rendition of ragtime piano. One had to be quick, of course, but it was possible to see a flicker of nostalgia touch the expression on the Judge's face as she reminisced of former times and friends long gone. But just as quickly her expression returns to the one she has kept steady yet sympathetic for three generations. No more, she pleads, play no more records.

These days private citizen Bosone has sharp recall of a fruitful life but even sharper convictions on the amelioration of the future. Her lyrical phrase, "Twilight slows the pace but sweetens the path," a path previously smooth or boulder-blocked, but never touched by shadows of ignominy, must refer to an easing up of the pace, not the creative urge.

Motivated by the words of Sam Walter Foss: "Let me live in my house by the side of the road/And be a friend to man," Reva has long since found that trying to live by this philosophy has resulted in both praise and criticism. But it has given her the confidence to "stand up and be counted" on vital issues. And all the dreams of that little girl in American Fork have been fulfilled, including the long-awaited award of an honorary doctorate from the University of Utah in June 1977! "Utah has really made it up to me!" Reva declares.

ON that memorable trip to Scandinavia and Russia she stood waiting for the hotel elevator one morning in Moscow. Crowded, it stopped at her floor. Reva pointed down but the young woman operator pointed up; it went on its way. A minute later the elevator door opened and she stepped in. As the only passenger, Reva noticed that the Russian woman's shoulders began to shake and she hid her face with a handkerchief. Weeping copiously, she dispelled Reva's notion that she might be suffering from an attack of hay fever, as the Judge occasionally did. Some deep hurt or unbearable sadness had evidently loosed the mooring of emotional control.

Suddenly Reva encircled her with her arms and although she couldn't sympathize in the woman's language, she comforted her until they reached the lobby floor. As the door opened Reva held her tightly and gazed into tearful grateful eyes with a look as meaningful as that of an American mother stretching an arm across a convex line of natural and language barriers to that of a Russian mother.

Then Reva Beck Bosone was on her way to confront with zest the happenings of an exciting journey.

INDEX